THE PROTESTANT REFORMATION
AND WORLD CHRISTIANITY

REFORMATION RESOURCES, 1517–2017

SERIES EDITORS

Norman A. Hjelm, Philip D. Krey, and William G. Rusch

The Protestant Reformation and World Christianity

Global Perspectives

Edited by

Dale T. Irvin

WILLIAM B. EERDMANS PUBLISHING COMPANY

GRAND RAPIDS, MICHIGAN

Wm. B. Eerdmans Publishing Co.
2140 Oak Industrial Drive N.E., Grand Rapids, Michigan 49505
www.eerdmans.com

26 25 24 23 22 21 20 19 18 17   1 2 3 4 5 6 7 8 9 10

ISBN 978-0-8028-7304-0

Library of Congress Cataloging-in-Publication Data

Names: Irvin, Dale T., 1955–   editor.
Title: The Protestant Reformation and world Christianity : global perspectives /
    edited by Dale T. Irvin.
Description: Grand Rapids : Eerdmans Publishing Co., 2017. |
    Series: Reformation resources, 1517–2017 |
    Includes bibliographical references and index.
Identifiers: LCCN 2017008127 | ISBN 9780802873040 (pbk. : alk. paper)
Subjects: LCSH: Christianity—21st century. | Reformation. | Protestantism.
Classification: LCC BR121.3 .P76 2017 | DDC 270.6—dc23
    LC record available at https://lccn.loc.gov/2017008127

Contents

Introduction

DALE T. IRVIN

Five centuries have now passed since Martin Luther sent a copy of *Disputatio pro declaratione virtutis indulgentiarum* (often translated as "The Ninety-Five Theses on the Power and Efficacy of Indulgences") to the Archbishop of Mainz in 1517. By all accounts the young German monk initially intended nothing more than to open up a dialogue in the form of a scholarly debate concerning a number of church practices that he considered improper. The debate soon took on a form that Luther never intended or imagined. Within a few years its reverberations were being felt across Europe, and eventually in other parts of the world. An era of reform opened up, not entirely initiated by Luther but certainly spurred on one way or another by his writings. Martin Luther, John Calvin, Ulrich (or Huldrych) Zwingli, and Thomas Cranmer had neither the first nor the last word when it came to determining the scope or meaning of the dialogues that coalesced to form the sixteenth-century Reformation(s) with which their names are so closely associated. To them we can add the names of Erasmus of Rotterdam, Johann Tetzel, Katharina von Bora, Kaspar Schwenckfeld, Thomas Müntzer, Michael Sattler, Katharina Schütz Zell, Heinrich Bullinger, Jeanne d'Albret, Andreas Karlstadt, Philipp Melanchthon, Francisco Jiménez de Cisneros, and a host of others. Some remained faithful members of the Roman Catholic Church. Others found themselves leading new communions or fellowships tagged as Lutheran, Reformed, Anabaptist, or Anglican. They were all part of the complex and powerful series of movements for spiritual and institutional reformation that swept through European Christianity beginning in the sixteenth century.

Understanding the Reformation (or Reformations) as a conversation that began in 1517 and has continued since to expand in terms of both time and space allows us to see it through the dialogical lens provided by the twentieth-century Russian literary critic, philosopher, and Orthodox Christian Mikhail Bakhtin:

> There is neither a first nor a last word and there are no limits to the dialogic context (it extends into the boundless past and boundless future). Even past meanings, that is those born in the dialogue of past centuries, can never be stable (finalized, ended once and for all)—they will always change (be renewed) in the process of subsequent, future development of the dialogue. At any moment in the development of the dialogue there are immense, boundless masses of forgotten contextual meanings, but at certain moments of the dialogue's subsequent development along the way they are recalled and invigorated in renewed form (in a new context).[1]

Both Protestant and Catholic Reformations were as much about interpreting the Christian past that European churches had inherited as they were charting a course for a global Christian future. The various theological positions that they staked out and explored through confessions of faith, articles of belief, treatises, books, pamphlets, letters, public statements of condemnation, biblical works of translation and exegesis, or more were never stable. The Reformation was not then and is not now a closed project. Scholars, religious leaders, and laypeople from all traditions continue today to debate in a variety of ways what these various documents meant

---

1. Mikhail M. Bakhtin, *Speech Genres and Other Late Essays*, ed. Caryl Emerson and Michael Holquist, trans. Vern W. McGee (Austin: University of Texas Press, 1986), 170.

in their own time and what they mean today. Karl Barth might indeed have been the first to actually use the Latin phrase *ecclesia reformata semper reformanda* (reformed and always needing to be reformed), as both Rebecca A. Giselbrecht and Vladimir Latinovic point out in their chapters in this volume, but it captures the sense of both open-endedness and renewal that characterizes the long history of the various movements of Christian reformation (Protestant and Catholic) that trace their lineage in one way or another through sixteenth-century Western Europe. As Giselbrecht writes, "our Reformation is not over."

Bakhtin pointed out that in the course of any historical movement, or what he calls "the development of the dialogue," there are an immense number of experiences and meanings that become lost or forgotten. It is in no small part the historian's task to try to recover as much of these as can be found in order to continue to enrich the ongoing dialogue. Bakhtin also noted that there are certain key moments in any historical movement that, in "the dialogue's subsequent development," are not only recalled, but "invigorated in renewed form." Given the changing nature of history, such (re)invigoration always takes place in new (or changing) contexts. In the process, old meanings are not simply repeated but neither are they necessarily erased. Rather, they tend to take on new contours of meaning with new implications. Reinvigoration and renewal are not only reformative. They are transformative as well.

The sixteenth-century Reformation in all its forms and expressions, Protestant as well as Roman Catholic, sought nothing less than the transformation of Christian faith. Five hundred years later, in a context of world Christianity, the transformation continues. Assisting in a transformational reading and interpretation of the Reformation from a variety of world Christian perspectives is the purpose of this volume. We do not purport this to be by any means a comprehensive study of the impact of the sixteenth-century Reformation upon world Christian history. We do not claim these six chapters to be exhaustive in terms of world Christian perspectives today upon the Reformation. The six chapters that make up this volume are more concerned with opening new directions in understanding and interpretation that emerge when the sixteenth-century

Reformation is seen from diverse contemporary global perspectives. Together the six authors are concerned with discovering what new meanings emerge from the Reformation that started with Luther in 1517 for world Christianity today.

In chapter 1, Charles Amjad-Ali explores the relationship of the early Protestant Reformation to Islam, doing so against the background of the history of conflict between Christian and Islamic empires. The Protestant and Roman Catholic Reformations of the sixteenth century took place while the Christian kingdoms of Portugal and newly united Spain were launching an era of conquest that would soon encircle the world. The nations of Western Europe, however, had not yet achieved global dominance. In 1453, only sixty-four years before Luther penned his Ninety-Five Theses, the armies of the Ottoman Sultan Mehmed II, a Muslim, had taken the city of Constantinople, bringing about an end to the Christian East Roman (or Byzantine) Empire. Four years after Luther published the Ninety-Five Theses the Ottoman ruler Suleiman I conquered Belgrade, in what is now Serbia. By 1529 his Turkish forces were at the gates of Vienna, in Austria.

In chapter 2, Joel Morales Cruz explores the relationship between a reformer of Christianity in the Americas with the reformers of continental Europe. Only twenty-five years before Luther penned his Ninety-Five Theses, the armies of Christian Spain had brought an end to the last Muslim kingdom in Iberia, in Granada. That same year, in 1492, Cristóbal Colón (or Christopher Columbus as he is better known in English) set sail to the west for what he thought would be Asia. The conquest that his and subsequent voyages unleashed brought an enormous region of the earth that came to be known as "America" or "the Americas" under Spanish rule. Spain's monarchs considered these territories to be colonies, under the amalgamated kingdom in Iberia. A Council of the Indies exercised administrative and judicial authority over the colonial regions and reported directly to the Spanish Crown, thereby maintaining royal control over governance and ensuring that the extracted wealth ended up in royal coffers. Catholic Christianity was established as the official religion of the Spanish colonies of Cuba, Puerto Rico, Santo Domingo, New Spain (Mexico), Guatemala,

Peru, and Chile. Operating under the privilege of *patronato real* (royal patronage), which gave monarchs the power to nominate all candidates for episcopal office, the Spanish Crown controlled the secular church (but not the orders). This allowed King Carlos of Spain, who in 1519 was elected Holy Roman Emperor as Charles V, to prevent any bishops from the dioceses in America from attending the Council of Trent, which opened in 1545. The matters that were to be addressed by Trent only concerned the churches of Europe, not those of America, he reasoned. The lasting effect of this divide has been to separate Bartolomé de Las Casas, who was primarily concerned with the reform of Christianity in America, from Luther, Calvin, Erasmus, and other sixteenth-century reformers concerned primarily with reforms of Christianity in Europe. Cruz challenges that divide and brings Las Casas into dialogue with the other reformers of the sixteenth century, opening up important new perspectives on both.

Chapter 3 is Rebecca A. Giselbrecht's exploration of how the Reformation changed the story of women in Christianity. One of the key commitments of the field of world Christianity in recent decades has been to recover the fuller story of women. The Christian movement has a long and tangled history of patriarchal domination and exclusion that has silenced the voice of women in its history. A number of excellent studies in recent years have taken up consideration specifically of the role women played in the sixteenth-century Reformation in Europe. Most have been forced by the absence of documentation regarding women's lives to focus on the exceptional women whose names were recorded, and in some cases whose writings were preserved. Giselbrecht takes a slightly different direction. She argues that the sixteenth-century Protestant reformers in Zurich as well as elsewhere believed women as well as men could approach God as individuals without a clerical mediator. This in turn led to two affirmations. First, she argues that equality before God led to notions of mutuality in marriage between one man and one woman. Second, in order to approach God everyone should be able to read the Bible, and this meant that women had to be educated. The ramifications of these commitments remain an unfinished project in our own age.

David D. Daniels uses chapter 4 to challenge the tendency of historians of the Reformation to treat Protestant churches and communions as being exclusively European until the nineteenth century. By the first decades of the seventeenth century, there were Protestants of Asian, African, and Native American descent. The issue of whether children of what were called "ethnic" peoples could be baptized before coming to the age of consent was brought before the Synod of Dort in 1618. Daniels argues that the theological debate about ethnic baptism signals a turning point in the late Protestant Reformation from being an exclusively European-oriented movement to a slightly more globally oriented movement, a shift that was prompted by pastoral concerns arising from the Global South.

In chapter 5, Peter C. Phan undertakes a broader historical overview of the efforts by descendants of the Protestant Reformation to spread their churches in Asia, efforts that often mixed evangelization with colonization. The Protestant Reformation first came to Asia on the ships of Dutch traders in the seventeenth century. The first full-fledged Protestant mission efforts in the early eighteenth century in Asia were undertaken by members of the Pietist movement in Protestantism. These efforts grew exponentially through the nineteenth and twentieth centuries with mixed results. Phan provocatively asks whether the impact of these efforts has been a blessing or a curse for Asia. His answer: a mixture of both, a response that he argues is itself grounded in the Reformation doctrine that human beings are *simul justus et peccator* (simultaneously justified and sinner). Like others in this volume, Phan argues that the way for the churches of the Reformation to move forward entails a fuller knowledge and understanding of the Reformation's past.

Looking back in order to look ahead is one of the common themes that tie this volume together. In chapter 6 Vladimir Latinovic argues that the legacy of the Reformation belongs to all Christian communions, and that all churches of the world can celebrate that legacy today. He also looks at the challenges faced by contemporary societies in the original European homelands of the sixteenth-century Reformation. Among the most important challenges to churches in Europe that claim to be descended from the Protestant Reformation is that posed by the growing number of Pentecostals in Europe, raising the question of whether the global Pentecostal movement is not a new reformation of our day. Latinovic's chapter serves not only as a conclusion to this volume, but also as an invitation to open the dialogue afresh. Perhaps it is time to post a new *Disputatio pro declaratione* in our own time and place.

1 Jews and Muslims in Europe

Exorcising Prejudice against the Other

CHARLES AMJAD-ALI

As part of the 500th anniversary celebrations of Calvin's birth in 2009, a special work of art was unveiled in Dordrecht, the Netherlands. Dordrecht, the site of the Synod of Dort in 1618–19, has a special significance for Reformed theology and the Reformation itself. Here Calvinism and its classical "five points" (viz., TULIP)[1] were established as the state religion of the Netherlands over against Arminianism. The artwork was commissioned by the city from a Moroccan artist, Aziz Bekkaoui, and was titled *Het Mekka van Calvijn* (*Calvin's Mecca*); it was a reflective glass cube apparently replicating the Ka'aba.[2] It displayed a link between Calvin and Islam conspicuously absent in academic works on Calvin, Reformed theology, and the Reformation in general. This monument generated deep emotions, controversy, and soul-searching in Holland (and Europe), and it produced intensely vitriolic attacks on Islam and Muslims. Calvinist identity became of critical importance in the

1. TULIP stands for total depravity, unconditional election, limited atonement, irresistible (or irrevocable) grace, and perseverance of the saints.

2. The center of Muslim pilgrimage (Hajj, one of the five pillars of Islam), in Mecca, Saudi Arabia. The unveiling of the artwork was repeatedly postponed. Ironically, the street signs pointing to the monument had two different arrows: one for Calvinists and another for non-Calvinists, perhaps shades of "double predestination."

1

highly secular political and sociocultural milieu of Holland. The then Prime Minister[3] even confessed openly in a political speech that he was a Calvinist—this in a context where openly confessing to being a Christian is a contested public stance. One of the main questions that surfaced during this controversy was what exactly do Calvin and the Reformation have to do with Islam?

The Resurgence of Islam as Epistemological Challenge

Following the collapse of the Soviet Union in 1991, Islam has emerged as the new binary enemy of the West. The best-known articulation of this was Samuel Huntington's "The Clash of Civilizations?"[4] Unfortunately, this phrase has since acquired ubiquity with little reflection on its historical accuracy, full meaning, and implications.[5] In Europe especially, Islam as the new enemy of the West is highlighted regularly across newspapers and magazines, and at conferences in universities and ecclesial centers. This debate is grounded in the epistemological conviction that religion is at best a residual superstition that will be eradicated with the full flowering of science and reason, and is also the source of all conflict and violence within and between societies. It is ironical therefore that the Christian identity of the West is instantly championed whenever dealing with the "*Muslim question.*"[6]

As the new enemy, Islam has forced itself into political and economic arenas, as well as the sociocultural consciousness and

3. Jan Peter Balkenende, prime minister of Holland from 2002 to 2010, was trained as a jurist but also taught theology at the Free University, Amsterdam.

4. Cf. *Foreign Affairs* 72, no. 3 (Summer 1993): 22–28. This was later converted into the popular book *The Clash of Civilizations and the Remaking of World Order* (New York: Simon & Schuster, 1996).

5. For a critical assessment of the history and widespread use of the phrase "clash of civilizations," see my *Islamophobia or Restorative Justice: Tearing the Veils of Ignorance* (Johannesburg: Ditshwanelo CAR2AS, 2006), esp. 2–5.

6. Besides the existential question posed by Muslim immigrants, who come mostly from ex-European colonies, the question has clearly been just below the surface in the challenge to the inclusion of Turkey in the European Union.

discourse of the West. It poses a threat to Western scientific rationality and raises a question in the West about whether it should take its Christian identity seriously. Islam poses a security problem and challenges the rights-based sociopolitical achievements in the West. These standards are increasingly threatened by the reversion to a "survivalist ethics": i.e., rights are placed in abeyance in the face of these threats. Islam also challenges the very survival of the modern Western nation-state—a product of the Reformation finalized in the Treaty of Westphalia (1648).

The *Het Mekka van Calvijn* debate not only symbolically brought all these issues to the fore; it demanded a critical look at the Reformation in relation to Islam. Epistemologically, this issue has been consciously, almost universally, ignored. This, in spite of the perception of Islam's widespread threat, deep impact, and major significance at the time of the Reformation. It is truly ironic given that some of the contemporary antipathy and sophistry against Islam is uncritically borrowed directly from the Reformation's vitriol.

Crisis of Meaning and the Emergence of the New Episteme

The Reformation had world-changing consequences in Europe. It thoroughly challenged the apparently singular architectonic political system of the "Holy Roman Empire" and the determining orthodoxy of Christianity as controlled through the papacy and the Catholic Church. Their diminution led to the emergence of plurivocal religious and moral authorities. The bishops acquired local ruling ecclesial authority, while the princes acquired the power of local political "emperors," precipitating the emergence of princely-denominational nation-states through the Treaty of Westphalia. This was achieved through the reconfirmation of the critical clause *cuius regio, eius religio* (whose region/realm, his religion) of the Peace of Augsburg (1555),[7] while at the same time epistemolog-

---

7. The Peace of Augsburg was between the Holy Roman Emperor, Charles V, and an alliance of Lutheran princes, the Schmalkaldic League; Calvinists and Anabaptists were not part of this settlement. The Treaty of Westphalia expanded

ically claiming the separation of "Church and State."[8] The latter was then thrust as a requirement for acceptability and epistemological validity in the contemporary political and religious world order.

The Reformation not only had religious, theological, and spiritual dimensions but it also impacted philosophical and political discourse. Politically it led to nationalistic tendencies, and philosophically and religiously to a high individualization. These produced in their wake liberal political theory with the *locus politicus* tied to a vying individuality and in religion to the imperative of individual personal faith and conversion. It was a period of major rethinking, not just of existing doctrines, theology, and the understanding of Christian faith, but of the theological epistemology as well as the sociopolitical nature of the church. These positions had evolved over eleven hundred years, from the early fourth century and the Edict of Milan in 313, the subsequent "conversion of Constantine," and finally, Christianity becoming the official imperial religion under Theodosius in 380. This sequence of events had provided the epistemological foundation for theology, ethics, social virtue, etc.

This much we learned in our theological and doctrinal formation, and in our church history. What we tend to overlook, however, is the critical role of Islam during medieval times and particularly during the Reformation.

---

the Peace of Augsburg to include the Calvinists, but even here the Anabaptists were excluded since they did not have a prince from within their persuasion to represent them at the Treaty. They were subsequently persecuted equally by all the princes of the other faiths (denominations), and thus migrated to the New World, finding no safe haven anywhere in Europe.

8. This was largely based on a rather poor hermeneutic of Luke 20:20-26 and the much-touted phrase "Render to Caesar what is Caesar's and to God what is God's." Cf. my "Confusing Power and Authority: A Case against Idolatrous Nationalism," in *Working Preacher*, on January 19, 2009, http://www.workingpreacher .org/craft.aspx?post=1646. For a more theological discussion of the separation of "Church and State" and "Religion and Politics," see my "The Religious Dimension of Social Change," in *Christian Ethics in Ecumenical Context: Theology, Culture, and Politics in Dialogue*, ed. Shin Chiba, George R. Hunsberger, and Lester E. J. Ruiz (Grand Rapids: Eerdmans, 1995), 268-78.

The Emergence of Islam and Its Challenge to Christendom

Born in the early seventh century, Islam expanded rapidly and took over almost all of the biblical lands, absorbing three of the five founding patriarchates (the Pentarchy) of Christianity.[9] It controlled most of the Mediterranean and the "Eastern" Roman Empire, as well as large portions of the "Western" Roman Empire. It occupied North Africa and ruled most of the Iberian Peninsula for eight hundred years; made forays into France and Italy; and attacked the Eastern Roman Empire (Byzantium), finally capturing Constantinople itself in 1453.

The threat and awe of Islam was further exacerbated during the crusades, which became a self-justifying *cause célèbre* for Christianity and played a very significant role in most aspects of European medieval life. From their very inception, the crusades were put on a religious and spiritual footing by Urban II in 1095 at the Council of Clermont, who linked them to Christian independence struggles on the Muslim Iberian Peninsula. In brief, the Crusades were a series of Christian "holy wars," initially between 1096 and 1270,[10] against the Muslims in larger Syria and Palestine and subsequently elsewhere in the region. Steven Runciman, one of the major historians of the crusades, correctly describes them as "a long act of intoler-

9. Viz., Jerusalem, Antioch, and Alexandria; later even Constantinople. Rome was the exception, though it too came very close to being captured. Sultan Mehmet II of the Ottoman Empire clearly had his eye on Rome, having already captured Otranto in 1480. However, he suddenly died and Turkish expansion stopped due to internal strife over his succession.

10. There were at least eight crusades, of which the first four are the most relevant. The battle cries of the first crusade, i.e., that "God wills it" and "to free the Holy Land of the Infidels," became established as the overt *raison d'être* for subsequent crusades. The first crusade was successful: Jerusalem was taken in 1099, establishing the crusader Kingdom of Jerusalem, which lasted until 1187. The second was a disaster. The third led to the Treaty of Ramla in 1192 allowing Christian pilgrimage to Jerusalem, despite a Muslim victory and continuing control of the city itself. In the fourth, in 1204, the Crusaders sacked Constantinople (some 250 years prior to its subjugation by the Ottoman Muslims in 1453), desecrating many Orthodox churches, including Hagia Sophia (built in 537), one of the most holy ecclesial sites in all of Christianity.

ance in the name of God, which is a sin against the Holy Ghost."[11] Others have argued that "[i]n a broad sense the Crusades were an expression of militant Christianity and European expansion."[12] It is obvious that besides religion, there were political and economic interests at play. What is seldom mentioned is that besides killing a vast number of noncombatant Muslims, the crusades also killed a huge number of Jews in Europe along the way as well as in the Near East. These genocidal massacres were justified on the grounds that such killings were not sinful because the ones killed were not Christians but infidels (not of the faith).[13] All this had a deep impact on the developments leading up to the Reformation.

After the euphoric success of the First Crusade, the subsequent failures to sustain it shook Christianity, given the ubiquitous religious notion that success and victory show that "God is on our side/ God is with us" (*Nobiscum deus/Gott mit uns*, etc.). Conversely, the Muslims were buoyed by the same idea, given their successes in these centuries. By the time of the Reformation, the Turks were at the gates of Vienna threatening the core of what is now known as Western Europe. The Holy Roman Emperor, Charles V, had there-

---

11. Steven Runciman, *A History of the Crusades*, 3 vols. (New York: Harper & Row, 1967), 3:480.

12. See http://history-world.org/crusades.htm.

13. Cf. Gustavo Perednik, a scholar of Judeophobia, who states that "the first half of this millennium witnessed genocides of Jews as the norm [the last millennium ended with the German/European Holocaust]. . . . [T]he main genocides were the first three crusades and the four Jew-murdering campaigns that followed them." Perednik also rightly points out that "Pope Urban II called for a campaign 'to free the Holy Land from the Muslim infidel.' . . . The crusaders decided to start their cleansing on the 'infidels at home,' and pounced upon the Jews all over Lorraine, massacring those who refused baptism. Soon it was rumored that their leader Godfrey had vowed not to set out for the crusade until he had avenged the crucifixion by spilling the blood of the Jews, and that he could not tolerate the continued existence of any man calling himself a Jew. Indeed, one common denominator of the genocides . . . was the attempt to wipe out the entire Jewish population, children included." So that "[b]y the end of the 13th century Jews had been expelled from England, France and Germany." See his "Judeophobia—Anti-Semitism, Jew-Hate and anti-'Zionism,'" a series of lectures based on his book *La Judeofobia: Cómo y Cuándo Nace, Dónde y Por Qué Pervive* (Mexico City: Tusquets, 2001), made available online at http://www.zionism-israel.com/his/judeophobia.htm.

fore called a diet at the imperial city of Augsburg in 1530, to ensure a unity of Catholic and Lutheran princes for a new crusade against this threat. The Augsburg Confession—a critical doctrine for Lutherans and the Reformation—was presented there in the context of crusades and the war against the Muslims. It was also the precursor to the 1555 Peace of Augsburg, and led to the 1648 Treaty of Westphalia.

Overall, these were seen as apocalyptic times by the Reformation founders. They anticipated cataclysmic persecution of the saints under Islam, which they perceived as a judgment of God—thus their highly negative anti-Islamic polemics. Their anti-papist rhetoric was because they considered Catholicism, and at times also the Jews, as the cause behind God's punishment through the rod of Islam.[14]

The Multireligious and Multicultural Context

Contrary to traditional wisdom, Europe at the time of Luther was neither monoreligious, nor monocultural; rather a sequence of historical developments over the previous centuries reflected a highly pluralistic context. These developments were still part of the collective memory, and in fact were the theological and epistemic grist for the Reformation. Spain had been under Muslim rule from 711[15] until the completion of the *Reconquista* of 1492, with the fall of Granada, the last Islamic state on the Iberian Peninsula.[16] After

14. The Muslims were ever-present in the reformers' condemnations, though weaker than those directed against the Catholic Church. The Jews had no power status except as a constant theological reminder of their link with Jesus, with no potential conversions to Christianity and the acceptance of Jesus as the Messiah. Perhaps subconsciously they reminded Christians of the failure to reach these objectives of Jesus's ministry and mission.

15. The year when the Muslim General Tariq ibn Ziyad (after whom Gibraltar is named, i.e., *Jabal Tariq*, the Mountain of Tariq) defeated King Roderic, the last of the Visigoth rulers of Hispania, and established Muslim rule on the Iberian Peninsula.

16. The year 1492 is now better recognized for Christopher Columbus and the "discovery" (i.e., colonization) of the Americas under the patronage of the Spanish monarchs.

1492, the most Catholic monarchs, Isabella and Ferdinand, force-fully converted the Muslims and Jews of Spain.[17] The Jewish expulsion started after their genocide of 1391,[18] and is seen as the turning point for the Spanish (Sephardic) Jewish existence in Europe.[19] This led to the Inquisition in 1478 to check the orthodoxy of the converts and finally to the expulsion of even the converted Jews that followed. The final expulsion of the Muslim converts from Spain began in 1609 and was completed in 1614.[20]

Despite this history of Islam in southern Europe, today northern and western Europe claim direct, unmediated continuity with southern and eastern Mediterranean ancient civilizations and the "mother" Greco-Roman civilizations. This sleight of hand conceptually and emotionally locates the Mediterranean[21] exclusively in

17. Muslim converts were referred to as Moriscos, i.e., Moorish, a term largely applied to the indigenous Spanish Muslim converts and not so much to those of Arab descent. Jewish converts were pejoratively called Marranos—meaning pigs, i.e., "filthy-dirty" and "unscrupulous." For Jews to be referred to as pigs, especially in the context of eight hundred years of Islamic rule (which has similar religious dietary laws), was obscenely offensive; their descendants therefore naturally preferred the term *Anusim*—Hebrew for "forced."

18. This genocide took place in different locations all across Spain: Seville, Cordoba, Toledo, Aragon, Catalonia, Majorica, Valencia, Palma, Barcelona, et al.

19. Estimates of the numbers of Jews expelled from Spain vary: Juan de Mariana, a Spanish Jesuit, estimates this number to be as high as 800,000; see his famous *Historiae de rebus Hispaniae*, a twenty-volume work published first in Toledo in 1592 (translated into English by J. Stevens, as *The General History of Spain* in 1699). Rabbi Isidore Loeb, founding editor of the Jewish journal *Revue des Études Juives*, estimates this number to be as low as 165,000. He also shows that some 90,000 (over 50 percent) of these refugees migrated to Turkey as they were welcomed by the Sultan. See "Le nombre des juifs de Castille et d'Espagne," *Revue des Études Juives* 14 (1887): 162-83.

20. In 1609 Philip III issued an Act of Expulsion of the Muslims (*Expulsión de los moriscos*) who were left behind after 1492, because he saw them as having loyalty to the Ottoman Turks and therefore as a subversive fifth column on the Iberian Peninsula. See esp. Mary E. Perry, *The Handless Maiden: Moriscos and the Politics of Religion in Early Modern Spain* (Princeton: Princeton University Press, 2005).

21. The term itself derives from the Latin word *mediterraneus* (*medi-*: "middle" or "between"; + *terra*, "land, earth"): i.e., "in the middle of earth" or "between lands," it being the sea between the then three known continents of Africa, Asia, and Europe. The Germans correctly name it *Mittelmeer*, i.e., the middle sea.

Europe, even though geographically it is located between Africa, Asia, and Europe. Through this historical manipulation they claim sole possession of this heritage, and thus to be the real successor of the Roman Empire.

What is critical to understand is that this perception of unbridged Mediterranean continuity and Europe's monoreligious status evolved largely out of a Constantinian Christendom model. The location of the capital of this Constantinian Christendom and empire bordered Asia, if it was not directly in Asia itself, i.e., on the Bosphorus. It had no real contribution from, nor was it ever a direct product of, the so-called European "barbarian" tribes[22] (except negatively in the threat they posed to Rome and the Roman Empire). In fact, it was their continued aggressions that led to the move from Rome to Byzantium (the New Rome on the Bosphorus) as the new capital of the empire in the fourth century. It is also important to recall that at the beginning of this period there is only one Roman Empire, no such mythical aberrations as Western and Eastern Roman Empires[23] as is oft romantically but falsely stated. It is also critical to note that it is here that Christianity becomes the religion of imperial Rome. Constantinople, therefore, is the original location of what came to be called "Christendom," rather than its accepted location in Western Europe.

22. Goths, Visigoths, Huns, Vandals, Franks, Angles, Saxons, etc. These tribes were variously located in eastern Germany, Pomerania to the Black Sea, Scandinavia, and the Caucasus to Central Asia, as well as the Norman Germanic tribes controlling Portugal and Spain (*Hispania*), southern Poland, Spain to some parts of North Africa and France, and Britain especially after the Romans left the area in 410 CE.

23. This myth was coined in modern European historiography to define the Western provinces and courts of the Roman Empire as a separate entity and to give them equal footing with the "Eastern Roman Empire," at Constantinople. The fact is that the capital was shifted from Rome to Byzantium by Constantine in 330 (renamed Constantinople after his death) and remained the capital of the Roman Empire till 1204 and the Fourth Crusade. However, we name Charlemagne's Carolingian rule five hundred years later (800–814) with the blessing of the Bishop of Rome (Pope Leo III), notwithstanding. For this historiography, see esp. Edward Gibbon, *The History of the Decline and Fall of the Roman Empire*, 6 vols. (London: Strahan & Cadell, 1776–89).

To Islam, which emerged after this shift, Constantinople was *the Rum*. It was they who became the true inheritors of this Roman Empire and of most of the Mediterranean, beginning with the initial period of Islamic expansion and conquest, crescendoing finally with the capture of Constantinople in 1453. With this, Muslims inherited the intellectual traditions of the Greco-Roman world, which later were transmitted to the West through Muslim scholars even for as central and pivotal a Christian theologian/philosopher as St. Thomas Aquinas. Sidney Griffiths rightly points out that

> Al-Farabi (870–950), Ibn Sina/Avicenna (980–1037), and Ibn Rushd/Averroes (1126–1198), are the Muslim philosophers with the most immediate name recognition . . . but they are far from being the only ones making major contributions. And, of course, their accomplishments sparked yet another translation movement in the eleventh and twelfth centuries, this time in the Islamo-Christian west, in places like Bologna, Toledo, and Barcelona, where eager minds translated philosophical texts from Arabic into Latin, and provided the impetus for the flowering of scholastic philosophy and theology in the works of Thomas Aquinas, Bonaventure, and Duns Scotus, through the earlier achievements of scholars such as Abelard and Albert the Great.[24]

So it was not by the sword that these great historical figures accepted the Muslim masters for their philosophy and their the-

---

24. Sidney H. Griffith, *The Church in the Shadows of the Mosque: Christians and Muslims in the World of Islam* (Princeton: Princeton University Press, 2008), 18. See also Majid Fakhry, *A History of Islamic Philosophy*, 3rd ed. (New York: Columbia University Press, 2004); Fernand van Steenberghen, *Aristotle and the West: The Origins of Latin Aristotelianism*, trans. Leonard Johnston (New York: Humanities Press, 1970); Charles Burnett, "The Translating Activity in Medieval Spain," in *The Legacy of Muslim Spain*, 2 vols., ed. Salma Khadra Jayyusi (Leiden: E. J. Brill, 1994), 2:1036–58; Burnett, "Arabic into Latin: The Reception of Arabic Philosophy into Western Europe," in *The Cambridge Companion to Arabic Philosophy*, ed. Peter Adamson and Richard C. Taylor (Cambridge: Cambridge University Press, 2005), 370–404; John E. Wansborough, *The Sectarian Milieu: Content and Composition of Islamic Salvation History* (Oxford: Oxford University Press, 1978). See also the present author's *Islamophobia*, specifically the first chapter.

ology. It was in the light of these masters that Thomas reexamined Christianity and insisted on the perspicuity of the sacred text, as was centrally held in Islam. This then influenced Luther's *sola scriptura* (and Calvinist centrality of the word of God—the Scriptures), which had little or no space for the mediation of *traditio*. On the other hand, it was Thomas's judgment and critique of these, his masters and teachers, and their Aristotelian philosophies, in *Summa de veritate catholicae fidei contra gentiles* (*Treatise on the Truth of the Catholic Faith against Unbelievers*),[25] which has determined our position on Islam and Muslims in the West, as well as on Aristotle in Protestant circles. These were Luther's predecessors and guides, leading up to the Reformation.

Large portions of central and eastern Europe also lived under sustained control of the Muslim Ottoman Turks. This started at least as early as the 1389 Battle of Kosovo. With some permutations, this status remained largely unchanged until as late as the First World War, i.e., a period of over five hundred years.[26] With the control of Constantinople in 1453, and all of Greece in 1460 (the cradle of the "western civilization"),[27] the Turkish Muslims had a comprehensive and persistent presence in this foundational part of Europe as well.

25. It has traditionally been dated to 1264, though some recent scholarship places it toward the end of Thomas's life, somewhere between 1270 and 1273. It is the success of this text that brings Thomas to papal notice and to the authorship of the *Summa theologica*.

26. This Turkish presence in Europe can be dated to the Battle of Maritsa in 1371, which the Ottomans won, or to as late as the Turkish victory in the Battle of Kosovo, in 1389. The latter has acquired a central role in Serbian folklore and is seen as the epic battle that heralded the beginning of bad luck for Serbia. This folklore played quite a significant role some six hundred years later in the Balkan wars of the 1990s leading to a genocide of the Muslims. The Ottoman Empire had also taken over the Greek areas of Thrace and much of Macedonia after the Battle of Maritsa. Sofia fell in 1382, followed by Tarnovgrad in 1393, and the state of Romania/ Hungary, after the Battle of Nicopolis in 1396. The Turkish victory over Hungarian forces in the Battle of Varna, in 1444, expanded their control over the Balkans and was of special concern to Calvin. See my article, "Debilitating Past and Future Hope: Calvin, Calvinism and Islam," *Reformed World* 61, no. 2 (2011): 120–33.

27. What is now modern Greece was also part of the Ottoman Empire from the mid-fifteenth century until its declaration of independence in 1821, a roughly three-hundred-year period historically known as *Tourkokratia* or "Turkish rule."

The two long-term multireligious contexts (i.e., Islamic and Jewish) in the western, central, and eastern parts of "Christian" Europe belie any exclusive monoreligious claim of Christianity. This forces us to reevaluate our present epistemic foundations in light of the significance of this multireligious experience and its concomitant dialogical practices. It further demands from us a more critical reexamination of this history, and a "demythologizing" of it for a more honest theological and philosophical task. The three monotheistic religious traditions certainly borrowed from one another in Muslim-ruled Spain, benefiting especially from the blooming of philosophy and the medieval sciences in Muslim Spain and the Middle East. There was more "tolerance" and coexistence, which is now beginning to be recognized, even when some scholars question whether this *convivencia* could actually be defined as "religious pluralism."[28] This completely changed after 1492.

Pre-Reformation Engagement with Islam

By the twelfth century, Islam was becoming the object of intellectual inquiry because of the immediacy of its threat to the West. These scholarly approaches were almost entirely negative. To give a few examples of the understanding of Islam in medieval scholarship available to the Reformation:

1. Peter the Venerable (c. 1092–1156) made an intellectual start to combat "the heresy" of Islam. He wrote *Summa totius heresis Saracenorum* (*The Summary of the Entire Heresy of the Saracens*) and *Liber contra sectam sive heresim Saracenorum* (*Refutation of the Sect or Heresy of the Saracens*). He also solicited the first translation of the Qur'an into Latin.
2. Robert Ketton (1110–1160) did this first seminal Latin translation of the Qur'an, ironically named *Lex Mahumet Pseudoprophete* (*The Law of Muhammad the Pseudo-Prophet*), c. 1143.[29]

28. See, for example, Stephen O'Shea, *Sea of Faith: Islam and Christianity in the Medieval Mediterranean World* (New York: Walker, 2006).

29. Adam S. Francisco rightly states that "Robert's translation is best described

3. Roger Bacon (c. 1214–1294) reluctantly acknowledged that he was deeply influenced by Islamic scientists and Jewish scholars in the tradition of Ibn Sina, Ibn Rushd, and Musa bin Maimun (Moses Maimonides).

4. Thomas Aquinas (c. 1225–1274), as already noted, wrote *Summa contra gentiles*—a philosophical apologetic, even polemic, against the Jews and Muslims (Moors) in Spain, and in defense of Christianity.[30] He also targeted the Greek masters (whom he later used in *Summa theologica*, particularly Aristotle) and Islamic scholars, especially Ibn Rushd, with whom he remained engaged throughout his life.[31] Some of his central epistemological and hermeneutical roots and contributions were deeply influenced by Islam.

5. Ramon Llull (c. 1232–1315) was a missionary to the Muslims in North Africa and wrote *Liber del gentile e dels tres savis* (*Book of the Pagan and the Three Sages*, 1277), in which a Jew, a Christian, and a Muslim each make an apologetic of their respective religion to a Pagan.[32]

6. Ricoldo of Montecroce (c. 1243–1320) was a Dominican missionary to Muslims in Baghdad. He wrote the *Contra legem*

as a paraphrase and, likewise, that it served to fuel the majority of medieval anti-Muslim polemics"; see his *Martin Luther and Islam: A Study in Sixteenth-Century Polemics and Apologetics* (Leiden: Brill, 2007), 12.

30. It is worth mentioning that while dealing with revelation, the Vatican Council of 1869–70 employed almost verbatim Thomas's treatment on the subject in this work. I find it very fascinating that most of the Christian polemics against Islam make some reference to, or repeat the argument of this work even today, without either having read this material or having any knowledge of the work itself or even of its existence.

31. He later wrote two further works against Ibn Rushd and radical Aristotelianism: *De unitate intellectus, contra Averroistas* (The Unicity of Intellect, against the Averroists; 1270) in which he blasted Averroism as incompatible with Christian doctrine; and *De aeternitate mundi contra murmurantes* (On the Eternity of the World, against Grumblers; 1270–72), which dealt with the controversial Averroist and Aristotelian theory of the *beginninglessness* of the universe.

32. Samuel M. Zwemer (who taught mission at Princeton Theological Seminary and later had a mission institute at Fuller Seminary named after him) considered Llull to be the first missionary to Muslims. Cf. *Raymond Lull: First Missionary to the Moslems* (New York: Funk & Wagnalls, 1902).

Saracenorum (*Against the Religion of the Saracens*), a comprehensive refutation of Islam, which was translated into German by Martin Luther in 1542. Ricoldo attempted to translate the Qur'an, although it is not known whether he completed it.

7. Juan de Segovia (c. 1400–1458) was concerned about finding the best way of converting Muslims to Christianity. For this he commissioned a translation of the Qur'an into Castilian, which he then translated into Latin; presumably it forms the basis for his *De mittendo gladio divini Spiritus in corda Sarracenorum* (*On Driving the Sword of the Holy Spirit into the Hearts of the Saracens*)—a refutation of the Qur'an.[33]

8. Nicholas of Cusa (c. 1401–1464) wrote *De pace fidei* (*On the Peace of Faith*), shortly after the Turkish capture of Constantinople in 1453. He argued that the true faith can be manifested in different religions, specifically including Islam, although Christianity is, of course, the greatest of these. He also wrote *Cribratio Alchorani* (*Sifting the Koran*, c. 1460), a detailed review of Ketton's Latin translation of the Qur'an, which he used to prove the superiority of Christianity, but he did treat Judaism and Islam as sharing in the truth. Despite this openness, Nicholas fully supported Pope Pius II's call for a new crusade against the Turks, even when crusades were being broadly questioned.

9. There was a tradition that viewed Islam as a mirror provided for the critical self-reflection of Christendom, and as a rod of God, just as Assyria was for Israel in Jeremiah and Isaiah.[34] This attitude was especially present in the works of John Wycliffe (c. 1320–1384) and to some extent in Erasmus of Rotterdam (c. 1466/69–1536).

While Peter the Venerable, Ketton, Bacon, Aquinas, and Nicholas of Cusa lived exclusively in the context of "Christian Europe," Llull lived and worked in Spain and North Africa, Ricoldo of Montecroce worked in Baghdad, and John of Segovia in Spain, i.e., in an

---

33. See Leonard Patrick Harvey, *Islamic Spain, 1250 to 1500* (Chicago: University of Chicago Press, 1990), 79–85.

34. Esp. Isaiah 10:5 and Jeremiah 2:46.

Islamic context. What is surprising is that they were allowed to operate in these Muslim contexts without being seriously threatened, especially since many of their texts were quite derogatory toward Islam. This may reflect an unacknowledged level of tolerance in the Islamic context, which certainly was not always reciprocated toward the Muslims living in Christian contexts. However, it should be recognized that the schools of Ibn Sina, Ibn Rushd, and Al Ghazali, etc., were able to operate in Paris and Naples, epistemologically influencing almost all of Europe.

The Islamic Problem

The existence of Islam posed far-reaching problems for medieval Christendom and for the Reformation at every level. It posed a practical political problem in terms of needing to discern between the competing possibilities of crusade, conversion (mission), coexistence, and commercial interchange. And the mystery of its existence was a theological problem: What was Islam's providential role in history? Was it a symptom of the world's last days or a stage in Christian development? A heresy, a schism, or a new religion? The product of a highly venal and morally corrupt person (viz., Muhammad) or even the devil himself? An obscene parody of Christianity? Or a system of thought that deserved to be treated with respect? As a geographically and numerically growing post-Christian religion, it challenged the claim to the absolute and final efficacy of Christianity. It also challenged the Christian claim (and its Jewish antecedents) of being God's special chosen/providential people. It claimed both a continuity with, and an abrogation of, the "Judeo-Christian heritage," and an ultimate fulfillment of these religions. All this was deeply perplexing and caused a crisis of faith for the West and for Christianity.

Norman Daniel, a philosopher, political theorist, and ethicist at Harvard University, writing about the Western "scientific" approach toward Islam, rightly advises us that "even when we read the more detached scholars, we need to keep in mind how medieval Christendom argued, because it has always been and still is part of the makeup of every western mind brought to bear on the subject."[35] From a very different perspective, Colin Chapman, an evangelical missionary who spent time in the Near East School of Theology and London Bible College, writes that "[a]t the time of the Reformation, Protestants saw Islam alongside Roman Catholicism as embodiments of the Antichrist, while Catholics saw in Islam many of the features they hated most in the Protestants. Then, with the coming of the Enlightenment, the rationalists took their turn to denigrate Islam and pour scorn on the Prophet."[36] What is consistent in these two critical quotes, from highly divergent sources, is the ubiquitous anti-Islamic attitude and negative judgment that has been the West's epistemic normative over several centuries, even though these Western interlocutors themselves have different and antagonistic ideological starting points toward each other.

Given medieval Christianity's wishful belief that after Constantine's conversion (a clear sign of God and proof of Christianity's efficaciousness) Europe was a monoreligious milieu, it therefore lacked any real epistemological resources to counter Islam. On the whole, Europe had neither the knowledge of the main sources of Islam nor the linguistic abilities to access them. This was true despite some three hundred years of crusades and quite a long duration of dwelling in the Middle East, as well as several centuries of dealing with Muslim neighbors within Europe. Their cultural prejudices and the fear of contamination (syncretism) generated by the church in its polemics for the crusades kept the West steeped in ignorance and at the same time increasingly frightened of Islam. The plethora of anti-Jewish polemical literature failed to provide an adequate epistemology to deal with the challenges posed by Islam because Judaism was a pre-Christian religion and as such could simply occupy the space of *praeparatio evangelica* (preparation for the gospel). Islam, as a post-Christian religion, however, had to be understood differently: through a biblical prism, as part of the negative apocalyptic elements

35. Norman Daniel, *Islam and the West: The Making of an Image* (Edinburgh: Edinburgh University Press, 1960; rev. ed. 1993), 326.

36. Colin Chapman, *Islam and the West: Conflict, Coexistence or Conversion?* (London: Paternoster, 1998), 11.

signaling the end of the world, or as a mirror for self-critical reflection, or as the rod of God punishing Christendom for its transgressions. Islam was willfully misunderstood and deliberately misrepresented (which now forms a millennia-long hermeneutical tradition of its own, with its own effective history—*Wirkungsgeschichte*). In different places, Luther argued each of these positions. Conversely, Calvin barely mentions Islam and the Muslims, but when he does he mostly follows Luther's assessment, and whenever he does make his own judgment, it is invariably negative.

Islam and Judaism in the Reformation

The anti-Jewish and anti-Islamic sentiments prevalent during the Crusades continued into the Reformation period, as is evident in Luther's writings and later in Calvin. Both seriously polemicized against Islam, but even more significantly, they both saw Islam as a judgment of God upon a highly corrupt and venal Christianity, especially Roman Catholicism. Therefore Luther called Islam "the rod of God." Writing as early as 1518 Luther says, "To fight against the Turk is the same as resisting God, who visits our sin upon us with this rod."[37] So in response to Pope Leo X's call for a new crusade against the Ottoman Turks, Luther, in *Resolutiones disputationum de indulgentiarum virtute*, argues: "Many, however, even the 'big wheels' in the church, now dream of nothing else than war against the Turk. They want to fight, not against iniquities, but against the lash of iniquity and thus they would oppose God who says that through that lash he himself punishes us for our iniquities because we do not punish ourselves for them."[38] His opposition to the crusades was not because of any

---

37. See Sarah Henrich and James L. Boyce, "Martin Luther—Translations of Two Prefaces on Islam: Preface to the Libellus de ritu et moribus Turcorum (1530), and Preface to Bibliander's Edition of the Qur'ān (1543)," *Word & World* 16, no. 2 (Spring 1996): 250–66; see esp. 252, footnote 3 quoting from the *Explanations of the Ninety-Five Theses* in *Luther's Works*, trans. Harold J. Grimm and Helmut T. Lehmann, vol. 31 (Philadelphia: Muhlenberg and Fortress, 1957), 79–252, esp. 91–92.

38. See *Explanations of the Disputation Concerning the Value of Indulgences*, popularly known as the *Explanations of the Ninety-Five Theses*, 92.

pacifism toward Islam but rather because of his vociferous opposition to the corruption of the sale of indulgences that financed these crusades. Following the defeat of Belgrade (1521) and Hungary (1526) by the Ottomans, Luther had already called upon the Holy Roman Emperor, Charles V, to wage war against the Turks.[39] Nonetheless, as late as 1529, in *On War against the Turk*, he still describes the Turks as the "rod of God's wrath" by which "God is punishing the world."[40]

Luther saw Islam as a deceitful and murderous religion advocating utter disregard for marriage, and as the enemy of Christianity. However, he felt that many of these failings were not unique to the Turks, but were traits equally prevalent in the papacy, among the Jews, and even among the radical reformers. He saw Islam, along with Catholicism, as "the second horn on the head of the devil." For Luther, the Turks were thus both the rod of God's wrath and also of Satan. Both these seemingly paradoxical positions vis-à-vis Islam were maintained by Luther and followed by Calvin.[41] As George Forell argues, "For Luther the devil was always God's devil, i.e., in attempting to counteract God the devil ultimately serves God."[42] So Satan (and thereby the Turks) was being used by God for God's purposes. This was further confirmed by an unjust war carried out exclusively for aggressive purposes (which is the devil's *modus operandi*), rather than defensively. Thus the Turks were, according to Luther, the instrument "with which God is punishing the world as he often does through wicked scoundrels, and sometimes through godly people."[43]

Francisco points out that Luther rarely talks about the Turks without also mentioning the papacy:

39. Some have even suggested that the Reformation hymn, "A Mighty Fortress Is Our God" (c. 1527–29), based on Psalm 46, was written in the context of the Turkish siege of Vienna in 1529.

40. As quoted by Henrich and Boyce, "Martin Luther—Translations of Two Prefaces on Islam," 252.

41. See Amjad-Ali, "Debilitating Past."

42. George Forell, "Luther and the War against the Turks," in *Martin Luther, Theologian of the Church: Collected Essays*, ed. William Russell (St. Paul: Luther Seminary, 1994), 127.

43. *On War against the Turk*, in *Luther's Works*, 46:170. See Francisco, *Martin Luther and Islam*, 80.

His colleagues recorded him as suggesting that both were the Antichrist. "The Pope is the spirit of the Antichrist, and the Turk is the flesh of the Antichrist. They both help each other to choke [us], the latter with body and soul, the former with doctrine and spirit."[44] In his own writings . . . he viewed the Pope as the Antichrist whereas the Turks were another sort of demonic aberration. Along with the rest of the Muslim world, they were followers of the beast of Apocalypse 20:10, which was Muhammad. The situation, according to Luther's exegesis of the passage was thus: Muhammad's kingdom (the beast) reigned in the East and the papacy (the false prophet of Antichrist) reigned in the West. Both were poised under the command of Satan waiting for orders to commence the final assault upon the church. "Because the end of the world is at hand," he wrote, "the Devil must attack Christendom with both of his forces." Yet, interestingly, and probably due to proximity, Luther almost always viewed the papacy as the bigger threat than Muhammad and the Turks. He often remarked that compared to the Pope, "Muhammad appears before the world as a pure saint." Nevertheless, both played an integral role in his eschatological view of history and his assessment of the nature of the Turkish threat.[45]

In spite of all this, Luther is one of the earliest of the major Western theologians to acknowledge the critical role of Islam, even as he faced its threat and imminent conquest of Europe. This is present in many of his writings and not, as is so often portrayed, exclusively in his *On War against the Turk*. Luther advised that "in whatever way possible the religion and customs of 'Muhammadanism' be published and spread abroad."[46] It is particularly fascinating to recall that Luther toward the end of his life in 1543 was critically

---

44. *D. Martin Luthers Werke: Tischreden*, 6 vols. (Weimar: Bohlau, 1912–21), 1:135.15–17: "Papa est spiritus Antichristi, et Turca est caro Antichristi. Sie helffen beyde einander wurgen, hic corpore et gladio, ille doctrina et spiritu"; cf. also 3:158.31–35.

45. Francisco, *Martin Luther and Islam*, 83–84.

46. Henrich and Boyce, "Martin Luther—Translations of Two Prefaces on Islam," 255.

instrumental in the publication of a new translation of the Qur'an into Latin by Theodore Bibliander.[47]

Bibliander, upon Luther's request, published a reworked version of Ketton's Latin Qur'an. In 1542, Luther used his influence to persuade the Council of Basel to lift the ban on this translation, which they did on the condition that both Luther and Melanchthon write prefaces to it. Bibliander's Qur'anic translation was finally published in 1543 along with these prefaces. Henrich and Boyce summarize: "The main burden of Luther's preface . . . was to argue once again for the clear presentation of the teachings of Muhammad so that by contrast they might be more readily refuted by the clear teachings of the church about Christ, the incarnation, his death for our sins, and the resurrection, and so that Christians might thereby be armed in conflict with the enemy by a sure and certain knowledge of the central tenets of their own faith."[48] For Luther regarded the Qur'an as a "foul and shameful book,"[49] and sought to translate it in order to expose its perversities.

Besides these warnings and critiques, Luther at the very end of his preface writes:

In this age of ours how many varied enemies have we already seen? Papist defenders of idolatry, the Jews, the multifarious monstrosities of the Anabaptists, *Servetus*, and others. Let us now prepare ourselves against Muhammad. But what can we say about matters that are still outside our knowledge? Therefore, it is of value for the learned[50] to read the writings of the enemy in

47. Born in Bischofszell, Switzerland, Theodor Buchmann is known by his Greek name of Theodore Bibliander, a common practice (along with Latin) to raise the status of the person in middle Europe.

48. Henrich and Boyce, "Martin Luther—Translations of Two Prefaces on Islam," 256.

49. *Luther's Works*, 46:176.

50. Therefore, contrary to his emphasis on *lingua franca*, Luther wanted the new translation of the Qur'an in Latin and not German, holding to the traditional distinction between *lingua sacra* and *lingua popularis*. This was perhaps more a way of maintaining the distinction between the *lingua intelligentia/academia* and the *lingua popularis*.

order to refute them more keenly, to cut them to pieces and to overturn them, in order that they might be able to bring some to safety, or certainly to fortify our people with more sturdy arguments.[51]

So Luther's approach was to attempt to overcome the existing lacuna of knowledge vis-à-vis the religion of the Turks. According to Southern, this was because "he looked forward to the probability that Christendom would be engulfed in Islam"[52] and thus Christians should prepare themselves to live under this enemy. Luther had earlier argued, in his preface to *Libellus de ritu et moribus Turcorum* (*Tract on the Rites and Customs of the Turks*, 1530):[53]

> Since we now have the Turk and his religion at our very doorstep our people must be warned lest, either moved by the splendor of the Turkish religion and the external appearances of their customs or displeased by the meager display of our own faith or the deformity of our customs, they deny their Christ and follow Muhammad.[54]

Earlier in the text he argues,

> [W]e see that the religion of the Turks or Muhammad is far more splendid in ceremonies—and, I might almost say, in customs— than ours, even including that of the religious or all the clerics. The modesty and simplicity of their food, clothing, dwellings, and everything else, as well as the fasts, prayers, and common gatherings of the people that this book reveals are nowhere seen among us . . . which of our monks, be it a Carthusian (they who

51. Henrich and Boyce, "Martin Luther—Translations of Two Prefaces on Islam," 266, emphasis added, as Servetus is of critical importance in Calvin's encounter with Islam.

52. R. W. Southern, *Western Views of Islam in the Middle Ages* (Cambridge, MA: Harvard University Press, 1962, 3rd printing 1982), 105–6.

53. A tract originally published in 1481.

54. Henrich and Boyce, "Martin Luther—Translations of Two Prefaces on Islam," 260.

wish to appear the best) or a Benedictine, is not put to shame by the miraculous and wondrous abstinence and discipline among their religious? Our religious are mere shadows when compared to them, and our people clearly profane when compared to theirs. *Not even true Christians, not Christ himself, not the apostles or prophets ever exhibited so great a display.* This is the reason why many persons so easily depart from faith in Christ for Muhammadanism and adhere to it so tenaciously. I sincerely believe that no papist, monk, cleric, or their equal in faith would be able to remain in their faith if they should spend three days among the Turks.[55] . . . *Indeed, in all these things the Turks are by far superior.*[56]

Very high praise indeed! Though clearly for a negative *telos*. As such, he saw nothing of value in Islam; in spite of its moral piety and good behavior, it could not be salvific, for salvation only comes through Christ. Thus he displays the overall medieval tendencies to always judge Islam negatively, though at times he does reluctantly assert a more positive interpretation.

In his earlier writings Luther did not explicitly endorse or condemn the various military measures taken against the Turks, as such, but he rejected completely the idea of a *new crusade*. When George Spalatin solicited his opinion in 1518 vis-à-vis the papal plans for another crusade against the Turks, he responded,

If I rightly understand you, you ask whether an expedition against the Turks can be defended by me on biblical grounds. Even supposing the war should be undertaken for pious reasons rather than for gain, I confess that I cannot promise what you ask, but rather the opposite. . . . It seems to me if we must have any Turkish war, we ought to begin with ourselves. In vain we wage carnal wars without, while at home we are conquered by

55. Despite all his negativity about Islam, here Luther unwittingly sees conversion to Islam based on its virtue and morality rather than the usually assumed cause of such conversion based on the sword.

56. Henrich and Boyce, "Martin Luther—Translations of Two Prefaces on Islam," 259, emphasis added.

spiritual battles. . . . Now that the Roman Curia is more tyranni-
cal than any Turk, fighting with such portentous deeds against
Christ and against his Church, and now that the clergy is sunk
in the depth of avarice, ambition and luxury, and now that the
face of the Church is everywhere most wretched, there is no hope
of a successful war or of victory. As far as I can see, God fights
against us; first, we must conquer him with tears, pure prayers,
holy life and pure faith.[57]

Luther's denouncement of the papacy and its demand for a
popular crusade/holy war in the face of imminent Turkish inva-
sion had already angered the Catholic Church. In 1518, Luther went
so far as to publicly declare "that the Pope was not only a 'tyrant'
of Christianity but also the 'Antichrist.'"[58] He made matters worse
when, in 1520, he hyperbolized that the true "Turks" were the pope's
servants, his "lackeys and whores."[59] The pope's response to this
sustained attack was to threaten to excommunicate Luther in 1520.
Among Luther's many alleged heretical and scandalous teachings,
denounced by the papacy in the bull *Exsurge Domine* (1520), was
a summary of an early statement he had made with regard to the
Turks: "[T]o fight against the Turks is to fight against God's visita-
tion upon our iniquities."[60]

Luther's response to the papal bull of excommunication was
to maintain that

This article does not mean that we are not to fight against the
Turk, as that holy manufacturer of heresies, the pope charges. It
means, rather, that we should mend our ways and cause God to

57. *Luther's Correspondence*, 1:140–41, as quoted in Francisco, *Martin Luther
and Islam*, 68.

58. Francisco, *Martin Luther and Islam*, 69, quoting *Eyn Sermon von den newen
Testament*, in *Luther's Works*, 35:107.

59. *Luther's Works*, 35:90.

60. "Exsurge Domine," in *Quellen zur Geschichte des Papsttums und das rö-
mische Katholizismus*, 2nd ed., ed. Carl Mirbt (Tübingen: J. C. B. Mohr, 1901), 184.
Pope Leo X also sent a letter to Elector Frederick accompanying the bull, claiming
that Luther "favors Turks." See Francisco, *Martin Luther and Islam*, 70n11.

be gracious to us. We should not plunge into war, relying on the pope's indulgence with which he has deceived Christians in the past and is deceiving them still. . . . All the pope accomplishes with his crusading indulgences and his promises of heaven is to lead Christians with their lives into death and with their souls into hell. This is, of course, the proper work of the Antichrist. God does not demand crusades, indulgences, and wars. He wants us to live good lives. But the pope and his followers run from goodness faster than from anything else, yet he wants to devour the Turks. . . . This is the reason why our war against the Turks is so successful—so that where he formerly held one mile of land he now holds a hundred. But we still do not see it, so completely have we been taken by this Roman leader of the blind.[61]

This does not mean that Luther was a pacifist, something for which he strongly condemned the Anabaptists. Rather, he endorsed a military response against the Turks. See, for example, the *Türkenbüchlein*—the so-called Turkish writings, the most well known of which is *Vom Kriege wider die Türken* (*On War against the Turks*) in 1529. He writes the latter in order to counter those "stupid preachers amongst us Germans . . . who are making us believe that we ought not and must not fight. Some are even so foolish to say that it is not proper for Christians to bear the temporal sword or to be rulers . . . some actually want the Turk to come and rule because they think our *German people are wild and uncivilized*."[62] With Suleiman I's conquest of Belgrade in 1521 and the Kingdom of Hungary in 1526, and the (repelled) Ottoman attack on Vienna in 1529, the threat of Ottoman occupation of Western Europe became very serious indeed. It was not so much a question of a crusade against the Turks (i.e., an offensive attack on Turkish territory outside of Europe), but rather now a very real possibility of having to defend their territory against Ottoman occupation.

61. *Luther's Works*, 32:89–91, as quoted in Francisco, *Martin Luther and Islam*, 70. The pope officially excommunicated Luther in 1521 via the bull *Decet Romanum Pontificen*.

62. *Luther's Works*, 46:161–62, emphasis added.

In *On War against the Turk*, Luther reconfirmed that his earlier position (i.e., that Christians must fight their wars by spiritual means, through repentance and reform) was because the pope promoted this war as a Holy War (crusade) to be undertaken in the name of Christ, which he found blasphemous. He then argues they must fight the Turks, but only as part of their *secular* vocation: not as a crusade, a holy war against the Turkish religion, but rather a secular war, led by secular leaders, against an invader. If one were to go to war against heresy, one would have to start with Roman Catholicism. "Let the Turk believe and live as he will, just as one lets the papacy and other false Christians live."[63] Now, he urged everyone to take up arms against the Turks, not as a religious issue but as an issue of vocation. In *Eine Heerpredigt wider den Türken* (*An Army Sermon against the Turks*), 1530, Luther encourages Christians to embrace the vocation of soldiery, because "[s]uch a person should know that they were merely defending themselves 'against the Turks in a war started by them,' which they were entitled and even obliged to do . . . for in battling the Turks one was 'fighting against an enemy of God and a blasphemer of Christ, indeed, the Devil himself.'"[64]

Two of the central tenets of Luther's theology (i.e., the Two Kingdoms, and the concept of *vocatio Dei*) were, I believe, deeply

---

63. *Luther's Works*, 46:185–86.

64. Francisco, *Martin Luther and Islam*, 77, quoting *Eine Heerpredigt wider den Türken* in *Luther's Werken* 30/2:173.4–5, 9. This argument by Luther has been used by some contemporary Lutherans pushing for a reworking of the "just war theory" outside the Catholic parameters; see esp. the "Foreword" by Charles Lutz to John H. Yoder's *When War Is Unjust: Being Honest in Just-War Thinking* (Maryknoll, NY: Orbis, 1996), and Gary Simpson, *War, Peace and God: Rethinking the Just-war Tradition* (Minneapolis: Augsburg Fortress, 2007). These Lutherans, among many others, find pacifism an anathema to Christian faith, based on Luther's concept of soldiery as a vocation. So for different reasons Lutherans and Catholics both have a theological place for a just war theory. Both are against the pacifism of the Anabaptists, Quakers, et al., which they see as violative of church doctrine. Elsewhere I have argued that this doctrine has no foundation in the biblical witness (especially the New Testament) or the church's *traditio* as such, but is rather based on Cicero's seminal position on this subject, which should be irrelevant for a theology claiming *sola scriptura*. See my "Jihad and Just War Theory: Dissonance and Truth," *Dialog: A Journal of Theology* 48, no. 3 (Fall 2009): 239–47.

influenced by the Turkish threat and the responses it generated from the Catholics invoking the crusade, or, conversely, the pacifism of the Anabaptists. The latter, while agreeing with Luther that Islam was indeed the rod of God to purge Christianity of its sin and calumny, saw his resistance against the Turks as un-Christian, and against God's ordination and design. Unlike the Anabaptists, who were not worried about how they were perceived, Luther still needed the support of the people, especially his princely friends, and thus his correspondence with the Reverend Spalatin mentioned above. Therefore, he develops a very novel and creative idea of seeing a broader notion of *vocatio Dei*, rather than the extant exclusive understanding restricting vocation to sacramental priestly duties. It is through this notion of soldiery as a vocation, and the vocation of a soldier, that Luther reconfigures the notion of just war theory away from the Catholic notion of a religious war, and refutes the Anabaptist position of total pacifism. For Luther, therefore, at issue is not so much a definition of warring itself, but of two sets of governance—civil and religious, as well as the notion of the Christian vocation being larger than residing exclusively in the priesthood. Warring is thus in the domain of the civil governance and to be initiated and conducted by this side of the two kingdoms and not to be undertaken as a holy war or crusade initiated by the church.

Calvin's Attitude toward Islam

The Turkish threat must have been very real for Calvin, since he was only twenty when the siege of Vienna took place. Furthermore, Hungary, which had been under constant threat by the Ottomans since their victory at the Battle of Mohacs in 1526, was of particular existential importance to Calvin. For Hungary had a strong Lutheran, and later Calvinist, presence, and reformers elsewhere in Europe provided significant funding for the war there against the Ottoman Turks. So when Francis I of France in 1536 made a Franco-Ottoman alliance with Suleiman the Magnificent, against the Holy Roman Empire, it caused Calvin serious consternation, further exacerbated by the fall of Buda in 1541.

All this is to say that it is quite surprising that Calvin, a humanist with legal training, shows only a very cursory understanding of Islam. People like Jan Slomp[65] predictably justify Calvin on the grounds that he had little opportunity to come into contact with Muslims and to know Islam. This, however, does not explain the sheer lack of inquiry, or simple curiosity, apologetics, and even polemics, vis-à-vis the most persistent and longstanding enemy and threat to Europe, especially in light of Luther's immense "intellectual curiosity." Calvin clearly shows the influence of medieval polemics, and like Luther, largely rearticulates them, but with little or no appreciation for Islam whatsoever. So Calvin follows Luther's tack that Europe should defend itself against the Turks without an aggressive war or crusade-like situation, and the church should organize days of prayers and penitence.

A major stigma on Calvin's career in Geneva was the execution of Michael Servetus,[66] burnt as a heretic in 1553. Servetus, a Spaniard, was truly a renaissance man, well educated in many fields, and best known for his contributions to theology and medicine, a field heavily influenced by Muslims. His theology ran him afoul of Calvin, because he decried Trinitarian monotheism in order to make a Christian apologetic to meet the needs of Jewish and Islamic unitarian monotheism.[67] The Islamic influence behind his non-Trinitarian Christology has not received due scholarly attention, nor have Calvin's anti-Islamic sentiments, which clearly lie behind this travesty. During Servetus's trial, he was asked why he had studied the Qur'an and whether or not he believed it to be full of blasphemies.[68] This question, most probably authored by

65. Jan Slomp, "Calvin and the Turks," in *Christian-Muslim Encounters*, ed. Yvonne Yazbeck Haddad and Wadi Z. Haddad (Gainesville: University Press of Florida, 1995), 126–42.

66. Servetus was already evaluated very negatively by Luther, as mentioned above.

67. In 1531 he published *The Errors of the Trinity*.

68. See "The Complaint of Nicholas de la Fontaine against Servetus, 14 August, 1553," in *Translations and Reprints from the Original Sources of European History*, vol. 3 (Philadelphia: University of Pennsylvania History Department, 1907), 12–16, esp. 16: "*In the articles of the Procureur General are to be found several charges. . . .*

Calvin, indicates the perception of Servetus's heresy, for which he was ultimately executed, being informed by, and linked with, Islam. Further, Servetus critiqued Calvin's exclusion through double-predestination, which he felt violated the inclusive grace of God, and his understanding of inclusive Christology, which he said made grace available for both the Muslims and the Jews.

Both Calvin and Luther, though highly critical of Islam, encourage Christian believers to greater faithfulness by prescribing the zeal of Muslim faith practice. This acquires particular importance in Calvin because of his emphasis on sanctification, and perhaps the "third use of the law," which is reminiscent of the Muslim orthopractic obligations of piety, righteousness, and sanctification. Of course this recommendation does not come at any point as an overall appreciation of Islamic faith, doctrine, etc., and the condemnations are usually associated with the papists. What is interesting to note is that there seems to be little evidence in Calvin's work to suggest that Christians should either preach to Muslims or try to convert them. This lack of missionary zeal is equally valid for the papists and the Jews, all being apostates, and as such God's problem not ours.

Calvin's equation of the Turks and the papists is also based on their search for truth outside of the Scriptures, which is a litmus test applied equally against Turks, papists, and Jews. While for the latter this attack is based on their apostasy in denying the fulfillment of the Old Testament, the former two are accused of seeking sources outside the Bible as having revelatory power, and as sources for doctrine, theology, and guidance for faith praxes. For the Catholics, this extra-scriptural source is tied to their understanding of the sacramental role of the church as well as the Petrine office. For the Muslims, it is the Qur'an and Muhammad. Therefore for Calvin,

---

Among these are the following: 21. *Item*, whether he did not know that his doctrine was pernicious, considering that he favors the Jews and Turks, by making excuses for them, and if he has not studied the Koran in order to disprove and controvert the doctrine and religion that the Christian churches hold, together with other profane books, from which people ought to abstain in matters of religion, according to the doctrine of St. Paul. 22. *Item*, whether the said book Koran is not a bad book, full of blasphemies."

all three have to be attacked not only because they are wrong and apostate but also because they deny two things central to his theology: (1) the centrality and coherence of the Scriptures in themselves; and (2) the God of the Scriptures, which is the Father, the Son, and the Holy Spirit.

Interestingly, in terms of epistemology, Calvin has more similarities with the Muslims than with papists and even Lutherans, dare I say.[69] For him, the canonical Scripture, as the word of God, seemed to acquire a status that Luther was never willing to give it, despite the latter's emphasis on *sola scriptura*. Luther had developed his own *Antilegomena* of Hebrews, James, Jude, and Revelation, claiming they violated key Protestant doctrines such as *sola gratia* and *sola fidei*. Unlike the Catholics, and along with Luther, Calvin acknowledged no source of revelation and grace other than Jesus, and vicariously the Scriptures. At times though, Calvin seems to elevate the text to such a high revelatory status that the secondary *logos tou theou* (the word of God, i.e., the Scriptures) almost seems equal to the primary *logos tou theou* (i.e., Jesus Christ). In Islam, the Qur'an is the primary *logos tou theou* (*kalam allah*), but this is the direct word of God unmediated through human agency except the Prophet Muhammad who simply recited the message (*iqra*—from which comes the word "Qur'an") given to him by the angel of God; he had no role in writing it. Again unlike Luther, Calvin demands a certain piety and sanctification for the believers normally referred to as the "third use of the law" (which for Luther was clearly an anathema against the comprehensive power of grace, which he articulated in his call of *sola gratia* and *sola fidei* [by grace alone and by faith alone] the latter itself being the gift of grace). Thus Calvin's understanding of sanctification and piety is similar to that held in Islam.

Despite his lack of theological curiosity toward Islam, Calvin is particularly hostile toward Muhammad, regarding him as a de-

---

69. See the works of James Anthony Froude, *Calvinism: An Address Delivered at St. Andrews, March 17, 1871* (New York: Charles Scribner & Co., 1871), and especially the great missiologist Samuel Zwemer, "Calvinism and Missionary Enterprise," *Theology Today* 7, no. 2 (July 1950): 206–16.

ceiver and corrupter who had led the Turks away from Christianity, toward a twisted and distorted heresy.[70] Thus Calvin described him as the "lawless one" of 2 Thessalonians 2:8.[71] He links Muhammad to the pope, calling him "the companion of the Pope," because both preach false doctrine and poison the minds and souls of the people.[72]

Nonetheless, it is quite possible to see parallels between Muhammad and Calvin. This is most clearly manifested in the way they conceived the relevance of their preaching and teaching for constructing their society, community, and even the state, which means the centrality of the divine injunction for the proper order of things.

A further point to note is that there has been continual bad interpretation of the Reformed double-predestinarian doctrinal heritage, especially in the US[73] and in Afrikaner Apartheid structures in South Africa. In both contexts Christians claiming a Calvinist heritage saw themselves as God's exclusively chosen people with the right to others' land and even labor (slavery), and they saw the original people as being under the permanent curse of the negating predestination. One finds Muslim scholars and apologists adopting a similar double-predestinarian approach in their present theorizing about Islamic states, the Muslims, and the modern world. They base their approach on a bad interpretation of the doctrine of *dar-ul-Islam* (the house of Islam) and *dar-ul-Harb* (the house of war), leading to internal and external policies similar to those followed by the early Calvinists.

Another issue that brings Calvin and Muslims together is the popularized social contribution, as seen through the works of Max

70. *Joannis Calvini, Opera Quae Supersunt Omnia*, ed. Wilhelm Baum, Eduard Cunitz, and Eduard Reuss (Neukirchen: Neukirchener Verlag der Buchhandlung des Erziehungsverein, 1863–1900), 54:138. From here on referred to as CO.

71. CO 52:197.

72. CO 53:340; also cf. CO 47:335.

73. Will Herberg, a Jewish theologian, rightly argues that in America everyone in significant ways, whether Jewish, Catholic, or Protestant, falls prey to this double-predestinarian theology and its justification. See Will Herberg, *Protestant, Catholic, Jew: An Essay in American Religious Sociology* (Garden City, NY: Doubleday, 1955).

Weber, especially *The Protestant Ethic and the Spirit of Capitalism.*[74] Weber sees a direct connection between Calvin's theology and emerging capitalism. When Calvin's social construct is deprived of his theological asceticism, it produces a rapacious capitalism and the iron cage of bureaucracy. Some Muslim scholars have argued that Islam has a similar ascetic ethics, and following Weber's approach, have regarded themselves as Islamic Calvinists, and see the blessings of God as a reward for their ascetic piety.[75] I think that Calvin actually makes a twofold move simultaneously: (1) to ask all Christians to develop a monastic morality; and (2) to do so without this morality becoming celibate asceticism. So in fact Calvin does away with the difference between the religious orders and the secular priests of the Catholic Church, for he sees the morality of the religious orders as the one applicable to all Christians as a part of the third use of the law, piety and sanctification. This understanding is very similar to that of Islam, which though seeing celibate asceticism as absolutely unacceptable, believes moral piety to be an absolute imperative.

Implications for Jews and Muslims Today

What is the relevancy of Reformation attitudes for Turks and Jews today? If the horrific appropriation of Luther's anti-Jewish sentiments by the Nazis is any indicator, critical awareness of the situation of the Muslim immigrants in Europe becomes vital. Germany acts as a paradigmatic microcosm for the rest of Europe. With the emergence of the totally new transcendent "united European identity" (*à la* US) overcoming the old Westphalian nationalist identities, the question of "the Other" becomes critical. This particularly applies to non-European immigrants (nationalized or otherwise), especially Muslims, and specifically the Turks in Germany. This has

74. Translated by T. Parsons (New York: Charles Scribner's Sons, 1976).

75. See Dorian Jones, "Islamic Calvinism and Industrialisation Meet in Turkey" (17 April 2007), at http://www.commongroundnews.org/article .php?id=20708&lan=en&sp=0, and Aasiya Lodhi, "Turkish Toil Brings New Form of Faith" (13 March 2006), at http://news.bbc.co.uk/2/hi/business/4788712.stm.

become even more crucial since September 11, 2001, with the ever-expanding Islamophobic rhetoric. The contemporary presence of Islam, and its growing radicalization, poses serious questions and challenges some of the fundamental assumptions behind liberal democracy and the human rights regime that has evolved over the past few centuries in Europe. Issues such as freedom of speech versus hate speech (e.g., the derogatory images of the Prophet Muhammad and the associated terroristic essentialization of Islam, *Charlie Hebdo*'s freedom of press and speech, and the parameters of hate speech against foreigners); the character of religious freedom in a post-Christian secular context; a question about the character of law (e.g., the issue of the scare-mongering sophistry of the imposition of Shariah law by Muslims upon secular Europe); the freedom of religion and expression embodied in the right to wear the veil versus the state imposition of a dress-code; the rise of (neo-Nazi) organizations like *PEGIDA*[76] and its xenophobic politics; nationalist political parties and their extreme xenophobia like Geert Wilders's *Partij voor de Vrijheid* and Marine Le Pen's *Front National*; etc. Such issues demand a serious reevaluation of democracy, the accepted human rights standards, as well as the recognition of the reconstructive role of immigrants in European history after the Second World War, and the appropriate compensatory justice in evaluating these contributory constructive roles.

Given the horrific history of the German Holocaust, with some level of cooperative commission by most of Europe, or at least their acquiescence through silence and omission, it is rightly not acceptable to make anti-Jewish statements or to deny the Holocaust;[77] these are justly perceived as hate crimes. The same cour-

76. *Patriotische Europäer gegen die Islamisierung des Abendlandes*, or Patriotic Europeans against the Islamization of the West.

77. Though when this valid restriction against the vilification of a people or individuals, i.e. Jews, is expanded to cover the state, i.e. Israel, moral or otherwise, it entails taking away the right of ethical discourse itself, which is a *sine qua non* for modern democracy and transparent and accountable governance. So if any critique of the state of Israel, even for its most immoral acts, is seen as a pejorative judgment against Jews, there is a serious confusion of categories. If this is not challenged, then the issue of restorative justice that lies behind this position is itself seriously

tesy, however, is not extended to the Muslim minorities that now actually reside in Europe. The highly negative language, imagery, and rhetoric that were once applied to the Jews are now used with impunity against Muslims and Islam, with little or no approbation against such practices.

In 2009 it was estimated by Germany's Federal Office for Migration and Refugees that there were 4.3 million Muslims in Germany (i.e., 5.2 percent of the overall population). Around 63 percent of these were of Turkish descent (i.e., 2.7 million, constituting 3.0 percent of the total population). About 65 percent of these Muslims were fully German citizens. And with the new refugee crisis of 2015, the situation is quickly changing to include more Muslims. This gives some sense of the contemporary numerical context of religious minorities in Germany, which becomes especially critical when compared to the Jewish population in pre–World War II Germany: "In pre-war central Europe, the largest Jewish community was in Germany, with about 500,000 members (0.75 percent of the total German population)."[78] If this small number of Jews was found unacceptable from 1933 onwards, and therefore there was widespread acceptance of the concentration camps and even genocide,[79] one wonders where the current, much larger, Turkish and Muslim presence could lead to, if some trigger is set off. Like the earlier *Judenfrage* (the Jewish Question) we are now facing the *Muslimfrage* (the Muslim Question), and the worry is that it could

---

damaged, if not totally nullified, and the idea of critical virtuous thought and citizenship itself is put into serious question. The lack of these rights was central in generating the crimes against the Jews in the first place. So when a critique of the state is seen as anti-Semitic and all critical conversation is shut down, then we have a major confusion between the people (*dēmos*) and the state (*basileia*). This curtails the core value of the ability of moral discourse against the state and its coercive and moral overreach.

78. See "Jewish Population of Europe in 1933: Population Data by Country," in the United States Holocaust Memorial Museum's *Holocaust Encyclopedia*, at http://www.ushmm.org/wlc/en/article.php?ModuleId=10005161.

79. For the comprehensive involvement of the German populace in this morally dark period in German history, see Daniel J. Goldhagen, *Hitler's Willing Executioners: Ordinary Germans and the Holocaust* (New York: Alfred A. Knopf, 1996).

be converted to a more violent structured removal of the contemporary "Others," like that exercised against the Jews during the Second World War.

In the contemporary context, the Turks in Germany are, on the one hand, a vulnerable, weak, and dependent ethnic and religious minority, like the Jews of Luther's (and Hitler's) times. They are at times treated with capricious disregard and high moral and social coercion. Because of the causal link of being initially a "lower/laboring class" and vulnerable ethnic minority, what Luther and the Reformation perceived about the *Ottoman* Turks does not apply directly to the contemporary *German* Turks. However, what he wrote about the Jews could be quite easily applied to them.

On the other hand, they are Muslims and thus, after the end of the Cold War and collapse of the Soviet Union, are the new binary enemy. They are therefore essentialized and stereotyped as part of the "War on Terror," and as a result the status of the Turks in Germany has undergone a major shift since September 11, 2001 (as is the case for all Muslim immigrants across Europe). From being a vulnerable, blue-collar labor force, and therefore somewhat tolerated for economic and social convenience, Muslims have now come to represent the new *Inbegriff der Feindschaft* (enemy-ness) with almost apocalyptic implications for what Western social values stand for, and therefore they are now seen as a threat and challenge to this "normative virtuous life."

Here, therefore, Luther's texts on the Ottoman Turks can be applied rather directly. This entailed a major shift, and with it new sets of prejudices: Islam and Muslims are no longer seen as a weak and vulnerable minority living in Europe in culturally and socially specific ghettos; rather now they are a highly hyperbolized threatening and very powerful enemy, both inside and outside, which could take over Europe at very short notice and impose their law (*Shariah*) on the local citizens and destroy the European values and achievements. So vis-à-vis the current European Islamic presence, both of Luther's approaches toward the Jews and the Turks have application and possibilities.

Prejudice against the Other and the Grace of God in Christ

In this chapter, I have attempted a hermeneutic of Luther's and Calvin's texts vis-à-vis the Jews and the Muslims (Turks), the historical events in which their writings emerged, and the overall context of their work, in order to radicalize the Reformation and shed critical light on their pre-judgments (the European *prejudicium*—to use Hans-Georg Gadamer's wonderful concept)[80] against "the Other." Behind this hermeneutical task is concern for the development of Reformation theology with the focus on the religious "Other(ness)" of the Jews and the Muslims (Turks) during that period, *and* what this then means for our own times. We must go beyond both the sanctification of the Reformation texts and events for generating doctrinal and dogmatic material and certitude, and also the self-justifying attitude we develop toward these Reformation texts. Rather the task should be to provide critical clues for our own self-understanding in our situation and in our time for a more virtuous approach to the contemporary "Other," so that justice and peace prevails.

In the Reformation fathers we see a high level of antipathy not just toward Islam, which of course has always been present even prior to the Reformation, but also toward the pope (Catholicism), Anabaptists, and Judaism. They use appalling, and for our present ears anachronistically crude language, idioms, and vocabulary. No amount of current justification or rationalization can, or should, protect these major figures of theology and church history vis-à-vis their vitriol and calumny. Those who do so end up giving either some very puerile arguments to defend them, or come across as still totally prejudiced with their petrified orthodoxy, having no ethical *nous* and little or no consciousness of the contemporary constraints of language, idiom, and metaphor. In the post-ecumenical and post-conciliar church, and a church living in post-Christendom (a fact oft stated, but seldom epistemologically recognized and followed), we cannot afford a theology that begins with exclusion, whatever the status of double-predestinarianism is in contemporary Calvinist

80. See his *Truth and Method* (New York: Seabury, 1975).

scholarship. We have experienced the horrendous implications of such exclusion even in the history of our times, and so can never see it as having any worth or place when doing theology from the foot of the cross.

Reformation theology, more than anything else, rightly emphasizes the sufficiency and universality of the grace of God in Christ. It also prepares us to openly acknowledge the overall inclusive character of the gospel of Jesus Christ and the centrality of the *missio Dei* in the context of that inclusivity. The Reformation understood this, preached it, and even developed mantras to this effect, but the Reformation was still a child—even though the last gasping child—of Christendom. Both the major reformers, Luther and Calvin, had drunk deeply from that fountain. So even though they talked about *sola gratia* and *sola fidei*, this was used for exclusivizing purposes rather than the radical inclusivity that such a theological concept must entail, for it is not based on human efforts, volition, or even ecclesial sacramental presence, but is located in the reconciling God of 2 Corinthians 5:17–21 and the kenotic God of the Philippian hymn (Philippians 2). This inclusivity has to be part of our piety, our sanctification, and should be seen as a Christian imperative and part of the third use of the law.

In recent history the shifting focus of theology, ecclesiology, and missiology has been seriously involved in the retrieval both of the ecumenical vocation as well as the imperative of inclusivity. Thus we have begun a very constructive dialogical relationship with the Catholics. For this we must be grateful to God. Even more radically, over the past seventy years or so, we have recognized the continuing sin that has taken place against Jews in the church for some seventeen hundred years, and its vilest full manifestation in the Holocaust. However, the latter is not always a true ecumenical discourse but rather it is often only undertaken out of guilt, which still undergirds our attitude toward the state of Israel, and therefore our total inability to challenge the very vices that we condemn in our recently coined, hyphenated understanding of the continuity of the Judeo-Christian faith.[81] For me the imperative is to develop

---

81. After much research, and challenges to my graduate students, the earliest

a sympathetic ear of inclusion, and a dialogical and vocational partnership for the sake of the world that God loves and for God's shalom/salaam. I hope this becomes part of the new imperative for understanding Reformation theology and part of its sanctification. Normally when I pose this to my colleagues and friends in the context of Islam, I am quickly reminded this will only happen when Islam also seeks it. This answer truly grieves me because our sanctification and piety cannot be based on reciprocity or *quid pro quo* theology; instead it must be a part of our faith expressing itself, and not dependent on what others do. Whether this is an imperative for Muslim faith praxis, piety, and sanctification is for them to decide and to struggle with, but it is clearly required of us, as part of the core imperative and the dialectic of love of God and love of neighbor. Even the worst antinomians among us have to recognize the absolute quality of these two commands. And yet when it comes to Muslims, whom we have maligned and hated for some fourteen hundred years, even at our best moment in history, the Reformation, we did not show any compassion or humanity toward them but continued unabated in our prejudices and our hatred. Should we continue in this prejudice and hatred, hiding behind the fact that it is part of our Reformation confessions, tradition, history, and heritage, or should we look to this same Reformation through its call for *ecclesia reformata, semper reformanda* (the church reformed and always to be reformed) to overcome these prejudices and seek out a brave new world? Just as we now see our Catholic and Jewish brothers and sisters as an integral part of our own theological biographical imperatives, isn't it also now time to consider Muslims as equally part of a contemporary biographical and theological reality, and see it as our theological and missiological imperative with that inclusive eye? Further, we must recognize the truth of their history: that Islam is not a new entrant on our horizon because of new immigrants, and the colonial legacy. Rather we have been intertwined in the foundational moments of our contemporary history and thought,

---

reference to anything Judeo-Christian that I have been able to find was in 1939. Prior to this that concept does not seem to exist and whenever Judaism was mentioned it was done so highly negatively.

especially as the churches of the Reformation. Such a task is both exciting and challenging, and may even jeopardize our security, and our sense of worth over against the other. But such an understanding comes from the depth of the theology of the cross, with its foundation in Golgotha and not in some monarchical pattern generated through Constantinian Christianity and its concomitant Christendom. It is not generated out of power to dominate and to win, but with the power to love and to die for, with a resurrection and Pentecostal hope for all.

2   Spaniards in the Americas

Las Casas among the Reformers

JOEL MORALES CRUZ

In 1517, a young priest angrily listed his demands before the church. His soul was aflame with prophetic indignation at the belligerent abuses he had witnessed, the exploitation of innocent souls in the pursuit of greed committed in the name of Christ. He pleaded his case with passion, aware that what were at stake were the very nature of the gospel and the well-being of his fellow humans. This scene is familiar to most of us who remember the origins of the Protestant Reformation, but this time the actors are different. The year that Martin Luther famously posted "The Ninety-Five Theses on the Power and Efficacy of Indulgences," Bartolomé de Las Casas (1484–1566) had left the island of Hispaniola for Spain to seek out Cardinal Jiménez de Cisneros (1436–1517).[1] Since the death of King Fernando the previous year, Cisneros had ruled Spain with a heavy hand before Fernando's grandson, the sixteen-year-old Carlos, later Charles V—Holy Roman Emperor—ascended the throne. But now he was dying, and Las Casas rushed to his side to seek his help on behalf of the dying and decimated native peoples of the New World.

---

1. Whether Luther posted them on October 31, 1517, on the door of the Castle Church or posted them by mail to Archbishop Albrecht of Brandenburg continues to be a scholarly debate.

The 500th anniversary of the Ninety-Five Theses by Martin Luther is an appropriate opportunity for retrospect and contemplation on the events that sundered the Western medieval church. Much has changed on this religious stage in five centuries. In that time not only has Protestantism splintered into innumerable self-dividing denominations and traditions, but the Roman Catholic Church itself undertook, in the Second Vatican Council, some of the very reforms that Martin Luther and his contemporaries demanded.[2] Additionally, Christianity, in its Catholic, Orthodox, and Protestant incarnations, has become a truly worldwide faith whose axis has shifted from northern Europe to its former colonies in Africa, Asia, and Latin America.[3] It is thus altogether fitting that we should explore the Reformation from these modern perspectives. In particular, we will seek to present a Latin American/Latin point of view, focusing on the role and contributions of the "Protector of the Indians," Bartolomé de Las Casas.

Traditional surveys of the Reformation emphasize the usual names: Martin Luther, Ulrich Zwingli, John Calvin, Menno Simmons, and Thomas Cranmer. More recently, contributions of women such as Katharina Schütz Zell, Argula von Grumbach, and even Katharina von Bora Luther have been explored. If the Catholic Reformation is included, mention is made of the Council of Trent, Ignatius of Loyola, and perhaps Teresa of Ávila. Yet strangely absent from this roll call of eminent figures is Bartolomé de Las Casas. Why? Several ideas come to mind.

In a field of study that tends to focus on systems of thought and where theological giants walked the earth, Las Casas is not known for his insights in the "Queen of Sciences." His most famous writings, in fact most of the corpus of his work, consists in the telling of history as propaganda in service toward the defense of the native peoples of the Americas.

Unlike his contemporaries, Las Casas did not begin a new

2. Such as the liturgy in the vernacular, the dissemination of the Bible, and communion in both kinds (bread and wine) to the laity.

3. Philip Jenkins, *The Next Christendom: The Coming of Global Christianity* (New York: Oxford University Press, 2002).

church, tradition, or religious order. He was no pious mystic or visionary. For most of his life he remained a Dominican friar, passionate in his calling to speak out on behalf of his beloved Indians. While engaging theology and ecclesial structures, he was involved in what many today would call "social justice issues."

Martin Luther never lived far from his place of birth. John Calvin spent most of his life in Geneva. Las Casas's sphere of influence, however, was the burgeoning Atlantic world. He regularly crossed the ocean between Spain and the Americas to fulfill his mission. Thus he is not someone quickly associated with the European Reformations. Nonetheless there are solid reasons for including Las Casas among the reformers, particularly if we reconsider our notions of a sixteenth-century Reformation and place him within that larger context.

Spain and Reformation

While the concept of a quincentenary marking the birth of Protestantism is an occasion for reflection, by definition it is one that privileges the reform movements of the late medieval/early modern periods that emerged from sixteenth-century northern Europe. The discussion around Luther's life, action, and legacy places Germany as the center of the Reformation—with Protestant Switzerland and England in close orbit.[4] As a result, the church reform movements that occurred in Spain and elsewhere are relegated to the periphery, if remembered at all. Yet what would happen if we stepped back and recentered those sixteenth-century Reformations? What if, for our purposes, the epicenter lay not in Wittenberg but in the kingdoms of Castile and Aragon as a newly united Spain stepped forward to create the modern era?

The concept of a reformation is one that has its roots in the classical period in the sense of returning to a better or more pristine

---

4. A significant exception to this rule is found in George Huntston Williams, *The Radical Reformation*, 3rd ed. (Kirksville, MO: Truman State University Press, 2000), where the author begins his survey in Spain.

condition. The conciliar movement of the fourteenth-century Western church urged an ethical reformation, one "in head and members." Late medieval writers appealed to the assumption that church and society had fallen on decadent times and that it was imperative that individuals return to an idealized past. In the sixteenth century, this concept was expanded to call for renewal in institutions and doctrine, as well as behavior.[5] Even before Luther's time, critics blasted corruption, nepotism, decadence, and various and sundry deadly sins from the clergy to the pope.[6] Spain was no different. The marriage of Isabella of Castile (1451–1504) and Fernando of Aragon (1452–1516) became the foundation for a united Spain. The monarchs, in particular Isabella, threw themselves into a reform of government and society. They brought the kingdom's debt and finances under control, reorganized the government, and reduced a rampant crime rate.[7] In the centuries of holy struggle against the Islamic presence in the southern part of the peninsula, Catholicism had become an integral feature of national identity. In 1492, with the support of the Church, Spain emerged victorious against the Muslim Kingdom of Granada, imbued with a sense of divine election and mission. The expulsion of the Jews in 1492 was part of that effort to create an ideologically united, pure Catholic state and coincided with Columbus's first voyage across the Atlantic.[8]

Yet the Catholic Church was not only the vehicle of reform but its object as well. Central to the efforts of the Catholic monarchs to this institution was Francisco Jiménez de Cisneros. Originally a secular churchman climbing the ecclesiastical ladder, at the age of

---

5. Carter Lindberg, *The European Reformations* (Oxford: Blackwell, 1996), 9.

6. Lindberg, *The European Reformations*, 41–55.

7. John Edwards, *Ferdinand and Isabella: Profiles in Power* (Harlow, UK: Pearson Education, 2005), 27–47.

8. Helen Rawlings, *Church, Religion, and Society in Early Modern Spain* (New York: Palgrave, 2002), 50. For more on the Spanish Reconquista and the voyages of exploration, see Joseph F. O'Callaghan, *Reconquest and Crusade in Medieval Spain* (Philadelphia: University of Pennsylvania Press, 2004); Hugh Thomas, *Rivers of Gold: The Rise of the Spanish Empire, from Columbus to Magellan* (New York: Random House, 2004); Henry Kamen, *Empire: How Spain Became a World Power, 1492–1763* (New York: HarperCollins, 2003).

forty-eight he gave up his worldly belongings and joined the Franciscan order, taking on a rigorous asceticism that he maintained the rest of his life. In 1492, Cisneros was called upon to serve as confessor to Queen Isabella, a position of trust that she relied upon not only for her spiritual counsel but for his advice in matters of state, including perhaps her decision to expel the Jews. Three years later Isabella secured for him the Archbishopric of Toledo, the seat of Catholicism in Spain. Unwilling to accept the position, Cisneros nonetheless submitted, but underneath the pomp and spectacle of his office maintained his austere lifestyle.[9]

With the backing of the queen and permission of the pope, Cisneros set out to reform the religious and secular orders, by pressure and force if necessary. Friars and monks were directed to give up their concubines, priests to preach on Sundays and reside in the town of their parishes; worldly goods were confiscated and sold to fund charitable institutions; in short, a program of religious austerity was imposed so forcefully that it was recounted that some friars fled to Africa with their companions and converted to Islam.[10] His zeal for a purified, Catholic Spain is evident in his tampering with the Treaty of Alhambra, which guaranteed to the Muslims of Granada religious toleration. Accompanied by the Inquisition, Cisneros journeyed to Granada in 1499 and forced the mass conversion of 50,000 of its population, giving them the choice between baptism and exile and setting the stage for the expulsion of Spain's Muslims in 1506.[11] After the death of Isabella, Cisneros remained loyal to Fernando through multiple court intrigues and was rewarded with the cardinal's hat and his appointment as Grand Inquisitor in 1507.[12]

Cisneros, however, represented more than the militant face of Christendom. In 1499, he secured a papal bull from Alexander VI

---

9. Rawlings, *Church, Religion, and Society*, 149; M. K. Van Lennep, *La Historia de la Reforma en España en el Siglo XVI*, trans. Jorge Fleidner (Kalamazoo, MI: Subcomisión Literatura Cristiana, 1984), 36–38.

10. Marcel Batallon, *Erasmo y España*, trans. Antonio Alatorre (Mexico City: Fondo de Cultura Económica, 1937, 1950, 1996), 2–10; Van Lennep, *La Historia de la Reforma*, 39–40.

11. Rawlings, *Church, Religion, and Society*, 15.

12. Rawlings, *Church, Religion, and Society*, 149.

reorganizing the school at Alcalá de Henares, first established in 1293, into a full university whose degrees would be recognized throughout Europe. Now named the Complutensian University, throughout the sixteenth century it became a seat of humanism and scholarship across Europe.[13] Cisneros edited and published the first printed editions of the Mozarabic Rite and breviary, a version of the Latin Mass dating to the seventh century and peculiar to Spain.[14] His greatest intellectual accomplishment, however, was the creation of the Complutensian Polyglot Bible, which he undertook at his personal expense in order to revive the study of the Scriptures. Cisneros amassed a collection of biblical manuscripts and invited the top scholars of his day to gather at the university to edit and compile what would eventually become a six-volume set containing the Hebrew, Greek, Aramaic, and Latin versions of the Old and New Testaments in parallel columns, complete with dictionaries and lexical aids. The Greek New Testament of this collection, though predating that of Erasmus of Rotterdam's (1456–1536) 1516 influential edition, did not see the light of day until 1520 through an accident of technical bureaucracy.[15]

The role of Erasmus of Rotterdam in relation to the reform movements of Spain is difficult to deny and hard to completely gauge. The scholarly pursuits of Christian humanism, with its emphasis upon a return *ad fontes*, to the original sources of Christian inspiration—the Hebrew and Greek biblical manuscripts and the writings of the church fathers—were clearly valued by churchmen such as Jiménez de Cisneros. Beginning in 1516, Erasmus of Rotterdam in particular was celebrated among Spanish humanists for his Greek New Testament.[16] The other side to Erasmus, however, was his biting critique of the Renaissance papacy, ecclesiastical structures, monasticism, and clerical abuse, and his emphasis on

13. Batallon, *Erasmo y España*, 10–22.
14. Lynette M. F. Bosch, *Art, Liturgy, and Legend in Renaissance Toledo: The Mendoza and the Iglesia Primaria* (University Park: Pennsylvania State University Press, 2000), 62; Richard Hitchcock, *Mozarabs in Medieval and Early Modern Spain: Identities and Influences* (Farnham, UK: Ashgate, 2008), 109–10.
15. Batallon, *Erasmo y España*, 22–43; Rawlings, *Church, Religion, and Society*, 29.
16. Batallon, *Erasmo y España*, 72–73.

the *philosophia Christi*, the simple Christ-centered piety independent of ritual.[17] However, by 1520, the year Martin Luther's famous three treatises were published, some began to question Erasmus's connections or influence upon the German reformer.[18] In 1527, a faction critical of Erasmus, made up of Dominicans and Franciscans, voiced their opposition to him at a meeting of theologians, inquisitors, and others gathered at Valladolid.[19] The attack on the popular humanist came to nothing, but in 1529 the departure of the emperor for Italy along with his humanist retinue and the implication of Erasmian influence on the *alumbrados* sect created an opportunity for anti-Erasmian individuals in the Church and the Inquisition to persecute followers of the Dutchman.[20] On a larger scale, the protestations of German princes in 1529 at the Diet of Speyer set off alarm bells at the prospect of a heretical, seditious, and disunited Christendom in mortal danger from the Ottoman Turks.[21] This panic resulted in a crackdown on humanist, heretical, or questionable individuals and movements by an authoritarian, conservative, and powerful faction within Spanish Catholicism.[22]

For the first decades of the sixteenth century Spain was a cauldron of reformist ideas, alternate spiritualities, and lay devotion. Two popular movements that illustrate the diversity within the reform movements of Spanish Catholicism deserve special mention: the *alumbrados* and the Spanish Protestants. Though there is some question as to the origins of the *alumbradismo* (Illuminism) movement—whether they were inspired by the writings of Erasmus or originated among the Franciscans and then spread into the order's lay tertiaries and their associates, scholars agree that this was

---

17. Batallon, *Erasmo y España*, 72–77.

18. *The Babylonian Captivity of the Church, The Address to the German Nobility,* and *The Freedom of the Christian.* Cf. Batallon, *Erasmo y España*, 117–32.

19. Batallon, *Erasmo y España*, 236–40, 242–78.

20. On the translation of Erasmus's works into Castilian, see Batallon, *Erasmo y España*, 279–315. On Erasmus and the *alumbrados*, see Batallon, *Erasmo y España*, 117–18; on Erasmus and the imperial court, see Batallon, *Erasmo y España*, 230–36.

21. Rawlings, *Church, Religion, and Society*, 30–31.

22. Rawlings, *Church, Religion, and Society*, 31–49.

a wholly native movement that emerged in Castile.[23] Its adherents prioritized meditation and prayer over ceremony as the means to union with God. Because of their surreptitious nature and because their core beliefs circumvented the formal avenues of the Church toward salvation, the *alumbrados* were persecuted by the Inquisition beginning in 1524. Later, due to their critique of the institutional means of grace and their emphasis upon the individual's private relationship with God, they were implicated in the "Lutheran heresy."[24]

One writer who was associated with Illuminism and Protestantism was Juan de Valdés (1509–1541). Educated at the Complutensian University, Valdés became especially known within his lifetime for his *Dialogue on Christian Doctrine* (1529), in which he excoriates the abuses of the Catholic Church and like Erasmus, with whom he corresponded, emphasizes a Christocentric piety and good works.[25] The *Dialogue* was popular in lay and clerical circles for a number of years until it appeared on the Index of Prohibited Books under suspicion for heresy. Valdés fled to Naples, where he gathered a circle of followers and continued to write on biblical interpretation and the philology of the Spanish (Castilian) language until his death.[26]

The ideas of Martin Luther were not immediately condemned in Spain. It is not known when or where Luther's books first made their way into the peninsula, but they were most likely limited to university circles. There is evidence that by 1521, some of his works were being translated into Castilian and used by *conversos*, Jewish and Muslim converts to Catholicism who were often targeted by an Inquisition suspicious of their sincerity. The situation was such that

23. Alastair Hamilton, *Heresy and Mysticism in Sixteenth-Century Spain: The Alumbrados* (Toronto: University of Toronto Press, 1992), 25–50; Lesley Twomey, ed., *Faith and Fanaticism: Religious Fervor in Early Modern Spain* (Aldershot, UK: Ashgate, 1997), 62–63.

24. Hamilton, *Heresy and Mysticism*, 51–75; Rawlings, *Church, Religion, and Society*, 28–32; Robert Scribner, Roy Porter, and Mikulas Teich, eds., *The Reformation in National Context* (Cambridge: Cambridge University Press, 1994), 203.

25. Batallon, *Erasmo y España*, 316–63; Jose C. Nieto, *Erasmo y la Otra España: Visión Cultural Socioespiritual* (Geneva: Librairie Droz, 1997), 102–6, 377–81.

26. Hamilton, *Heresy and Mysticism*, 40–42; Christopher Black, *Church, Religion, and Society in Early Modern Italy* (New York: Palgrave, 2004), 3–12; cf. Scribner et al., *The Reformation in National Context*, 208.

Adrian of Utrecht (1459–1523), then regent of Spain in Charles I's absence, ordered the ban on Lutheran books, an order echoed four years later by the Inquisitor General. Yet ironically, within the emperor's court, Luther's writings enjoyed some measure of popularity, in part for his calls to reform the abuses of the Church. This remained true when the imperial retinue returned to Spain in 1522 and even despite Luther's condemnation at the Diet of Worms a year earlier.[27] The emperor's departure in 1529 had empowered more conservative elements of the Church to police orthodoxy. Between the 1520s and the 1550s, there we find hints of Luther's influence in Spain: mention by the Inquisition of Protestant writings among the possessions of *alumbrados* captured in Toledo, similarities to Luther's thought in the writings of Juan de Valdés, and occasional discovery and seizure of Protestant books from the Low Countries at Spanish ports.[28]

Not until the late 1550s are there signs of Protestantism in Spain, specifically in evangelical cells in Seville and Valladolid. Beginning with the discovery of Protestant books and propaganda in Seville in 1557, a network of about a thousand individuals was revealed in both cities, led by prominent clergymen.[29] With the support of Philip I, the Inquisition harried these heretics and conducted a series of seven *autos-da-fé* in Valladolid and Seville between 1559 and 1562.[30] Some managed to escape and make their way to the centers of Protestant Europe, among them several friars from the Hieronymite Monastery of St. Isidore outside Seville, including Casiodoro de Reina (c. 1520–1594), who bequeathed to the Spanish-

27. Scribner et al., *The Reformation in National Context*, 202–3; Hamilton, *Heresy and Mysticism*, 72–73.

28. Andrew Pettegree, ed., *The Reformation World* (London: Routledge, 2000), 300.

29. While some have questioned the Protestant connections of these conventicles, their testimony points to definite Protestant beliefs such as justification by faith, a denial of the cult of saints and their images, and a Christocentric piety. Moreover, when discovered, some of these adherents fled to England and Protestant parts of Germany, Switzerland, and the Netherlands, forming Spanish-speaking congregations. Pettegree, *The Reformation World*, 301–3; Batallon, *Erasmo y España*, 522–29.

30. Rawlings, *Church, Religion, and Society*, 37–42; Pettegree, *The Reformation World*, 304.

speaking world that language's first complete translation of the Bible from the original languages, and Cipriano de Valera (c. 1532–1600), who revised Reina's Bible into its present recognizable form and translated Calvin's *Institutes* in 1597.[31]

Mention must also be made of Teresa of Ávila (1515–1582), John of the Cross (1542–1591), and Ignatius of Loyola (1491–1556), whose reform efforts, unlike those of the *alumbrados* or the Protestants, came to be embraced by the institutional Church. Yet the atmosphere of the times was such that they also experienced suspicion, danger, and even persecution by the Inquisition before their reforms—the establishment of the Discalced Carmelites and the Society of Jesus—were accepted.[32]

Spain and the Atlantic World

Spain's entrance onto the global stage and the creation of the Iberian Atlantic world in the sixteenth century did not develop in a vacuum separate from the nation's internal political and religious challenges. It is well known that Isabella and Fernando only deigned to listen to the petitions of Christopher Columbus after their subjugation of Granada in January 1492. The exploration and colonization of the Americas were the accidental response to Spain's desire to compete with Portugal in the search for Asian wealth. The fall of Constantinople to the Ottoman Turks in 1453 forced the Iberian kingdoms, situated between two large bodies of water, to seek alternate routes to the East. Their success resulted in the axis of European trade moving from the Mediterranean to the Atlantic.

Christopher Columbus sailed forth in search of a back door to the wealth of Asia, convinced of a divine mandate as the "Christ-

31. Van Lennep, *La Historia de la Reforma*, 95–240; A. Gordon Kinder, *Casiodoro de Reina: Spanish Reformer of the Sixteenth Century* (London: Tamesis, 1975); Raymond S. Rosales, *Casiodoro de Reina: Patriarca del Protestantismo Hispano* (St. Louis: Concordia, 2002); Paul J. Hauben, *Three Spanish Heretics and the Reformation* (Geneva: Librairie Droz, 1967); Nieto, *Erasmo y la Otra España*, 413–26, 461–508.

32. Michael Mullet, *The Catholic Reformation* (London: Routledge, 1999), 74–100, 181–82; Rawlings, *Church, Religion, and Society*, 35–37.

bearer" to take Christianity to whatever lands he encountered and to return with the means of a final crusade to liberate the Holy Land from Islam. He encountered more than what he bargained for, and his exploratory successors quickly determined that this was a New World filled with peoples, cultures, tongues, flora, and fauna never before known to any Europeans. In the meantime, Pope Alexander VI in 1494 divided these "discoveries," potential or real, between the Spanish and the Portuguese in the Treaty of Tordesillas. A year earlier, the papal bull, *Inter caetera*, required the evangelization of the native peoples as a prerequisite to the Conquest itself.[33]

The Spanish "discovery" of the inhabitants of the New World was earth-shattering. The existence of a new continent tore at the geographical conception of the continents, Europe, Africa, and Asia reflecting the perfect number of the Trinity. The Table of Nations in Genesis 10 did not account for these newly encountered peoples. On chancing upon the Taíno in 1492, Christopher Columbus described them as having "fine shapes and faces" and "handsomely formed." Quickly, though, he recognized their economic and religious potential: "[T]he people are ingenious, and would be good servants and I am of opinion that they would very readily become Christians, as they appear to have no religion." These two motivations, the religious and the pecuniary, repeatedly clashed throughout this early period. Religious orders sought to convert individuals through baptism, catechesis, the destruction of idols, and the teaching of the Commandments. However, Spanish imperial theology—that vision, developed throughout centuries of *Reconquista*, of Spain as holder of a unique place in salvation history to promulgate the gospel and rid the world of false religion through expansionist power—ran roughshod over the efforts of the friars. One of the more curious results of the subsequent debates over the legal and religious legitimacy of the Conquest was the *Requerimiento*, whereby from 1513, would-be colonizers were to read aloud a summary of salvation

---

33. Frank Graziano, *The Millennial New World* (Oxford: Oxford University Press, 1999), 26–31; on the Alexandrine bulls, see Luis N. Rivera, *A Violent Evangelism: The Political and Religious Conquest of the Americas* (Louisville: Westminster John Knox, 1992), 23–41.

history and the claims of the Spanish monarchs to the lands and to entreat the natives to conversion. Their "refusal" to submit and convert—given that the document was read in Spanish and sometimes even to barren beaches—provided the rationalization for taking the lands by just war.[34]

The first religious orders to break ground on the evangelization of the Americas were the Franciscans, the Dominicans, and the Augustinians. Many of these early missionaries and church leaders had been schooled in the humanist tradition in Spain. They produced the first grammars and dictionaries in the native languages of the Americas. Some, like Bernardino de Sahagún (1499–1590), studied native cultures and worldviews in order to better communicate the Christian message. Others, like Juan de Zumárraga (1468–1548) and Vasco de Quiroga (1470–1565), were inspired by Erasmus and Sir Thomas More to create the just society.[35] The Franciscans are of special note. The Spiritual Franciscans were a reform movement within the order that emerged after Francis's death in the thirteenth century. In reaction to the saint's extreme views and practices regarding poverty, the order split between the Conventuals, who practiced a relaxed monastic rule, and the Spirituals, who tried to stay true to the principles of their founder. Jiménez de Cisneros was a member of their order, and Columbus himself belonged to the Third Order and frequented their convent at La Rábida. Some parts of the order followed the teachings of Joachim of Fiore (c. 1135–1202), the medieval writer who divided time and history according to a Trinitarian scheme and who foresaw an eschatological age of the Spirit when the Order of the Just would replace the church. Thus, not only did the evangelization of the indigenous peoples of the Americas fulfill Spain's divine mandate to spread and preserve the Catholic faith, but among some such as the Spiritual Franciscans, it became a necessary precursor to Christ's second coming.[36] As Protestant-

---

34. Cf. Rivera, *A Violent Evangelism*, 32–41.

35. Rawlings, *Church, Religion, and Society*, 108.

36. Osvaldo F. Pardo, *The Origins of Mexican Catholicism: Nahua Rituals and Christian Sacraments in Sixteenth-Century Mexico* (Ann Arbor: University of Michigan Press, 2006), 2–3; for more on the Spanish *Reconquista* and the voyages of exploration, see O'Callaghan, *Reconquest and Crusade in Medieval Spain*; Thomas,

ism began to make inroads throughout northern Europe, however, the missionary enterprise was reinterpreted; God had entrusted the Spanish monarchs with the salvation of the Americas to make up for the apostasy of the Protestants.[37]

Las Casas the Reformer

Bartolomé de Las Casas belongs within this company of women and men who sought the reform and renewal of church and society in sixteenth-century Spain. His prophetic summons to an end of the exploitation of the native peoples of the Americas falls within the calls for moral and spiritual reformation that we find among the Erasmian humanists, the *alumbrados*, and the Cisnerian reforms. Las Casas's repeated challenges to the ecclesial, monastic, and academic structures of his day while working within their systems bring to mind the efforts of the Spanish Protestants to bring about religious change from their communities and monastic cells before their virtual extinction by the Inquisition. Finally, it was his insistence that the conversion of the Americas be undertaken in peace and love to not only obey the imperative to spread the gospel to the ends of the earth, but also to fulfill Spain's own mission and serve as the only justification for her presence in the New World. Space does not permit a full exploration of Las Casas's life.[38] Instead, a summary of incidents from his biography will serve to illustrate his prophetic and reforming call.

Rivers of Gold; Kamen, *Empire: How Spain Became a World Power*. See also Graziano, *The Millennial New World*, 42–44.

37. Rivera, *A Violent Evangelism*, 60–61.

38. For fuller treatments, see Lawrence A. Clayton, *Bartolomé de Las Casas: A Biography* (Cambridge: Cambridge University Press, 2012); Gustavo Gutiérrez, *Las Casas: In Search of the Poor of Jesus Christ*, trans. Robert R. Barr (Maryknoll, NY: Orbis, 1995); Lewis Hanke, *The Spanish Struggle for Justice in the Conquest of America* (Philadelphia: University of Pennsylvania Press, 1949); Juan Friede and Benjamin Keen, eds., *Bartolomé de Las Casas in History: Toward an Understanding of the Man and His Work* (DeKalb: Northern Illinois University Press, 1971); Francis Patrick Sullivan, SJ, trans., *Indian Freedom: The Cause of Bartolomé de Las Casas 1484–1566: A Reader* (Kansas City, MO: Sheed & Ward, 1995); George Sanderlin, ed., *Witness: Writings of Bartolomé de Las Casas* (Maryknoll, NY: Orbis, 1971).

In his youth, Las Casas was among the throngs of Seville gathered on the streets to witness the triumphal return of Christopher Columbus after his first voyage across the Atlantic. His father, seeking to make his fortune, joined the Genoese mariner on his second expedition in 1493. Las Casas himself arrived on Hispaniola in 1502 as a young man and was ordained there several years later.

Whereas the papal bulls granting the rights of New World exploration to Spain prioritized the task of evangelism, the desires of the Crown and the colonizers for worldly wealth tended to take precedence on the ground. The backbone of the colonial system was the *encomienda*, the grant of land and Indians to the colonists by the authorities in reward for service. In return for work, the *encomendero* was expected to provide for the natives' needs and evangelism. Of course, the situation quickly degenerated into outright slavery. Indians were subjugated and enslaved through violence.

Though individual priests or friars accompanied the first voyages of exploration to minister to the Spanish, it would not be until 1510 that members of the religious orders arrived in the New World for the express purpose of evangelizing the Indians. Friars of the Dominican order were the first on the island of Hispaniola and while, throughout history, many clerics would subscribe to and benefit from the imperial theology, these newcomers quickly decided they would not. Led by Pedro de Córdoba (c. 1460–1525), they became the first voices of conscience in the New World. The fiery 1511 Advent sermon of Antonio de Montesinos (c. 1475–1540) questioned the Christianity of the settlers in light of their exploitation of and cruelty to the Indians. "Are they not men? Do they not have rational souls? Are you not bound to love them as you love yourselves?" On the basis of a common humanity and the Christian ethical imperative, the Dominicans' protest threatened to subvert the economic reason for the Conquest.[39] Among his audience may have been the young Las Casas, who himself held an *encomienda*.

As a newly ordained priest, Las Casas served as chaplain on a number of expeditions to conquer nearby islands. Among them was Cuba, and the violence that he witnessed inflicted upon the

---

39. Clayton, *Bartolomé de Las Casas*, 56–62; Gutiérrez, *Las Casas*, 28–37.

Indians there in 1513 was seared into his memory.[40] He recalled it years later:

> Once, some Indians were coming out to us to receive us with victuals and gifts ten leagues from a great village, and when we came to them we were given a great quantity of fish and bread, and food and all else that they are able. But suddenly the Devil came upon the Christians, and in my presence, they took out their knives (with no reason or cause that might be alleged in justification) and slew about three thousand souls, who were sitting there before us, men and women and children. And there I saw such great cruelties, that no living man had ever seen the like of them before, or thought to see. . . . After all the Indians of this island were cast into the same servitude and calamity as those of Hispaniola, seeing all of themselves and their people die and perish without any help for it, some began to flee into the wilderness, others to hang themselves in desperation and lack of hope, and husbands and wives to hang themselves together, and with them hang their children. And because of the cruelties of one most tyrannous Spaniard (whom I met), above two hundred Indians hanged themselves. An infinite number died in this manner.[41]

However, Las Casas maintained his *encomienda* despite these experiences and, by his own admission, was so preoccupied by material interests that he neglected the spiritual instruction of the Indians under his care.[42] Not until the following year, 1514, did Las Casas come to what has been described as his "first conversion." He had already been admonished by a Dominican friar, most likely Pedro de Córdba, and denied absolution on account of his *encomienda*. While studying Ecclesiasticus, Las Casas came to a crisis of con-

40. Friede and Keen, *Bartolomé de Las Casas in History*, 72–73; Clayton, *Bartolomé de Las Casas*, 69–76; cf. 27–50.

41. Bartolomé de Las Casas, *An Account, Much Abbreviated, of the Destruction of the Indies with Related Texts*, trans. Andrew Hurley (Indianapolis: Hackett, 2003), 20–21.

42. Friede and Keen, *Bartolomé de Las Casas in History*, 73; Clayton, *Bartolomé de Las Casas*, 51.

science.[43] He immediately surrendered his *encomienda* and liqui-dated his property.[44] With the support of the Dominican friars on Hispaniola he returned to Spain to lobby on behalf of the Indians.[45]

There, despite opposition from the minister to the Indies—the bishop of Burgos, attempted bribes from prominent members of the Court, and eventually the death of King Fernando himself, Las Casas carried on. He was encouraged by the co-regent, Adrian of Utrecht, and pressed his petitions forward to Jiménez de Cisneros. The powerful but aging churchman listened attentively to Las Casas's tales of terror in paradise. He replaced the hostile and apathetic ministers in charge of administrating the colonies with his own men. Cisneros drew up a plan of reform that included the establishment of free Indian communities. Upon his return, unfortunately, Las Casas discovered to his frustration that legislating change was one thing but implementing it an ocean away was another altogether.[46]

Opposed by colonists and the Hieronymite friars who had been appointed to supervise the reforms, Las Casas, now "Protector of the Indians," returned to Spain in 1517. He was unable to meet with

43. "If one sacrifices ill-gotten goods, the offering is blemished; the gifts of the lawless are not acceptable. The Most High is not pleased with the offerings of the ungodly, nor for a multitude of sacrifices does he forgive sins. Like one who kills a son before his father's eyes is the person who offers a sacrifice from the property of the poor. The bread of the needy is the life of the poor; whoever deprives them of it is a murderer. To take away a neighbor's living is to commit murder; to deprive an employee of wages is to shed blood" (Ecclesiasticus [Sirach] 34:21–27 [NRSV]).

44. Clayton, *Bartolomé de Las Casas*, 76–81.

45. Friede and Keen, *Bartolomé de Las Casas in History*, 74–75; Clayton, *Bartolomé de Las Casas*, 82–95.

46. Friede and Keen, *Bartolomé de Las Casas in History*, 75–77; Clayton, *Bartolomé de Las Casas*, 95–106. Mention must be made that it was at this time that Las Casas, seeking to alleviate the burden of the Indians, first proposed the importation of "black and white slaves from Castile." His experience of African slavery at the time had been restricted to those he witnessed in the cities of Spain. However, in 1547, Las Casas was in Lisbon exploring the chronicles and journals of the early Portuguese explorers and encountered, perhaps for the first time, firsthand accounts of the capture and enslavement of Africans off that continent's coast. From that year, his attitude toward the use of African slaves made an about-face. He condemned the slave trade, though his priority remained the oppression of the New World natives. Clayton, *Bartolomé de Las Casas*, 135–39, 420–28; cf. Parrish, *Bartolomé de Las Casas*, 201–8.

the dying Cisneros and decided to seek out the aid of the young, untested new king, Charles I. When he was unable to convince Charles's new minister of the Indies, Juan Rodríguez de Fonseca, of the urgency of his pleas, Las Casas turned his attention to securing royal permission to found a settlement made up of Indians and Spanish farmers living in peaceful coexistence in Cumaná, on the Venezuelan coast. The priest sought to prove that the colonization and evangelization of the New World by nonviolent means could financially benefit the Crown while preserving the lives of the natives. A series of unfortunate events, from storms that scattered the missionaries to the inability to find suitable settlers, doomed the project. When slave-traders invaded the settlement to capture Indians, the latter responded in kind, destroying the colony.[47]

After the failure at Cumaná, Las Casas withdrew from public life, and, experiencing his "second conversion," entered the Dominican order in 1523. Shut up in the monastery in Santo Domingo, for several years Las Casas devoted himself to the study of the Bible, the church fathers, theology, and philosophy along with the spiritual practices of prayer and obedience.[48] About this time, the cleric began amassing his materials and writing the rough drafts that would become a memorial to the early years of exploration, conquest, and exploitation, the *Historia de las Indias*.[49]

Shaken into action once again, Las Casas spent the next several years traveling throughout the Caribbean and Central America on behalf of the order. Throughout this time, he continued to preach against the subjugation of the Indians, earning the hatred of the colonists. However, in 1534 he brought about the peaceful surrender of the rebellious Taíno leader, Enriquillo, who had led a number of armed revolts throughout Hispaniola since 1519.[50] These events doubtless honed the ideas and strategies that he put to paper in *De unico vo-*

47. Friede and Keen, *Bartolomé de Las Casas in History*, 79–81; Clayton, *Bartolomé de Las Casas*, 107–20, 166–95.

48. Clayton, *Bartolomé de Las Casas* 212–17.

49. *Historia de las Indias*, 3 vols., ed. Agustín Millares Carlo (Mexico City: Fondo de Cultura Económica, 1951, repr. 1995); cf. Clayton, *Bartolomé de Las Casas*, 217–19.

50. Clayton, *Bartolomé de Las Casas*, 229–34; Gutiérrez, *Las Casas*, 303–4.

cationis modo, his thesis on the motivations and means of spreading the gospel.[51] This tract formed the backbone of a series of memorials sent to Pope Paul III (1468–1549) by Las Casas and other like-minded churchmen. These efforts resulted in the 1537 bull, *Sublimus Dei*, which proclaimed the full humanity and rationality of the Indians and rebuked those who would deny them in order to enslave them.[52]

Las Casas traveled to Spain again in 1540 to petition for his missionary project in Tuzulutlán, Guatemala. In addition to recruiting missionaries for this ambitious project of evangelizing the Indians in this so-called land of war, Las Casas continued to present his petitions to Charles I for the reform of the colonial enterprise.[53] He described Indian slavery, pointed fingers at corrupt government officials, and attacked the *encomienda* system. Letters from church officials such as Juan de Zumárraga and Francisco Marroquín buttressed his arguments.[54] On Charles's departure, Las Casas began to follow Prince Philip, who was left in charge of the government. When the Council of the Indies reconvened in Seville, Las Casas was there. As a result, in 1542, Charles I passed the New Laws intended to prohibit the enslavement of the Indians and bring about the end of the *encomienda* system by forbidding its passing to the next generation after the death of the original *encomendero*.[55]

---

51. Helen Rand Parrish, ed., *Bartolomé de Las Casas: The Only Way*, trans. Francis Patrick Sullivan, SJ (Mahwah, NJ: Paulist, 1992); Clayton, *Bartolomé de Las Casas*, 234–40.

52. Friede and Keen, *Bartolomé de Las Casas in History*, 86–89; Clayton, *Bartolomé de Las Casas*, 237; Gutiérrez, *Las Casas*, 302–6.

53. Pedro de Alvarado had conquered Tuzulutlán with one hundred soldiers but was soon driven out by the Indians. When Las Casas preached against Indian slavery and for peaceful evangelization, outraged settlers challenged him to go to Tuzulutlán. This presented an opportunity to prove his thesis that the successful conversion of the Indians could be done without means of violence. While Las Casas most likely never ministered in the region himself, he actively promoted the project. However, Luis de Cancer (1500–1549), a Dominican priest and correspondent of Las Casas, did report success. Clayton, *Bartolomé de Las Casas*, 255–59, 262–64.

54. Juan de Zumárraga (1468–1548), first bishop of Mexico; Francisco Marroquín (1499–1563), first bishop of Guatemala.

55. Friede and Keen, *Bartolomé de Las Casas in History*, 92–97; Clayton, *Bartolomé de Las Casas*, 270–84.

In 1545, Las Casas accepted the post of bishop of Chiapas. Armed with authority from the Crown and the Council to implement the New Laws, he arrived in Yucatan in 1545. There and elsewhere in the colonies he encountered consistent hostility. The mastermind behind the New Laws, after all, was responsible for depriving them of Indian labor to extract the New World's riches. Moreover, the New Laws would deny their children and grandchildren the fruits of those efforts. To make matters worse, Las Casas prohibited the granting of absolution to *encomenderos* during Lent, 1545, unless they freed their Indians or gave them their just restitution. Churchmen in the colonies—and even some in the religious orders—denounced him to the Council of the Indies. Failing to enforce the laws he had lobbied for and faced with overwhelming enmity and threats, the bishop returned to Spain after only a year on the episcopal throne, never to return to the Americas.[56] Las Casas spent the rest of his years advocating for the full humanity of the Native Americans. He continued to follow the Court and to write and publish his histories and the conclusions he was drawing from the study of the Bible, theology, law, and his own experiences.[57]

A high-water mark in Las Casas's already long career came about in 1550 at the Valladolid Debate, organized by King Charles to argue the question of whether the Indians possessed rationality. Las Casas's opponent was the accomplished jurist, Juan Ginés de Sepúlveda (1489/90–1573). Though the proceedings of the Valladolid Debate have been lost, it is not difficult to reconstruct the participants' arguments from their writings. Sepúlveda, siding with the colonists, drew upon an Aristotelian understanding of humanity to justify the continued war against the Amerindians. Here, fully human beings possess *humanitas*, the capacity for morality and reason that allows them to create civilizations. Only those possessing those characteristics are deservedly free. Basing himself on descriptions of the Indians (of whom he had no firsthand experience), Sepúlveda declared that their barbarity, lack of morality, and idolatry made them less than human, lacking true humanity. As beings given to

---

56. Clayton, *Bartolomé de Las Casas*, 285–341.
57. Friede and Keen, *Bartolomé de Las Casas in History*, 97–103.

their baser instincts, they belong to another class of people—those who by nature are designed to be dominated by the civilized. Lacking rationality, morality, or civilization, they are fit only for slavery. Sepúlveda further argued that their conquest by the Spanish served as a positive good, preventing the practice of cannibalism or human sacrifice and placing them in a position to receive Christianity. Though Sepúlveda, in his treatise *Democrates Secundus* (late 1540s) had softened some of the language regarding the necessity of force in the conquest of the Indians in light of the papal pronouncement from the previous decade, his thesis regarding the enslavement and implied political usurpation of the Indians belies this.[58]

Las Casas drew upon his personal experiences among the natives, as witness to the wars of conquest, as well as his own biblical, humanist, and scholastic training. He began with an exhausting word-for-word reading of a five-hundred-page Latin treatise rebutting Sepúlveda's claims. In order to answer his assertions on the inferiority of the Indians, Las Casas relied heavily on his *Apologetic History*, describing the history and civilizations of the Indians and pointing out how they not only fulfilled Aristotle's conditions for full humanity but were in several respects superior to the ancient Greeks and Romans. He does not discount Aristotle's categories of humanity but simply notes that, by virtue of their culture, rationality, morality, and civilization, the Indians are not inferior beings. In answering the charge that human sacrifice proved the barbarity of the natives, he played an exaggerated game of philosophical gymnastics to remove culpability from the Indians. Admitting that they were probably in error, he nonetheless pointed out that in sacrificing fellow human beings, they truly understood the nature of sacrifice as demanding the best that one could offer. While repudiating the conquest of the Americas by means of violence, Las Casas had to

---

58. Joel M. Cruz, *The Histories of the Latin American Church: A Handbook* (Minneapolis: Fortress, 2014), 56–57; Friede and Keen, *Bartolomé de Las Casas in History*, 108–10; Clayton, *Bartolomé de Las Casas*, 342–52; Gutiérrez, *Las Casas*, 292–93; Lewis Hanke, *All Mankind Is One: A Study of the Disputation Between Bartolome de Las Casas and Juan Gines de Sepulveda in 1550 on the Religious and Intellectual Capacity of the American Indians* (DeKalb: Northern Illinois University Press, 1974).

step gingerly so as to not attack the rights of the Spanish Crown to colonize the continent. Not only did it risk treason but also a denial of papal authority, given that the rights of expansion and evangelization had been recognized by *Sublimus Dei*, whose pronouncements on the Indians he sought to defend. Here, the Dominican friar placed the emphasis upon Spain's mission to spread the gospel, repeating, as he had done masterfully in his 1537 treatise *De unico vocationis modo*, that the only legitimate means of evangelization was peaceful, appealing to reason, and acting in love. As Christ, the apostles, and their followers had gone forth to spread the good news without the use of arms, so should the Spanish.[59]

The debate with Sepúlveda resulted in the Crown granting him greater authority to recruit qualified missionaries for the New World. In 1546 he published perhaps his most infamous and most translated work, the *Brevíssima Relación de la Destrucción de las Indias*.[60] He never ceased his attacks on the *encomienda*, or editing and enlarging his *History of the Indies*.[61]

59. Though both Sepúlveda and Las Casas claimed victory after Valladolid, the decisions of the judges have been lost to history. Sepúlveda was unable to publish his works afterwards, perhaps due to his opponent's efforts. Las Casas, perceiving that not much at all had changed in the Americas, continued to pen, publish, prod, plead, and petition. The active enslavement of the Indians eventually ceased, in part due to new legislation and in greater part due to their extermination and the importation of African slaves. In the broader arguments regarding war, conquest, and the rights and responsibilities of combatants, the views of the Dominican theologian Francisco de Vitoria (c. 1483–1546), who proposed a universal standard of conduct based upon the "law of nations"—the foundation of international law—would prevail. Cruz, *The Histories of the Latin American Church*, 57; Clayton, *Bartolomé de Las Casas*, 352–86.

60. *A Short Account of the Destruction of the Indies*, composed of elaborated-upon excerpts from the larger *History of the Indies*, this book was translated and published repeatedly throughout Europe. A work of history as propaganda, its power lies in the repetitious nature of its stories; whether in Hispaniola, Cuba, Nicaragua, or elsewhere, the unimaginable atrocities committed by the Spanish are recounted like a pounding drumbeat, punctuated repeatedly by the author's own admission, "I saw this with my very own eyes." Clayton, *Bartolomé de Las Casas*, 395–98.

61. An interesting account for our purposes is Las Casas's defense of Bartolomé Carranza de Miranda (1503–1576), the archbishop of Toledo, who had been

Las Casas, who throughout his career always sought to balance the human needs of the native peoples with the prerogatives of the Crown to colonize new lands, began to question the entire colonial apparatus in the waning years of his life. Regarding the conquest of Peru, he argued that the whole enterprise was illegal and immoral, and that the Inca should be restored to their original positions and wealth.[62] If the *a priori* reason for Spain's presence in the Americas was the evangelization of its people (per the papal bull *Inter caetera*)—and if this was being either ignored or done at the point of the sword, then Spain had no legitimate right to be in the Americas and should give restitution to its native peoples or face the wrath of God.[63]

Las Casas: The Only Way

Even if Las Casas was not known for the *Brevíssima Relación* and its links to the Black Legend, and even if his *History of the Indies* had not become an important source of detailed information for the early settlement of the Americas, it is arguable that the Dominican friar would still retain his importance based solely upon his 1537 treatise, *De unico vocationis modo omnium gentium ad veram religionem* (*The Only Way to Attract All People to the True Religion*).[64]

---

seized by the Inquisition outside Madrid in 1559 and accused of Lutheranism. Las Casas had warned the archbishop of the plot laid against him by his ecclesiastical rivals, and during his trial defended him from the charges of heresy. Thus, while Las Casas was not sympathetic to Protestantism, here we have an overlap between his life and the rise and persecution of Protestant cells in the late 1550s. If nothing, it places the Dominican priest more squarely within the larger religious, social, and ecclesial movements of the sixteenth century. Rawlings, *Church, Religion, and Society*, 44–47; Friede and Keen, *Bartolomé de Las Casas in History*, 114; Clayton, *Bartolomé de Las Casas*, 398–420.

62. Clayton, *Bartolomé de Las Casas*, 429–45.

63. Friede and Keen, *Bartolomé de Las Casas in History*, 110–18.

64. *Brevissima Relación* has been recognized as an important factor in the development of the Black Legend—the idea, particularly propagated in northern Europe, that the Spanish colonial enterprise in the New World was exceptionally violent and barbaric, reflecting a particular nature or trait of the Spanish people.

The tragedy of the book is that all that remains to us of it are chapters five, six, and seven of Book One. The rest of the work has been lost. Nonetheless, it is possible to reconstruct Las Casas's thought in it, whose mild tone and persuasive efforts have been eclipsed by the urgent, fiery language of the *Brief Account*. Upon reading it one is struck by the common sense of it all; until one realizes that Las Casas was not working out some abstract theory, but responding to the real practice of conversion through the sword, and that the issues he raises dwell on the nature of the gospel itself and human freedom. For that reason, it remains an important work in summarizing the thought of Las Casas as well as serving as a seminal work in the history of Christian missions and theology.

> One way, one way only, of teaching a living faith, to everyone, everywhere, always, was set by Divine Providence: the way that wins the mind with reasons. It has to fit all peoples on earth, no distinction made for sect, error, even for evil.[65]

The first four sections of chapter five explain that all of the world's people are called to receive the gospel as a free gift. Therefore, all have the capacity to receive the faith. Las Casas explains therefore that the way to preach the Christian message to all people must be one that persuades the hearer and attracts the will. Missionaries and evangelists must act in such a way that makes people receptive to God's Spirit to move the individual to conversion. Las Casas emphasizes a faith that comes from understanding, a process of evangelism that respects the free faculties of the individual. Therefore, it is one that is patient, not rushing the person but accompanying them on their journey. This conflicted with the views of some missionaries in the New World, particularly the Franciscans, who favored the immediate baptism of the natives without prior instruction or catechism.[66] Las Casas uses the Bible, the church fathers, and the precedent of history to underline his

---

65. Parrish, *Bartolomé de Las Casas*, 68.
66. In light of the quickly approaching Second Coming of Christ, catechism had to take a back seat to conversion.

points, subtly addressing how the love of wealth has compromised the Church's mission. The method of peace and love will convince unbelievers that the missionaries have no underlying interest in overpowering or robbing them of their wealth.[67] Then in the next chapter, he contrasts the way of peace with the methods being used in the Americas where force, plunder, rape, and murder had arrived hand in hand with the missionaries. This, he notes, not only violates human freedom and dignity, but it also contradicts the very nature, mission, and instructions set forth by Christ and the apostles, who themselves exemplified peace.

> War brings with it cannon fire, surprise attacks, shore raids that are lawless and blind, violence, riots, scandals, corpses, carnage, butchery, robbery, looting, parent split from child, child from parent, slavery, the ruin of states and kingdoms, of lords and local rulers, the devastation of cities and towns and people without number. War fills here and there and everywhere with tears, with sobs, with keening over every pitiful spectacle possible . . . how opposed to the peaceful way of preaching the faith, how utterly opposed the violent way is. It is the dead opposite, the reverse of preaching the faith and drawing people gently into the flock of Christ.[68]

Las Casas anticipates the theologies of liberation and the African American Civil Rights movements of the modern era when he states in his concluding chapter that the means of nonviolence are also for the benefit of the oppressor. Those who would use force to impose the gospel commit mortal sin against God and their Indian brethren and risk their own souls.

> Mongers of war to convert show they are not submissive to God. Look at the unbelievable injustice, the criminal injustice they let loose in the wars on pagan peoples. They violate the law of God and every commandment. . . . And they destroy the bond

---

67. Parrish, *Bartolomé de Las Casas*, 69–116.
68. Parrish, *Bartolomé de Las Casas*, 117, 118; Gutiérrez, *Las Casas*, 159.

of human society when they kill people and have no reason to, when they strip, destroy, erase whole populations. Their sin is a mortal sin. . . . They are already damned.[69]

For Las Casas, the damned are not simply those who commit acts of war upon the innocent but also those who are complicit in the crime: those who do nothing to prevent the act, and those who abdicate their authority and protect the offender.[70] Here, the friar addresses the systemic, even institutional, causes of oppression. Las Casas does not stop with either the exposition of an ideal or the condemnation of the unjust. He moves forward, connecting the ideal of love of neighbor with the admonition to do justice.

> On peril of losing their souls, all who start wars of conversion, all who will in the future, all who assist in any way that we just said, all are bound to restore to the devastated pagan peoples whatever they took in war, permanent or perishable, and make up for whatever they destroyed. Make up totally.[71]

The Only Way is an exemplar of humanist sixteenth-century Reformation writing. Like his contemporaries, whether Cisneros, Luther, or Calvin, Las Casas returns to the sources (*ad fontes*) of Christian thought: the Old and New Testaments and the church fathers. Unlike the medieval scholastics who debated by amassing authorities to serve their arguments, Las Casas moves from one point to the next and invites the reader to follow the argument borne out by Scripture and reason. Yet, for a treatise that is rooted within both his academic and rhetorical context and the historical reality of the Spanish wars of conquest, *De unico vocationis modo* is incredibly contemporary as issues of human rights, justice, restitution, and their relation to Christian love and ethics occupy concerns of our time.

Observations of the 500th anniversary of the Reformation have been marked with sobriety more than celebration in recognition

69. Gutiérrez, *Las Casas*, 166.
70. Gutiérrez, *Las Casas*, 169–70.
71. Gutiérrez, *Las Casas*, 171.

of the sundering of Western Christianity. As mentioned above, the idea of a 500th anniversary makes one reformation in one place under one set of individuals the center of the idea. However, within a larger global context, reform was already in the air, proving the axiom of *ecclesia semper reformata*—the church always reforming. Bartolomé de Las Casas, in calling for the reform of Church and society to the virtue of love and the practice of justice, earns his place among the company of sixteenth-century reformers. Rather than confined to a church ministry or university town, Las Casas's ministry straddled an ocean that marked the beginnings of the modern world. The demographics of Latin America have changed since the sixteenth century and the children of the Protestant Reformation now form a sizeable minority alongside their Roman Catholic sisters and brothers in the region.[72] However, the violence and abuses that Las Casas witnessed toward the defenseless continue even if the methods and actors may be different—war, environmental destruction, economic disparity, injustice against women, the indigenous, people of African descent, and sexual minorities. It is important to reclaim Las Casas as integral to our observances and ideas of a sixteenth-century Reformation because his call for justice and love remain relevant throughout the world.

72. About 18.1 percent in the twenty Iberian-American nations that make up Latin America (including Brazil and the United States). Cruz, *The Histories of the Latin American Church*, 3.

3 Women from Then to Now

A Commitment to Mutuality and Literacy

REBECCA A. GISELBRECHT

New ideas swept across the European continent, overturned the old order on the British Isles, and challenged the world to reinterpret social systems, gender, and mores in light of humanist thought and the Reformations. Learning, innovations, and the imperative *ad fontes!* (back to the source—to the fountains of knowledge), along with Johannes Gutenberg's (1398–1468) printing press, made way for the irreversible momentum of modernity. From a Protestant perspective, the one corrupt religious system that required realignment had for centuries drawn its power and wealth from both men *and* women. Reform would, no doubt, also take the efforts of both genders. A look back at the enterprise reminds us that desire for true religion is much larger than imagined, and a rather messy proposition with a never-ending learning curve.

Metaphorically speaking, the sixteenth-century Protestant Reformation was a unique moment when a large key—the power of knowing—opened the old church and allowed a peek through the cloaked doors toward the kingdom of heaven. One of the novelties of this was the notion that men *and* women could enter the realm of faith as individual spiritual beings, each on their own accord without an earthly clerical mediator (1 Pet. 16:19).[1] Need-

---

1. Desiderius Erasmus and Silvana Seidel Menchi, "Iulius Exclusus," in *1–8 Or-*

less to say, the Reformation project, its hope and promise of more godly individual lives, will always remain open—*ecclesia reformata semper reformanda est* (the church, having been reformed, must always be further reformed)—because the world is plastic not static and always needs moral and social reforms to adjust lagging human rights, renew spiritual freedom, and remind us to love God and our neighbors.[2] As traditional Christian denominations fail in many of today's Western countries, and the number of persecuted Christians grows beyond those of any previous century, to ask what the Protestant reforms have done for women on a global scale and how this looks in our contemporary world seems crazy. Still, the purpose of this chapter is to begin thinking about it anyway.

Honestly, no matter how we stack the deck, the hierarchical androcentric bias of patriarchal epistemology and the historical narrative of the past five hundred years of church history make it no easy task to isolate what the Protestant Reformation did for women globally.[3] Some might sidestep the question and argue that female meaning-making is different anyway because the earth, the other, embodiment, and inclusion are women's topics.[4] Oth-

---

dinis Primi Tomus Octavus, ed. Silvana Seidel Menchi and Franz Bierlaire (Leiden: Brill, 2013), 223–97.

2. Theodor Mahlmann, "Ecclesia semper reformanda," in *Hermeneutica sacra: Studien zur Auslegung der Heiligen Schrift im 16. und 17. Jahrhundert* (Berlin: De Gruyter, 2010), 384–88. The words *Ecclesia semper reformanda est* originate with Jodocus van Lodenstein, were picked up by Karl Barth, and are the current motto of the French Reformed Church.

3. Feminist scholars have worked extensively on the question of gender equality and the Reformation. Here a sample of the classical literature on this includes Monika Gsell, "Hierarchie und Gegenseitigkeit: Ueberlegungen zur Geschlechterkonzeption in Heinrich Bullingers Eheschrift," in *Geschlechterbeziehungen und Textfunktionen: Studien zu Eheschriften der frühen Neuzeit*, ed. Rüdiger Schnell (Tübingen: Niemeyer, 1998), 89–118; Joan Kelly-Gadol, *Did Women Have a Renaissance?* (Chicago: University of Chicago Press, 1984), 19–51; Jane Dempsey Douglass, *Women, Freedom, and Calvin* (Philadelphia: Westminster, 1985); John Lee Thompson, *John Calvin and the Daughters of Sarah: Women in Regular and Exceptional Roles in the Exegesis of Calvin, His Predecessors, and His Contemporaries* (Geneva: Librairie Droz, 1992).

4. Feminist work enters these topics from many diverse perspectives, theolog-

ers might reach to social history, underscoring that women were and are suppressed and excluded from fully participating in public space; that they have been, and remain, disadvantaged throughout history and are yet in need of liberation.[5] Yet others would argue that, philosophically speaking, the polarities of gender talk must first be put aside.[6] These directions are correct and productive—to some extent. However, there is another minority perspective beyond pluralism and secularized society. There is still a room where the Christian perspective according to the biblical narrative fills space with a different reality.[7]

A theological perspective on the sixteenth-century Protestant interpretation of Scripture renders one of the central tenets of biblical faith to be an individual, personal, but also corporate responsibility for relating to God. As the Westminster Shorter Catechism states in the first answer to its initial question, "Man's chief end is to glorify God and to enjoy him forever." Thus, the freedom of an individual believer to practice a unique relationship with God: *sola scriptura, sola fide, sola gratia, solus Christus,* and *soli Deo gloria* is not a gendered—male—privilege. Protestant women are included in these tenets of the Protestant Reformation—the Reformation being a theological turn toward the biblical source where both men and women have the same spiritual rights *coram Deo.* Thus the notion of *sola scriptura* also denotes that Scripture interprets Scripture for

---

ical, sociological, philisophical, etc. To list them here would go beyond the scope of this work.

5. A few classics on the subject: Lyndal Roper et al., "Was There a Crisis in Gender Relations in Sixteenth Century Germany?," in *Krisenbewusstsein und Krisenbewältigung in der frühen Neuzeit: Festschrift für Hans-Christoph Rublack = Crisis in Early Modern Europe* (Frankfurt am Main and New York: Peter Lang, 1992); Kelly-Gadol, *Did Women Have a Renaissance?*; Elizabeth A. Clark, "The Lady Vanishes: Dilemmas of a Feminist Historian after the 'Linguistic Turn,'" *Church History* 67, no. 1 (1998): 1–33; Ute Gause, "Reformation, geschlechtergeschichtlich—auch ein notwendiger Nachtrag zum Calvinjahr 2009," *Zeitschrift für Evangelische Theologie* 4 (2010): 293–309.

6. Angela Berlis, Anne-Marie Korte, and Kune Biezeveld, *Everyday Life and the Sacred: Re/configuring Gender Studies in Religion* (Leiden/Boston: Brill, 2017).

7. The idea of a room of one's own is a classic notion central to the development of Feminist theory. See Virginia Woolf, *Mrs. Dalloway / A Room of One's Own* (1929; repr., Orlando: Houghton Mifflin Harcourt, 2010).

males and females. With Scripture at the center of faith and the church, barring various real handicaps such as class and physical or mental issues, the responsibility for a personal relationship with God is historically for Protestants a matter of education. The ability to read Scripture is one of the prongs on the key to knowing God.

Ad fontes was the underlying prompt for changing the world of women because to be literate and teach the Bible to children, staying faithful to the Word in society, and being a chaste, humble, and virtuous woman was key to the Reformation project. Thus, knowledge-sharing is an aspect of the Reformation that influenced women then and now on a global scale. It had staying power through the Renaissance and humanism, was emphasized in modernity and postmodernity, and is what gives vast power to technology, the economy, and the value of higher education to this day.

Individualism—*sola*, *solus*, and *soli*—the gestalt and content of current Middle European cultural values, is the result of how Reformation Christian ethics morphed as they were shaped by the Enlightenment individualism that lies at the core of basic anthropological notions.[8] In the process of the evolution of these fundamental values, as Michael W. Goheen reminds us, the spiritual vision grew more and more inward and "[t]he scope of the gospel thus narrows until all that is left is a personal relationship between God and the individual human."[9] Although individualism is a phenomenon that has adverse side effects—for instance, in Eastern Europe where the *communio sanctorum* is detached from the notion of faith on many levels—the necessity to read and write continues to define the roles of men and women on a global scale. The remarkable and noteworthy logic of the Protestant perspective is its truth claim and necessary requirement that all people everywhere are called to share the good news of the gospel with others. The missional nature of Protestantism is located at the center of the belief system. Protestant theology, then, must promote educating women in order to include them in the mission project of sharing knowledge of "the chief end of man." Thus, all females

---

8. Michael W. Goheen, *A Light to the Nations: The Missional Church and the Biblical Story* (Grand Rapids: Baker Academic, 2011), 13.

9. Goheen, *A Light to the Nations*, 13.

also participate in the *missio Dei*, which remains a global agenda of worship and sharing. *Sola scriptura* is both a vehicle and center of the salvation conflict that entails personal attention to the object of God's Word—the blueprint for redemption, sanctification, and a good life. An ongoing dialectic between each woman and man and the biblical God Almighty is a hallmark of the Protestant faith. In turn, the relational aspect of the church, the notion of the *communio sanctorum*, guarantees the global influence of the Protestant faith. As the Bible says, "People don't light a lamp and then put it in a closet or under a basket. Rather, they place the lamp on a lampstand" (Luke 11:33), and participation in the *missio Dei* is the Protestant reply, arguably since the Reformation. The longevity and vitality of the Protestant faith, in this sense, lies in the dissemination of the biblical Christian message that opened doors, not only for men, but also for women, to be spiritual, relational, and intelligent members of Christian and societal communities across the globe.[10] The Reformation conviction of the necessity of Scripture, of reading it, and of deepening our relationship with God, all result in the *certitudo* of faith.[11] Lived Protestant faith includes the hermeneutic criterion of the Great Commission to go into all the world.

The Tower of Babel: Unity and Diversity in Reforms

From a theological perspective, the Tower of Babel seems an apt biblical image or metaphor for how the valuation of the faith of both genders came to change the world as early modern Protestantism spread. The tower of the medieval religious elite fell, and the di-

---

10. Taking the stance that education was the most positive influence on women in the Reformation is not a blind embrace of misogyny that has remained part of historical reality to this day, nor should the volumes of arguments that women's lot in life was not improved be ignored. See Merry E. Wiesner, "Beyond Women and the Family: Towards a Gender Analysis of the Reformation," *Sixteenth Century Journal* 18, no. 3 (1987). Merry E. Wiesner's *Women and Gender in Early Modern Europe* (Cambridge: Cambridge University Press, 1993) is also authoritative on this subject and houses extensive sources on women in the Reformation.

11. Calvin, *Institutes* I.17.7–8.

versity of the individual as such grew and was disseminated incrementally so that eventually spiritual equality among all the saints became normative in the Protestant church. Unity and diversity are God's priorities.[12] Although the project is not complete, women's rights to education, then to vote, to equality in the workplace, and for ordination into ministry sprouted from the same seed, and in an ordered process became accepted institutionally within most Western cultures. Although the implementation of these remains somewhat contested in many parts of the world, the fundamental ethical values of gender equality are central to legal discourse, arrangements, and agreements inside and outside of the church, including the International Bill of Human Rights.[13]

The Protestant Reformation substantially interrupted medieval history with the bold idea that everyone should be able to read Scripture. The project took time. Nonetheless, at the inception of the various reforms, the power to interpret Scripture was embraced by the conservatives, the orthodox, and radical Protestants alike. The power of Protestant freedom, in contrast to the Roman tradition, gave each Protestant denomination, every church, the space to apply different measures to the imbalance of the gender status quo and the roles of women in the church. Still, spiritual equality, the nature of salvation and sanctification, was nonnegotiable equality, as we will presently see.

After establishing the philosophical and theological turn to include women as ensouled humans, I will limit my initial observations to a discussion of some of the novelties of the early Zurich Reformation and how the religious movement changed the lives and practices of women in middle Europe. Developing a view of the Zurich reforms and how Huldrych Zwingli (1484–1531) and Heinrich Bullinger (1504–1575) argued for their reform project, I will tease out

12. Terence E. Fretheim, "The Book of Genesis: Introduction, Commentary, and Reflections," in *The New Interpreter's Bible*, ed. Terence E. Fretheim and Daniel J. Simundson (Nashville: Abingdon, 1994). "The right kind of unity occurs only when the community encompasses the concerns of the entire world and encourages difference and diversity to that end" (414).

13. Also see CEDAW: UNFPA, "The Human Rights of Women," www.unfpa .org/resources/human-rights-women.

why I have come to believe that women were central and essential to the reformers' arguments for the Reformation. A look at Zwingli's and Bullinger's treatment of the biblical doctrine of the priesthood of all believers will set the stage for an examination of two aspects of the Protestant Reformation that serve as signposts along the path to women's spiritual equality in the church. The first is the notion of mutuality in marriage between one man and one woman. The other is the somewhat more forgotten mainstay of Protestantism ever since the Reformation—education—which I began to unpack in the introduction above. In my opinion, the key element of the global impact of the Protestant Reformation on women was how the new freedom to interpret Scripture slowly unlocked the dimension for sharing knowledge about who women are in God. Finally, I contend that the necessity for all men and women to be literate, for religious training and spiritual formation, makes education *the* most crucial Protestant priority, with sweeping global consequences for women.

Philosophical Roots of Gender and Spiritual Inequality

Gender inequality and exclusion are central to the normative religious conception of the relationship between the human body and the human soul. Let me expound a bit on the ideas of Plato (c. 423–348 BCE) and how the Greek philosopher's conviction that males are superior to females influenced biblical interpretation for centuries. By so doing, we will better understand the contours of the progressive development of the Protestant paradigm to include women as embodied thinking beings in the church and world. Early philosophical ideas often belittled women and promoted opposing polarities and serve as the ever-present background upon which women enter every form of discourse.

Plato categorized and valued the female gender when he wrote, "The identity of a woman or man comes from their mind (or soul) and not from their body."[14] Unfortunately, this seemingly

---

14. Prudence Allen, *The Concept of Woman*, vol. 1: *The Aristotelian Revolution, 750 B.C.–A.D. 1250* (Grand Rapids: Eerdmans, 1997), 61.

harmless statement instigated prejudice toward women as such. Plato continued, adding that a woman's soul makes her body weaker than that of a man. In contrast to Plato, it is notable that the Old and New Testament perspective speaks of men and women as spiritual equals. The embodied existence of people is presented as an inseparable unit, which is particularly evident in the gender-inclusive nature of Old and New Testament genealogies.

Contrary to this, Plato argued for gender polarity and a hierarchy of value—men above women.[15] Although he furthered women in education and encouraged their participating in public discourse, he placed limits on women's intellectual participation. He created the discriminatory rule that "[t]he limiting age for official appointments shall be forty for a woman, thirty for a man. The weakness of a woman's body simply means that she will need to study longer before achieving the height of wisdom necessary for her to become a philosopher guardian of the state."[16] Not the biblical perspective, but the theory of equality and physical differentiation have determined gender relations, male domination, and how power is perceived in Western culture.

Unfortunately, the seemingly insurmountable barrier to gender equality for woman set by Aristotle (385–322 BCE) was also adopted by Augustine of Hippo (354–430), by Thomas Aquinas (1225–1274), and finally by Christendom in general. Aristotle held that the female and the male are contraries; like his teacher Plato, Aristotle argued that a female is comparable to matter, and a male is form or spirit. Note that as Aristotle developed his hierarchical system, the earth, and therefore, everything female was at the bottom of the universe. Women are cold; men are hot. Women are deformed men, so that in procreation a woman contributes the material cause or body, while the male contributes the final cause or the child's soul.[17] The list of deficits continues with women being irrational and men rational, women mere opinion while men are knowledgeable. Women do not possess virtues. In fact, a woman is only virtuous when she associates with a man.

15. Allen, *The Concept of Woman*, 1:58–71.
16. Allen, *The Concept of Woman*, 1:68.
17. Allen, *The Concept of Woman*, 1:93–100.

Aristotle owned the sex-polarity position, which relegated women to private space and men to public space and constructed unbalanced gender-differentiated roles, education, and leadership hierarchies, and low social positions for women in Judeo-Christian thought.[18] Later, as the study of human anatomy highlighted the inadequacies of Aristotle's theories and did not hold water in light of scientific reasoning, the philosophical arguments remained. I believe the philosophy of gender polarity lurks behind the valuation of women in contemporary Western culture as evidenced in the pornography industry and human trafficking, but also the so-called glass ceiling for professional women.

The role of women in society and the possibilities of female leadership outside of the home in public space have been subject to the ebbs and flows of history. For instance, Plutarch's (46–125) theory of reincarnation provided a ladder for women to step up to equality with men at the spiritual level of the soul. Then Plotinus (205–270) associated the body with evil, and since the female is closer to the earth in Aristotle's hierarchy, women were then associated with evil and matter.[19] Rather than outline the rest of history here, it suffices to say that Augustine (354–430) and later Aquinas (1225–1274) adopted sex polarity, and—at least—women born common were treated accordingly.[20]

Yes, a way out of this later included entering a convent or becoming a religious. The role of a religious was a safe haven for women who wanted to be educated and participate in society rather than devote their lives to childbearing and the private space of their homes as wives and mothers. These women were, nevertheless, always subject to male supervision within the hierarchy of the church. The majority of women during the Middle Ages, however, were second-order humans.[21] Torjesen's description is incisive:

> Through her renunciation, a woman who embraced the ascetic ideal transcended the world of the body and sexuality. Fourth-

---

18. Allen, *The Concept of Woman*, 1:115.

19. Allen, *The Concept of Woman*, 1:200–205.

20. Allen, *The Concept of Woman*, 1:218–36, 384–402.

21. Although Augustine realized that men and women had similar heavenly callings and in this manner were in a spiritual sense equal, he prepared the way for complementary gender thought, but remained a proponent of gender polarity.

century writers on asceticism envisioned the virgin lifestyle as a return to the original state of human life, before the fall, sin, and sexual intercourse, as illustrated by this reconstruction.[22]

Embodied sexuality was not compatible with possessing knowledge. Then, female spirituality without sexuality was the price.

The Greek mind-body dualism stuck through the Middle Ages and evolved along with Western theology.[23] From the convent, where women were able to live scholarly lives, to the humanist rebirth of ideas and philosophies, to the fourteenth-century *Querelle des femmes* with Christine de Pisan (1365–1431), the two-pole ideology of Greek thinking continued to dehumanize women on a global scale.[24] Richard Mouw, writing on the New Testament, makes my point and aligns the question with Oscar Cullmann's crass observation, "Socrates died in a seemingly cheerful anticipation of the separation of his soul from his body. . . . Jesus on the other hand, sweats drops of blood in Gethsemane as he pleads with the Father to allow the cup of suffering to pass him by."[25] For many centuries, mind-body dualism and the lesser value of the female body restricted women's possibilities to acquire knowledge.

The revival of Aristotle's works in the thirteenth century, which became part of the required reading at universities throughout Europe, confirmed gender exclusion. Granted, as we shall see, not every male enjoyed school until after the Reformation either. The point is, popular opinion and powerful institutions presumed that women did not have what it takes to participate in spiritual or intellectual things because of their physical constitution. As we shall see, the impetus for reforming sex-polarity theory did not begin with

22. Karen Jo Torjesen, *When Women Were Priests: Women's Leadership in the Early Church and the Scandal of Their Subordination in the Rise of Christianity* (New York: HarperOne, 1993), 210.

23. See Nancey C. Murphy, *Bodies and Souls, or Spirited Bodies* (Cambridge and New York: Cambridge University Press, 2006), 11–16.

24. Christine de Pisan and Sarah Lawson, *The Treasure of the City of Ladies* (London: Penguin, 2003).

25. Richard J. Mouw, "The Imago Dei and Philosophical Anthropology," *Christian Scholar's Review* 43, no. 3 (2012): 260.

academic philosophy, but rather came from religious communities among Renaissance humanists and reformers.

The Priesthood of All Believers in the Zurich Reformation

A view of sixteenth-century Zurich puts this in perspective and provides a microcosm of what has been taking place globally ever since. The Zurich Reformation was propelled by the humanist movement spearheaded in the Helvetic Confederation by Desiderius Erasmus of Rotterdam (1466–1536). Both his work translating the Greek New Testament published in 1516 and intellectual arguments on education and women's roles should not be underestimated.[26] Beginning with Erasmus's vernacular translation of the Greek New Testament and his other works, Huldrych Zwingli, Heinrich Bullinger, and John Calvin (1509–1564) followed Erasmus's work to shape the Zurich Reformation. The significant influence of these men and the resulting impact of the Reformation on women is often overlooked.

During the Middle Ages, the Abbess of Fraumünster in Zurich was the leading political figure of the Zurich Council.[27] Female leaders managed convents throughout Europe mostly under the supervision of their male counterparts, and women mystics gained attention, while royal women and their children were in positions of power.[28] Looking to England, the power struggles and intrigues that involved women during the reign of King Henry VIII are well known. In light of the ruling class in Europe, one might wonder

26. Erika Rummel, *Erasmus on Women* (Toronto: University of Toronto Press, 1996); Christine Christ-von Wedel, *Erasmus of Rotterdam: Advocate of a New Christianity* (Toronto: University of Toronto Press, 2013), 368; Christina Christ-von Wedel, "Erasmus als Promoter neuer Frauenrollen," in *Hör nicht auf zu singen: Zeuginnen der Schweizer Reformation*, ed. Rebeccca A. Giselbrecht and Sabine Scheuter (Zürich: TVZ, 2016), 29–58.

27. Irene Gysel and Barbara Helbling, *Zürichs letzte Äbtissin: Katharina von Zimmern, 1478–1547* (Zürich: Neu Zürcher Zeitung, 1999).

28. The prime Genevan example of this in Jeanne de Jussie, *The Short Chronicle: A Poor Clare's Account of the Reformation of Geneva* (Chicago: University of Chicago Press, 2006), 208.

what difference the Reformation made to women and their societal roles.

The balance of equality certainly had to do with class and wealth in most of Europe, the scale tipping in the direction of the social elite. We must, however, note that Zurich had a different set of the elite as a confederation than Germany or other feudal systems. Nonetheless, I would argue that reforming the old church opened mutuality and inclusion and reintroduced the broader anthropological, theological discussion in the European mind—something that the old church with its papal hierarchy did not do then. What separated common women in and after the reformations from the Middle Ages is the thrust and ideation of the Protestant Reformation, which became a means of promoting equality between women and men in the private spheres of spirituality and marriage, by changing the modality of marital relations and educating women.[29] The same ideas became the engine in a process that eventually made public space more amenable to women.

Erasmus is a good starting point for examining the logical progression of women's roles in the Zurich Reformation.[30] As Erika Rummel argues in her summary of *Erasmus on Women*, he was a pivotal figure, who moved back and forth between the views held in the Middle Ages and more progressive modern ideas.[31] Erasmus moved within a new tradition that questioned the status quo and began to reexamine the stereotypes of female intellectual inferiority.[32] Why did the sixteenth century become the fulcrum for the flood of the last century's thought on female participation as spiritual beings in the *communio sanctorum*? Because the new social and ecclesial construct featured an ideological revival of the first-century notion of the priesthood of all believers, and this toppled

29. A public/private historical overview of women can be found in Jean Bethke Elshtain, *Public Man, Private Woman: Women in Social and Political Thought* (Princeton: Princeton University Press, 1981).

30. Christ-von Wedel, *Erasmus of Rotterdam*, 237–50.

31. Rummel, *Erasmus*; Christ-von Wedel, *Erasmus of Rotterdam*.

32. Of interest to our discussion is that Erasmus argued that girls should receive the same education as boys; see *Christiani matrimonii institutio* LB V 623B / CWE 69 232.

the corrupt Roman tradition with the hope of moving European culture toward a spiritually mature, that is, individually responsible, order of God-fearing people and politics.

Already in 1521, Zwingli was arguing for the priesthood of all believers before submitting his petition to allow priests to marry in 1522. Zwingli felt that not being able to marry hindered priests from living a holy life, which his own recourse to a prostitute illustrated.[33] In 1521 Zwingli wrote in reference to 1 Peter 2:5, "You yourselves are being built like living stones into a spiritual temple. You are being made into a holy priesthood to offer up spiritual sacrifices that are acceptable to God through Jesus Christ":

> Thereby Peter would have had to be forced with the sword to tes-
> tify that the bishops and priests were supposed to be princes and
> that they should reign according to worldly ways. This deserves
> to be axed down! On the contrary, Peter was of the opinion that
> all Christians are elected to the dignity of kings through our Lord
> Jesus Christ. Then all Christians no longer need any mediating
> priests to make sacrifices for them. Ultimately, each individual
> person is a priest, who brings spiritual offerings, in fact, should
> offer themselves completely to God.[34]

Within a different political system than Luther was bound to, in the Helvetic Confederation, Zwingli's argument for spiritual equality for men and women was based on a God-ordained relationship of marriage between men and women. Rather than celibacy, the Reformed pastors were to enjoy the *chastity* of marriage. The old system had clearly failed, evidenced by a great number of priests living with their women and children. They paid an indulgence to Rome to live in sin. These families were in an uncomfortable position that did not go without social repercussions.[35] Zwingli, therefore, inaugurated

33. Huldrych Zwingli to Heinrich Utinger: Emil Egli and Georg Finsler, eds., *Huldreich Zwinglis sämtliche Werke* (Berlin: Schwetschke, 1905), 110–12.

34. Huldrych Zwingli, "Die Klarheit und Gewissheit und Untrüglichkeit des Wortes Gottes, 1521," in Huldrych Zwingli, *Huldrych Zwingli Schriften* (Zürich: Theologischer Verlag Zürich, 1995), 146 (my trans.).

35. Heinrich Bullinger's own biography was imprinted by the situation in his

the priesthood of all believers mentioned above and the individual responsibility of each Christian saint before God for "bringing their own spiritual offerings . . . to God." The importance of what Zwingli wrote in 1521 is seldom connected with his petition to allow priests to marry in 1522, the Acts of the First Zurich Disputation of January 1523, and the Marriage Ordinance of 1525. His sixty-seven theses, in fact, make the clear demand that marriage is necessary. He did this all under the auspices of the priesthood of all believers.

After Zwingli was killed in 1531 in the Second Kappel War, his successor, Heinrich Bullinger, continued to profess and argue for the same spiritual gender equality as Zwingli. In his famous *Dekades*, a series of sermons from his nearly fifty years as Antistes of Zurich, he preached:

> We have the name of Christians of Christ, to whom being inseparably knit we are the members of that body whereof he is head. And because we are named Christians of Christ, who hath anointed us with the Holy Ghost, truly we also are kings and priests. Where you may see how great a benefit we have received of Christ, God and Man; for he hath made us kings and priests. . . . Furthermore if we be kings, we are lords over things, and are free, ruling, not ruled or in subjection: free, I say, from sin and everlasting death, and from all uncleanness; lords over Satan, prince of this world, and over the world itself.[36]

Bullinger preached his sermons mostly in Grossmünster for men and women, girls and boys; basically, the entire city of Zurich was under his theological influence. In another sermon, he clearly includes women as spiritual equals:

> All Christians truly, as well men as women, are priests, but we are not all ministers of the church: for we cannot all one with another

---

own family. His mother's brothers wanted to kill his father for taking her as a wife—in concubinage (134–71); and Carl Pestalozzi, *Heinrich Bullinger: Leben und ausgewählte Schriften—nach Handschriften und gleichzeitige Quellen* (Elberfeld: Friedrichs, 1858), 5.

36. Heinrich Bullinger, *The Fourth Decade*, trans. H. I. (Cambridge: Cambridge University Press, 1851), 289.

preach publicly, administer the sacraments, and execute other duties of pastors, unless we be lawfully called and ordained thereunto. This, our priesthood common to all, is spiritual, and is occupied in common duties of godliness, not in public and lawful ministries of the church. Whereupon one may and ought to instruct and admonish another privately, and while he so doeth, he executeth a priestly office; as when the good-man of the house instructeth his children at home in godliness; when the good-wife of the house teacheth and correcteth her daughters; to be short, when every one of us exhort every neighbour of ours to the desire and study of godliness.[37]

Although Bullinger put stipulations on the positional power of women within the hierarchy of the church, he is adamant that both men and women are spiritual equals. Whereas certain feminists rightly maintain that women were excluded from ecclesial positions within the system of the early Reformation church, the door was open for a change across the board that no longer gave the rights of spiritual privilege to a certain group of people set apart to serve the church as priests or nuns.[38] Now the entire population was charged with "common duties of godliness." Two unexpected and noteworthy aspects of the transition are worth mentioning. First, the few nuns left in Zurich took the opportunity to move to other regions that remained Catholic, which underscores a freedom of choice even for women in the early Reformation. Thus the Anabaptist group initially took the entire concept a step further than Zwingli and Bullinger so that their women were speaking, teaching, and we can assume participating in sacraments such as baptism in the early genesis of the tradition.[39] No doubt the key to new gender roles and women's position in society had been turned.

37. Bullinger, *The Fourth Decade*, 290.

38. The religious figure Jean de Jussie of Geneva is a good example of this. See de Jussie, *The Short Chronicle*.

39. Cf. Roland H. Bainton, "Margaret Hottinger of Zollikon," in *Women of the Reformation* (Minneapolis: Augsburg, 1977), 43–53; Auke Jelsma, "A 'Messiah for Women': Religious Commotion in North-East Switzerland 1525–26," in *Frontiers of the Reformation: Dissidence and Orthodoxy in Sixteenth-Century Europe* (Aldershot, UK: Ashgate, 1998), 41–51.

The chronological development of the notion of female spiritual worth and equality was still subject to the common values extracted from the biblical exegesis within the contexts of transition between the Middle Ages and the economy of the Reformation. Women were still to be humble, chaste, and silent—at least outside of the home.[40] However, both the institution of marriage and a perceived need for education to read Scripture, relate to God, and grow in virtue are two essential marks of the influence of Protestantism on women on a global scale. With the philosophical background and the new theological principle of equality in the spirit in place, we now turn our focus to how the Reformation influenced marital customs, and then to the continuing Protestant necessity for educating women, finally drawing on recent studies to support my argument that *semper reformanda* and spiritual gender equality are fundamental Protestant doctrines that still maintain influence globally.

Marriage and Mutuality

Zwingli based his argument and insistence on the marriage of priests on his argument that to marry was a religious, ethical priority because, otherwise, sexual impurity is normative.[41] In many of his works, the reformer calls the medieval Roman system of marriage unhealthy. He worked alongside the Zurich Council to set up a new Court for Marriage as well as put laws in place that improved women's nuptial rights. After Zwingli, Bullinger followed suit. Bullinger's *Eheschriften* will receive a bit more attention here because it was an educational tool and key instrument throughout Europe for spreading the redefined parameters of marriage upheld in the Zurich Reformation. First, however, a few instances of what

40. Here the "Series Editors' Introduction" to Margaret Leah King and Albert Rabil, *Teaching Other Voices: Women and Religion in Early Modern Europe* (Chicago: University of Chicago Press, 2007), deserves mention for the many publications from early modern women edited and commentated on by various scholars.

41. See Theses 28–30 in Zwingli's 67 Theses: Zwingli, *Huldrych Zwingli Schriften*, 297–315.

was going on in the Helvetic Confederation in the years of the early Reformation in the area of relations between men and women, marriage, and polygamy serve to underline the fragile condition of the institution of marriage at the inception of the reforms.

During the early years, moving from clerical marriage to polygamy came into play because the parameters of inter-gender relationships and holy matrimony were unclear and in flux. The boundaries were unclear as Huldrych Zwingli wrote to Joachim Vadian (1484–1551) in March of 1526. Zwingli wrote to ask Vadian, the mayor and St. Gallen reformer, because some gossip about St. Gallen was agitating the people of Zurich. Rumor had it that the Anabaptists in Appenzell, outside of St. Gallen, were practicing communal sex. Zwingli requested that Vadian take action to stop the libertine practices.[42] Although the Anabaptists in St. Gallen were thereafter squelched and dispersed or reintegrated into the Reformed Church, the Anabaptists who overran Münster in Germany between 1534 and 1535 not only maintained their libertine ways but also propagated polygamous practices. Their intentions were to erect a common theocracy under the leadership of John of Leyden (1509–1536).[43] Leyden is said to have introduced radical polygamy at Münster—himself the husband of sixteen women. The Münster Rebellion was eventually suppressed. Due to the various scandals, and because Zurich was well aware of what was going on in Münster and concerned that the reforms would end in chaos, the Anabaptist persecution followed. The cases in question also led Zwingli and the council to attend to the rules of matrimony.

In 1532, reimagining marriage was a European conundrum reaching such proportions that Charles V (reigned 1550–1558) tried to resolve the situation by making bigamy a capital offense in Germany, Austria, and Spain.[44] Despite the ambivalence, opportunistic individuals like the Landgrave Philip of Hessen (1504–1567)

42. See Bainton, "Margaret Hottinger of Zollikon," 24–29.

43. Roland H. Bainton, "The Immoralities of the Patriarchs According to the Exegesis of the Late Middle Ages and of the Reformation," *Harvard Theological Review* (1930): 39–49.

44. Walter Köhler, "Die Doppelehe Landgraf Philipps von Hessen," *Historische Zeitschrift* 94, no. 3 (1905): 385–411. A look at the court of Henry VIII in England

embraced the practice of polygamy anyway.[45] Philip reasoned with both Luther (1483–1546) and Melanchthon (1497–1560) that his first wife and mother of his six children, Christine, drank and smelled bad.[46] Philip was convinced that his own infidelity to Christine could be remedied, if only he could marry another woman. Philip's potential defection to Catholicism was such a threat to the reform that Luther, Melanchthon, and Martin Bucer (1491–1551) acceded to Philip's wishes and signed the Wittenberg Deliberation, which allowed Philip to marry Margarethe von der Saale in 1540, while he was still married to Christine. Despite promises of secrecy, word of this polygamy got out. Luther commented that polygamy is not right but certainly preferable to divorce.[47]

After the debacle of Philip of Hessen's second marriage, the preacher Johannes Lening (1491–1566) wrote a complete apologetic tract in support of polygamy titled *Dialogus Neobuli* that was circulated throughout Europe in mid-August of 1541 under the pseudonym Huldricus Neobulus.[48] The problem of polygamy continued to plague Bullinger even in the 1560s as the outcome of the Bernardino Ochino (1487–1564) tragedy.[49] The seventy-six-year-old Ochino, pastor of the Italian congregation in Zurich and companion of the Zurich and Genevan reformers, was expelled from Zurich and died within a year in Austerlitz, Moravia, a haven for Anabaptists and

---

(1491–1547) removes any doubt that polygamy was causing social unrest in numerous regions of Europe.

45. Köhler, "Die Doppelehe Landgraf Philipps von Hessen," 393.

46. Köhler, "Die Doppelehe Landgraf Philipps von Hessen," 402–3; John L. Thompson, "Patriarchs, Polygamy, and Private Resistance: John Calvin and Others on Breaking God's Rules," *Sixteenth Century Journal* 25, no. 1 (1994): 12–13.

47. For more on Philip of Hessen and polygamy, see John Alfred Faulkner, "Luther and the Bigamous Marriage of Philip of Hesse," *American Journal of Theology* 17, no. 2 (1913): 206–31.

48. See Mark Taplin, *The Italian Reformers and the Zurich Church, c. 1540–1620* (Aldershot, UK: Ashgate, 2003), 157; H. J. Selderhuis, *Marriage and Divorce in the Thought of Martin Bucer* (Kirksville, MO: Truman State University Press, 1999), 159n206.

49. The Italian Waldensian was pastor to the Italian religious refugees that were exiled and remained in Zurich; see Karl Benrath, *Bernardino Ochino von Siena* (Braunschweig: C. A. Schwetschke und Sohn, 1892).

other outcasts. Beza's letter to Ochino admonishing his *Dialogi XXX* served as the foundation for his *Tractatio de polygamia et divortiis* published in 1568 and *Tractatio de polygamia* published alone in 1573, as a reprint in 1582, and published in Dutch in 1595. Calvin's successor's arguments against polygamy clarified the theological and legal foundation of Christian monogamy.[50] Marriage between one man and one woman took years to become an institution according to a reinterpretation of the reformers' exegetical model: *sola scriptura*.

Handbooks on marriage had always been a literary tradition, but even more so after the church made marriage a sacrament in the twelfth century.[51] Bullinger published his handbook to provide matrimonial guidelines amidst the aforementioned uncertainty that gripped people of all social standings regarding the reformed institution of marriage. It seems that the Anabaptist outcasts, the Landgrave Philip von Hessen, Luther and Melanchthon, and the citizens of Zurich all lacked a common plumb line for measuring the changes in relations between the sexes. In a comparison of Bullinger's *Vollkommne underrichtung* (1527) and his *Der christlich eestand* (1540), the editor of the most recent publication of these texts, Detlef Roth, notes that Bullinger employed an entirely different style and methodology of argumentation in his second treatise

50. Benrath, *Bernardino Ochino von Siena*; Theodoro Beza, *De haereticis a civili magistratu puniendis libellus, adversus Martini Belliifaraginem* (Geneva: Oliva Roberti Stephani, 1554).

51. Detlef Roth, who edited Bullinger's *Eheschriften*, also discussed the entire work in a scholarly article. See Emidio Campi and Detlef Roth, eds., *Pastoraltheologische Schriften* (Zürich: Theologischer Verlag Zürich, 2009). Bullinger modeled his handbook on marriage on Erasmus, *Christiani matrimonij institutio*, Juan Luis Vives and Juan Justiniano, *Libro llamado Instrucion de la muger christiana. El qual co[n]tiene como se ha de criar vna virgen hasta casarla: y despues de casada como ha de regir su casa: y viuir prosperamente con su marido. y si fuere biuda lo que es tenida a hazer* (Caragoça: Casa de Bartholome de Nagera, 1555), and Juan Luis Vives, Richard Hyrde, and Thomas Berthelet, *A very fruteful and pleasant boke callyd the Instruction of a Christen woman: made fyrste in latyne* (London: in [a]edibus Thom[a]e Berth. regij impressoris. cum priuilegio ad imprimendum solum., 1541), [6], 138 [i.e. 140] leaves. Also see Rüdiger Schnell, *Geschlechterbeziehungen und Textfunktionen: Studien zu Eheschriften der frühen Neuzeit* (Tübingen: M. Niemeyer, 1998), 1–58; Charles William Pfeiffer, "Bullinger and Marriage" (PhD diss., St. Louis University, 1982), 125–54.

on marriage.[52] Roth attributes this change to Bullinger's position as Antistes in Zurich in conjunction with his involvement in the various cases brought before the Zurich marital council, which as pastor he was obliged to read to his congregation on Sundays.[53] Establishing scriptural conventions for the behavior of women and men was also a process reignited by the Reformation. Bullinger addresses almost every aspect of relations between men and women in his handbook and so, as the case of Philip of Hessen demonstrates, divorce was also an issue.[54] Another landmark of the Zurich Reformation was that divorce was also possible for women in untenable circumstances of unfaithfulness and abuse—an improvement for women from the laws of the Middle Ages.

From a social history perspective, one may also ask what role the mature Bullinger's eleven years of marriage and by this time almost the same number of children played in developing his theology of marriage for the handbook. Considering Bullinger's private and professional experiences, it seems consistent that his first marital instruction manual, the *Vollkommne underrichtung* of 1527, emphasizes parity and mutuality between conjugal partners.[55] However, in light of his experience, the second handbook of 1540 places more emphasis on the legal and moral foundations for male and female behavior, catalogs regulations and conventions, while seeking authoritative definitions in order to institutionalize marital relations.[56]

All euphoria aside and without being one-sided, mutuality and spiritual equality are theological ideals; thus social historians

---

52. Detlef Roth, "Heinrich Bullingers Eheschriften," *Zwingliana* 31 (2004): 281–82.

53. Roth, "Heinrich Bullingers Eheschriften," 291–96.

54. A small assessment of a meeting of the Marriage Court from 21 February 1543 with words from Bullinger is among some fragments at the ZB Archives in Zurich, Ms F 154, no. 6, "Von dem verkünden der Een und Kylchgang, ob man scheyden möge. Ob man den geschiedenen die Ee erlauben . . . döröftfe. Von Straff des Eebruchs . . ." (Trans: In regard to announcing a marriage and going to church, whether one may get a divorce. Whether a divorced person may remarry. . . . The punishment for adultery.)

55. Gsell, "Hierarchie und Gegenseitigkeit."

56. Roth, "Heinrich Bullingers Eheschriften."

and German-language scholars from secular environs often argue against the case that the Protestant Reformation influenced marital relations in a good way and lament the lack of research on religious women in the Reformation.[57] In an article in *Sociological Theory* on Marianne Weber's *Authority and Marriage* we read:

> Protestantism did raise marriage, as a work of God, above celibacy, as the work of humans; but it also allowed sexual love only under the blemish of "evil desires," which originate not from God, but from the devil. In the case of such desire God merely "looks through the fingers" in marriage because, as Luther says, there it is compensated by many kinds of listlessness and torment.[58]

She then profusely cites Luther.

Susan Karant-Nunn, another social historian, working on women in the German Reformation, has the same contentions concerning women and the Luther Reformation, pointing to the witch hunts, Anabaptist persecution, and also what Luther said about women to make the point that the Protestant Reformation did not improve women's roles whatsoever.[59] Perhaps it is best to conclude that marriage was the testing ground for theories on marriage during the early Reformation as Scripture was reinterpreted by the reformers. For those who were protected by the laws on mar-

---

57. Gause, "Reformation, geschlechtergeschichtlich—auch ein notwendiger Nachtrag zum Calvinjahr 2009," 293–309. Noteworthy are the writings on this subject as early as 1992 in Roper et al., "Was There a Crisis?"; Scott H. Hendrix and Susan C. Karant-Nunn, *Masculinity in the Reformation Era* (Kirksville, MO: Truman State University Press, 2008), ix–xix; Susanna Burghartz, *Zeiten der Reinheit—Orte der Unzucht: Ehe und Sexualität in Basel während der Frühen Neuzeit* (Paderborn: Ferdinand Schöningh, 1999).

58. Marianne Weber, "Authority and Autonomy in Marriage," translation with introduction and commentary by Craig R. Bermingham, *Sociological Theory* 21, no. 2 (2003): 88.

59. See Susan C. Karant-Nunn, "Was tut ein Mann und wie soll eine Frau sein? Diversität in den Geschlechterrollen," in *Hör nicht auf zu singen. Frauen der Schweizer Reformation*, ed. Rebecca A. Giselbrecht and Sabine Scheuter (Zürich: Theologische Verlag Zürich, 2016).

riage in Zurich regulating legal responsibility for children, banning child marriage, and requiring consent of marriage from both partners, the Reformation was undoubtedly helpful. Finally, putting all value judgments and exceptions aside, the Reformation standards for marriage between one man and one woman were undoubtedly authoritative and seemingly satisfactory for all of Western culture until very recently.

Protestant Women and Education

The thread between marriage and educating women is not as thin as one might assume. Returning to the image of the Tower of Babel, spiritual equality and legal frameworks for marital conventions spread across Europe, alongside the necessity to read Scripture. The unity in diversity of place and cultures was the stunning global thrust to educate women everywhere so they could, in turn, educate their children. The Reformation and the spiritual equality of both genders are central to the Protestant necessity to educate women.

Continuing to focus on the Swiss Reformation as our example, we see that the *Historisches Lexikon der Schweiz* explains that girls in higher social situations in Switzerland were educated in convents during the Middle Ages. Although there were parochial schools after the thirteenth century, it is unclear whether or not girls attended these.[60] From the fifteenth century on, girls from the upper class were able to attend private schools in almost every large city in the Helvetic Confederation, now Switzerland. A *meistressa d'escola* taught girls. Girls and boys enjoyed the same rudimentary education in rural areas until the nineteenth century. The records from the countryside are, however, less conclusive.

According to Zwingli, boys had to go to school for four or five hours daily and learn a profession; girls only went to school. Anne-Lise Head-König tells us that schools were only open in winter. She

---

60. The information here is translated from Anne-Lise Head-König, "Mädchenerziehung," Historisches Lexikon der Schweiz, www.hls-dhs-dss.ch/textes/d /D48195.php.

maintains that mothers played a vital role in teaching reading in any case. By the seventeenth century, girls' educations were catching up with those of boys in Reformed Zurich, and by the second half of the eighteenth century, girls and boys in 50.5 percent of the 263 rural areas studied had an equivalent reading level, while 44.5 percent of the boys had a higher education. It is worth noting that reading and writing were different: over 20 percent of the boys could write, but only 10 percent of the girls. Head-König makes the observation, "In the Catholic regions the number of girls that went to school is much lower, mostly below the level of boys."[61] Girls of the bourgeois class in Catholic cities were often taught in private institutions or in convents. At least in Reformed Switzerland, the importance of education is historically documented.

Although there are many examples of mothers teaching their children to read and memorize the Bible, one of the letters sent to Heinrich Bullinger by Anne Hooper from London on April 3, 1551, concerning his god-daughter Rachel Hooper, who was baptized on March 29, 1548, is particularly endearing. Rachel was only three or four years old.

> First then, you must know that she is well acquainted with English, and that she has learned by heart within these three months the form of giving thanks, the Ten Commandments, the Lord's Prayer, the Apostles' Creed, together with the first and second Psalm of David. And now, as she knows her letters, she is instructed in the catechism.[62]

The impressive efforts of Rachel Hooper represent a mother-and-daughter achievement and a Protestant trend. The priority of education and reading in Protestantism continued to significantly influence the roles of mothers, daughters, and the rest of the family members, opening the door to knowledge and relationship with

61. Head-König, "Mädchenerziehung" (my translation).
62. Hastings Robinson, *Original Letters Relative to the English Reformation, Written During the Reigns of King Henry VIII, King Edward VI, and Queen Mary: Chiefly from the Archives of Zurich* (Cambridge: Cambridge University Press, 1846), 107.

God. Therefore, higher education and eventually the ordination of women as ministers of the church spring from the same well.

Public higher education was another hurdle for women that a Protestant woman was eventually able to overcome. The first woman in Europe to be educated in an institute of higher learning was the German-born Anna Maria van Schurman (1607–1678). Although she was required to sit in a cage during lectures so as not to distract the male students, she attended the University of Utrecht beginning in 1636. In 1659, she wrote *Whether a Maid May Be Called a Scholar?* The excerpt of her tract below follows the tradition of the *Querelle des femmes*, which was discussed above as an argument surrounding the inclusion of women as equal members of humanity with men. The question she asked was the same posed from the Middle Ages onward: *Ob die Weiber Menschen seyn, oder nicht?* (Whether women are persons or not).[63] The answer is now clear: the education of women as promoted and facilitated by the Reformation moved past the question toward a real response, and gender equality continues to be achieved through educational inclusion. Van Schurman indicates that she is at least convinced of women's humanity and intellectual "desire for self-improvement."[64]

> My deep regard for learning, my conviction that equal justice is the right of all, impel me to protest against the theory which would allow only a minority of my sex to attain to what is, in the opinion of all men, most worth having. For since wisdom is admitted to be the crown of human achievement, and is within every man's right to aim at in proportion to his opportunities, I cannot see why a young girl in whom we admit a desire for self-improvement should not be encouraged to acquire the best that life affords.[65]

63. Gisela Bock, *Frauen in der europäischen Geschichte: vom Mittelalter bis zur Gegenwart* (Munich: C. H. Beck, 2000), 16; Valens Acidalius, *Disputatio nova contra mulieres, qva probatur eas homines non esse* (Wittenberg/Leipzig: S.I., 1595).

64. Anna Maria van Schurman, *The Learned Maid or, Whether a Maid May Be a Scholar?*, trans. Clement Barksdale (London: John Redmayne, 1659), 55.

65. Van Schurman, *The Learned Maid*, 55.

Van Schurman's spiritual journey from Calvinism to becoming a member of the Labadist community established by the mystic Jean de Labadie (1610–1674) is a pattern for female Protestant spirituality that can be traced throughout the past five hundred years—her spirituality trumped her desire for fame or fortune and ended in self-denying service to others. Still, the point here is that her educational opportunities were part of a linear progression of intellectual freedom for women due to the Protestant humanist tradition. As Bo Karen Lee explains, "Though the core of her thought would remain Calvinistic, van Schurman expanded her categories, embracing the thought and spirituality of both nascent Pietism and Catholic mysticism."[66] Her education allowed her greater freedom of choice. She is an early example of a global phenomenon.

The debate on gender order was in no way defined in the early seventeenth century, nor has it reached its climax on a global scale. However, a tendency for including women in spiritual matters, and practices such as prayer, was mostly unrestricted. The idea of hierarchical equality or positional power from a leadership or socio-cultural perspective is another area of progressive inclusion. Here too, including women in church leadership and pastoral ministry has always varied within the diversity of Protestantism. Indeed, a tendency toward increasing women's social participation, as we will see in my conclusion and survey of contemporary literature on this subject, depends on education. Mary Stewart Van Leeuwen, who argues extensively for gender reconciliation from a Protestant perspective in *After Eden,* claims:

> All agree that the theological and ethical core of Christian faith supports the liberation and affirmation of women. It is this core that functions normatively for feminist interpretation and use of the Bible, just as John Calvin's emphasis on God's promise of grace served as his interpretive core.[67]

66. Bo Karen Lee, "I Wish to Be Nothing," in *Women, Gender, and Radical Religion in Early Modern Europe*, ed. Sylvia Monica Brown (Leiden: Brill, 2007), 189–218, 196.

67. Mary Stewart Van Leeuwen, *After Eden: Facing the Challenge of Gender Reconciliation* (Grand Rapids: Eerdmans, 1993), 141.

In accord with the historical progression of increasing educational opportunities and women's freedom to join the public sphere, the University of Zurich, in one of the Protestant Swiss cantons, serves here as a final example of what slowly occurred globally through education. Women began to study at the University of Zurich in 1864, but they could only audit classes and not receive a degree. In 1913 Laura Elisabeth Rosa Gutknecht started to study theology.[68] She passed her boards in 1917 and was certified as a theologian. Although she worked in a church, preaching and teaching until she retired in 1953, she was never ordained. The ordination of women in the Swiss Evangelical Reformed Church did not take place until 1963. In 2016, more than 65 percent of the students at the Theological Seminary at the University of Zurich were female.

Indeed, a long road lies ahead before the doors to equal cultural valuation are completely open for all women everywhere to walk through. The historical progression of increased female participation in public space, at least in Western culture during the past five hundred years, cannot be denied.[69] To avoid sounding presumptuous, the word "progress" requires a definition. In our temporal context, progress is a positive step toward self-determination in a social group. A Christian definition of progress is sanctification, or moving toward God and godliness. Coming from the dualistic polarity of the past, the theological notion of the priesthood of all believers is a bridge and progressive theological contrast to the Aristotelian philosophical notion of women that still influences female self-identity and the global understanding and valuation of women. *Nota bene*, the idea of women being spiritually equal to men changed gender relations in many ways. Given the New Testament presupposition that all Christians are equal before God, the progressive nature of social change toward gender inclusion

---

68. Ines Buhofer and Irene Gysel, *Rosa Gutknecht: Pfarrhelferin am Grossmünster 1919–1953—eine Dokumentation* (Zürich: Helferei Grossmünster, 1995). All of the data concerning Rosa Gutknecht are contained in this little pamphlet in German.

69. Stephen Edelston Toulmin, *Cosmopolis: The Hidden Agenda of Modernity* (Chicago: University of Chicago Press, 1992), 167–74.

in Western cultures on a practical level is one result of existential exegesis and *sola scriptura*.

Gender Equality through Education

Considering the fact that it is challenging to scrape together literature on educating women in the Reformation, the research on Protestant missionary efforts to educate women, and the social results of these efforts that have been published in recent years, are remarkable. Mostly women are studying the topic of Protestant missionary efforts to educate women around the globe in places like Korea, India, Ireland, and Africa, to name a few locations. In her 1987 article in *Comparative Education*, "World Religions, Women and Education," Ursula King laments that "much more is known about the education of women in Christianity than in other religions." She concludes that "[t]he examples considered above also highlight the important contribution women religious have made to female education, in previous ages and in modern times, if one thinks of the large number of women missionaries and female teaching orders." Without outlining the wonderful projects of the Catholic Church to educate women globally, I want to stay focused on the Protestant efforts, which I have already argued had a scripturally based reasoning and an intrinsically missional imperative for spiritual gender equality since the Reformation. Around the same time, in 1988, Herbert R. Swanson wrote in *The Journal of Social Issues in Southeast Asia* on missionary influence in Thailand:

> For the first members of the "new generation," living in middle-class American Protestant missionary homes and institutions intensified and focused social change and grounded the missionaries' religious agenda in a much broader experience of new work habits, ways of ordering time, means of systematization, and a sense of discipline. All of this contributed to removing mission school girls from their traditional socio-cultural system and its restrictions on women's education. The domestication of Christian girls in missionary homes and institutions taught them

how to live and work in organizational settings unknown in traditional society. Those homes and institutions prepared girls culturally for professional employment, and then provided the first significant source of jobs available to trained, salaried women.[70]

Swanson reports on the phenomenon of mission that created educational networks, classes, and programs for women since the seventeenth century—*naturally* "to facilitate the Christianization of northern Thai society."[71] He underscores my point that Protestantism and education go hand in hand and have thereby furthered gender equality in spiritual and, eventually, socially oppressive aspects of cultures on women.

In her 2004 study, "Religiosity as a Determinant of Educational Attainment: The Case of Conservative Protestant Women in the United States," Evelyn Lehrer demonstrates a clear correlation between religious participation and completing both high school and college in the United States.[72] The same dynamic is reported in Korea, where Chong Bum Kim argues that the impact of Protestant mission schools was "especially dramatic for Korean women, who previously had no formal system of education."[73] She quotes Yi ch'an-yŏng in a footnote:

At the time (of the founding of women's schools) in our nation, shackled by the customs of Confucian feudalism, women's rights were completely ignored, and they did not even possess the opportunity for learning. But as Christianity came in, it emphasized the need to implement both male and female education based on the modern Christian idea of men and women as equal in Christ.[74]

70. Herbert R. Swanson, "A New Generation: Missionary Education and Changes in Women's Roles in Traditional Northern Thai Society," *Sojourn: Journal of Social Issues in Southeast Asia* 3, no. 2 (1988): 187–206, 198–99.

71. Swanson, "A New Generation," 187.

72. Evelyn Lehrer, "Religiosity as a Determinant of Educational Attainment: The Case of Conservative Protestant Women in the United States," *Review of Economics of the Household* 2 (2004): 203–19, 211.

73. Reza Chong Bum Kim, "For God and Home: Women's Education in Early Korean Protestantism," *Acta Koreana* 11, no. 3 (2008): 9–29.

74. Quoted in Chong Bum Kim, "For God and Home: Women's Education in

Notably in the same Korean context, the phenomena of the glass ceiling and historical amnesia regarding the achievements of women in church history still exist—as they have since the Reformation in early modern Europe and at the highest levels of leadership in today's global corporate environments and institutional hierarchies.[75] I conclude this section with the results of a study on education in India and another on the impact of Protestantism on the construction of female identity in Lebanon, both of them conducted in the field of political science. The first demonstrates that the data concerning educating females and Protestantism have also captured the imaginations and interest of secular scientists. The article "Competitive Religious Entrepreneurs: Christian Missionaries and Female Education in Colonial and Post-Colonial India" was published in 2012 in the *British Journal of Political Science*. It has a powerful message about the influence of British colonialism on education compared to Christian missionary education within the same scope. The authors conclude that it was not the British who had "large effects . . . on education" but rather the influence of Protestant missionaries made a greater imprint on "human capital."

The case of female identity among Muslim women in Lebanon is fascinating in relation to Christian-Muslim relations and how Christian education influences the "Construction of Female Identity" in Lebanon. The study focuses on the years between 1860 and 1950, noting that the missionary movement of that era followed the cliché of "women's work for women."[76] The notion discussed

Early Korean Protestantism," 10; Yi ch'an-yŏng, *Survey of Korean Christian Church History* (Seoul: Somangsa, 1994), 169–70. Cf. Lee-Ellen Strawn, "Protestant Bible Education for Women: First Steps in Professional Education for Modern Korean Women," *Journal of Korean Religions* 4, no. 1 (2013): 99: "Not only did these opportunities provide many Korean women with basic literacy skills but the advanced training for certified Bible women status represented the initial steps in women's professional education."

75. Christine Sungjin Chang, "Hidden but Real: The Vital Contribution of Biblewomen to the Rapid Growth of Korean Protestantism, 1892–1945," *Women's History Review* 17, no. 4 (2008): 575–95, 591.

76. Ellen Fleischmann, "The Impact of American Protestant Missions in Lebanon on the Construction of Female Identity, 1860–1950," *Islam and Christian-Muslim Relations* 13, no. 4 (2002): 411–26, 412. Fleischmann notes in footnote 10,

above concerning the central role that women played in educating their children in the sixteenth century continued in this case to be the premise and foundation of Christian values and mission. Ellen Fleischmann suggests that "home life, character and service to religion" were the main vision that the missionaries wanted to transfer to their students.[77] In concluding her brief survey, which is in no way exhaustive of recent scholarship on the influence of Protestant education on women around the globe, Fleischmann summarizes what I meant by the "progressive influence" of Protestantism on women globally:

> The missionaries could take credit in character building, but the irony is that missionary women provided role models for different kinds of characters from the modern homemakers they were trying to create through the educational system.[78]

The missionary women's identity as professional women rubbed off on their students, and many of the students went on to higher education or joined the workforce in some way or other. The implications of contemporary scholarship suggest indeed that at least one of the major influences of the Reformation on women has come through efforts to educate women to read, later to write, but in general to be able to think for themselves, due to the necessity of knowing God through Scripture.

Toward a Better End

Learning and knowledge are powerful keys to more gender equality. In the sixteenth century, the power of education and knowing was transferred from a religious monopoly and extended to all people for the common good. The Reformation was about setting things

---

"This was the title of a journal published by the Women's Foreign Missionary Society of the Presbyterian Church."

77. Fleischmann, "The Impact of American Protestant Missions," 417.

78. Fleischmann, "The Impact of American Protestant Missions," 420.

right, according to Scripture. It is ironic that the rediscovery of oppressive philosophical thought but also the theological ideas of the church fathers eventually brought intellectuals and religious leaders to revisit Scripture and climb down from their high towers to fight for social change.

Freedom to think and participate, at least in spiritual things, were slowly perceived as human rights. Thus, unity in diversity took on its own dynamic. It would be shortsighted to suggest that the Protestants educated the world—wrong to forget all the efforts of other groups, particularly the many Catholic institutions and orders. Nonetheless, the reformers did seize the kairos moment of transition. These men and women did so first because of their belief that the Word of God must be accessible to everyone. Later, other men and women spread the gospel to all people everywhere in response to the *missio Dei*.

Women's right to societal belonging as private and public citizens is now uncontested in most contemporary Western societies, and equality discourse is global. Philosophy and theology required correctives to achieve this. From a biblical perspective, the chronology of this present system will end with Christ in the eschaton. However, the Christian story—our reformation—is not over. The Reformation ordering of marriage with mutuality and the layers of the marital and family institution are in flux; they are still subject to change. We celebrate that women joined the workforce due to missionary work, but we must also remember that children and families need attention to flourish. Global technology is knowledge sharing, is education, but it is also a power behind inhuman violence, detached drone warfare, and various social pathologies. Our world still needs reformation. So we continue to reform and be reformed in a never-ending cycle of learning and education in God's ways, slowly progressing, as women and men, toward a better end.

4 The Global South

....

The Synod of Dort on Baptizing "Ethnics"

DAVID D. DANIELS

Lodging the late Protestant Reformation as a topic within the study of world Christianity can offer novel perspectives to the study of the emergence of Protestantism by excavating the interdependencies or interconnections within the history of the Protestant corridors in Europe and the Protestant nodes (or outposts) in Africa as well as Asia and the Americas between 1517 and 1665. Studying African Protestants along with other Protestants of the Global South during the late Protestant Reformation as a topic within the academic discipline of world Christianity challenges the reigning historiography of the Protestant Reformation. The reigning historiography interprets the Protestant Reformation as a European event, focusing exclusively on the activities of "white" European Protestants while being either uninterested or conceptually incapable of inserting African Protestants as well as Protestants indigenous to Asia and the Americas into the narrative of the Reformation. The study of world Christianity pursues alternatives to this dominant historiographic trajectory.

A critical site for this historical investigation was the Synod of Dort (1618–19), a pan-European Reformed Protestant conference, where a debate ensued about the baptism of what the English delegation called the "ethnics" or non-Christians from the Global South. The Synod of Dort debated two Reformed Protestant positions on baptizing ethnics, a topic prompted by an actual South Asian case. While the South Asian ecclesial context elicited the "sacramental" or pastoral issue, African Christians supplied the social content that informed "ethnic" as a term for European Protestants. By 1600, the Catholic history of baptizing African ethnics in recognizable numbers after 1444 was known in key circles.[1]

Through interrogating "On Baptizing the Children of Ethnics," a document of the Synod of Dort, as an expansion of the debates about baptism among Reformed Protestants during the late Protestant Reformation, we will argue here that Reformed Protestantism shifted during the Synod of Dort from being solely a European-oriented movement to a slightly more globally oriented movement that was shaped by the pastoral concerns of the Global South as well as by those of Europe.

"Ethnic" as a Term at the Synod of Dort

As a theological document and an ecclesial act, "On Baptizing the Children of Ethnics" is the product of a robust pan-European Reformed Protestant debate on the scope of baptism; the issue of baptism loomed large during the Protestant Reformation. Voluminous historical investigations probe the Reformation debates about the age of baptismal candidates, whether infant or adult; the mode of baptism, whether pouring and sprinkling or immersion; and the theology of baptism, whether a sacrament or an ordinance. Vastly underexamined within Reformation studies are debates about Protestant baptismal practices related to the baptism of non-Christian Africans, Asians, and Native Americans.[2]

---

1. On a discussion of the Synod of Dort and ethnic baptism, see Robert Carl-Heinz Shell, *Children of Bondage: A Social History of the Slave Society at the Cape of Good Hope, 1652–1838* (Hanover, NH, and London: Wesleyan University Press / University Press of New England, 1994), 334–48, 350–56, 362–65; and Yudha Thianto, *The Way to Heaven: Catechisms and Sermons in the Establishment of the Dutch Reformed Church in the East Indies* (Eugene, OR: Wipf & Stock, 2014).

2. "De ethnicorum pueris baptizandis" (1618); for example, see Hughes Oliph-

In broaching the baptism of the children of ethnics as a theological topic and ecclesial issue at the Synod of Dort, the delegates could have availed themselves of two axes of religious polarities. Where should ethnics be plotted on these axes? Should they be plotted on the *Christian-infidel* axis or the *Christian–primal religion* axis? Plotted along the *Christian-infidel* axes were Jews and Muslims since they allegedly knew of Christ but rejected him as the messiah and God incarnate. Along the *Christian–primal religion* axis were plotted religions ranging from the traditional religions of the Aztecs, Akans, and Maori to Hinduism and Buddhism. Being plotted on the *Christian–primal religion* axis placed the ethnics outside the hostility that Christians directed toward Jews and Muslims because of their religious infidelities. While African Muslims along with European and Asian Muslims received the scorn of Christian Europeans, African ethnics, in particular, escaped most of the hostility targeted toward Jews and Muslims.[3]

Prior to rehearsing the theological debate regarding ethnic baptism, there needs to be a discussion of the word "ethnic" to characterize the religion of these particular non-Christians. "Ethnic" as a term was first populated by Africans during the late medieval era within Europe, especially on the Iberian Peninsula. By the time of the opening of the Synod of Dort, Roman Catholic priests had been baptizing African ethnics and their children in the Kongo, Angola, Benin, Warri, Senegambia, Cape Verde, São Tomé, and Mutapa among other sites in Africa. Additionally, Ethiopian Orthodox priests had baptized ethnics in the non-Christian communities of the Ethiopian empire. Consequently, African ethnics filled the initial social content that informed "ethnic" as a term preceding and during the late Protestant Reformation.[4]

---

ant Old, *The Shaping of the Reformed Baptismal Rite in the Sixteenth Century* (Grand Rapids: Eerdmans, 1992).

3. George M. Frederickson, *Racism: A Short History* (Princeton: Princeton University Press, 2002/2015), 26–39. "Primal" was selected over the terms "heathen" and "pagan," even with the limitation that world religions such as Hinduism are not categorized as primal religions.

4. See Adrian Hastings, *The Church in Africa, 1450–1950* (Oxford: Clarendon, 1994).

English Protestant authors began translating the term as "ethnicks" rather than heathens or pagans even before the Synod of Dort in 1618. During the sixteenth century, there were references to "An ethnicke and pagan kyng" as well as an "ethnicke philosopher." Robert Fludd (1574–1637) classified ancient Greek philosophy as "ethnick philosophy." According to Colin Kidd in sixteenth- and seventeenth-century English parlance, ethnic pertained to religious matters. Kidd drew this conclusion from Thomas Blount's *Glossographia*, which Blount compiled in 1618–19. However, Blount had more negative connotations than Fludd and others. Blount defined "ethnick" as "heathenish, ungodly, irreligious: And may be used substantively for a heathen or gentile." Based on the Greek word *ethnos*, it had been translated in English as "ethnics," "nation," "heathen," or "pagan." As a term of religion, it was regularly employed as the opposite of Christians and Jews. Consequently, "ethnick" was not used as a derisive term but, in contrast to Christianity which was the true, godly religion, it was a term that referred to the religions beyond Christianity, Judaism, and Islam. John Hales employed the term without any derision. Hales, an observer at the Synod of Dort, wrote an eyewitness account chronicling the debate about baptizing the children of non-Christians in the form of letters written during the Synod. He translated into English the Latin word *ethnicorum* as "ethnick."[5]

The enslavement of African peoples especially complicates all historical analyses of African ethnics and of the encounters between Africans and Europeans during the era prior to the rise of modern racism. Clearly, by the early seventeenth century a large segment of the transatlantic slave trade markets were sub-Saharan Africans. Yet,

5. *Oxford English Dictionary*, 1545 Udall, Erasm. Par. Pref. 3; 1581: Marbeck, Bk. of Notes 61; Robert Fludd, *Mosaical Philosophy, Grounded upon the Essentiall Truth or Eternal Sapience* (London: Humphrey Moseley Printer, 1659), 30 at https://archive .org/stream/mosaicallphilosoooflud/; Colin Kidd, *British Identity Before Nationalism and Nationhood in the Atlantic World, 1600–1800* (Cambridge: Cambridge University Press, 2004), 34; "Mr. Hales Letters from the Synod of Dort to the Right Honourable Sr. Dudley Carlton, Lord Embassador &c.," in John Hales, *Golden Remains of the ever memorable Mr. John Hales of Eton College &c.* (London: Printed for Tim. Garwaithe and the Little North Doore of St. Paul, 1659), 189f. (renumbered as page 1f.).

the global slave trade industry at that time included Eastern Europeans, Eurasians, "white" Muslims, South Asians, and Native Americans in addition to Northern and sub-Saharan Africans. Therefore one could argue that slavery in the early to mid-seventeenth century functioned differently than it would operate within the system of modern racism during the later seventeenth and subsequent centuries. Consequently, prejudice against Africans or Asians during the Long Protestant Reformation should be distinguished from what constitutes modern racism as a socio-economic-political system.[6]

Ethnic Baptism at the Synod of Dort

The Synod of Dort convened an international ecumenical council of Reformed Protestants. Delegations from England, Scotland, the Swiss cantons, Geneva, the Palatinate, Hesse, Nassau-Wetteravia, Bremen, and Emden joined the Dutch delegates at the city of Dort in their deliberations. A French delegation was selected, but the French monarch refused to allow them to attend the Synod. Apparently uninvited were the Reformed Christians in Eastern Europe such as those in the Polish-Lithuanian Commonwealth, Bohemia, Hungary, and Transylvania. By the time of the debate about baptizing the children of ethnics, there were approximately eighty-four delegates constituting the Synod. The Dutch delegation numbered fifty-eight, including fifteen elders and four professors; the foreign delegates numbered around twenty-six. The British delegation was composed of one bishop and three professors of theology. John Hales held the status of an observer.[7]

At the Synod, two opposing positions surfaced responding to

6. Christoph Witzenrath, ed., *Eurasian Slavery, Ransom and Abolition in World History, 1200–1860* (Burlington, VT: Ashgate, 2015); Richard B. Allen, *European Slave Trading in the Indian Ocean, 1500–1850* (Athens: Ohio University Press, 2014); Barbara L. Solow, ed., *Slavery and the Rise of the Atlantic System* (Cambridge: Cambridge University Press, 1991).

7. Aza Goudriaan and Fred van Lieburg, eds., *Revisiting the Synod of Dordt (1618–1619)* (Leiden: Brill, 2011); some accounts list slightly over one hundred delegates to the Synod.

the query from the Global South regarding the baptism of ethnic children: an inclusionary position that welcomed the baptizing of ethnic children; and an exclusionary position that prohibited it. The debate revealed European Reformed Protestantism to be more of a contested site in world Christianity than is often assumed. Voting privileges were limited to the Dutch delegates because Reformed polity only allowed for a national ecclesial governing body or structure to legislate connectional and local congregational life. Thus, the more global Reformed Protestant perspective on this pastoral and theological topic that emerged from the Global South lost out to the more "ethnocentric" perspective of the Dutch Reformed Protestant community.

Arising from the Global South in the Asian country of Indonesia (Spice Islands) and having implications for African ethnics, this baptismal query had currency because during this era the Roman Catholic Church, with its wider global reach than Protestant churches, had approved the baptism of ethnics of all ages. Catholics regarded baptism as a sacrament available to all people, including infants whose parents were not Christians, and challenged the more limited Reformed perspective, which held that Christian parents committed to raising up the child in the Christian faith were a prerequisite for baptism.[8]

Being religiously ethnic was for the Reformed delegates at Dort a defining theological factor. The dilemma that required theological interrogation revolved around whether ethnic children under the age of discretion could be baptized. During the debate about "On Baptizing the Children of Ethnics," the delegates identified four cohorts: ethnic adults, ethnic adolescents, ethnic children, and ethnic infants. Unanimity existed on extending the right of Christian baptism to ethnic adolescents and adults who professed the Christian faith; the voting and nonvoting delegations agreed that these two cohorts could receive baptism. The question was: Could infants and children born to ethnic parents be baptized?[9]

---

8. Dienke Hondius, *Blackness in Western Europe: Racial Patterns of Paternalism and Exclusion* (New Brunswick, NJ: Transaction, 2014), 146.
9. Hales, *Golden Remains*, 17 (letter of 3 December 1618).

Various issues needed to be addressed related to the topic. Did pre-adolescents possess the capacity and right to make their own religious choices, especially since they were legal dependents of adults? Was where they lived consequential? Did it matter if they resided in the household of their ethnic birth parents? Was it more acceptable if they lived in a Christian household? If these pre-adolescent ethnics were "legally" adopted and resided in a Christian household in which the Christian head of the household and the spouse were the "legal" parents, was the legal adoption analogous to a spiritual adoption? Would these adopted ethnic children have the same right to baptism as children born to Christian parents? Ethnics who were "legally" or "rightfully adopted" were distinguished from ethnics who were illegally placed into a Christian household. Illegal placement included ethnic children being taken without parental consent through kidnapping, being taken as captives in war, or being found abandoned. Even with the parents' consent, their status was compromised if they were given or sold to a Christian family since it might be unclear if the birth parent knew such a transfer included changing religions. As stated above, African, Asian, and Native American infants and pre-adolescents born to parents who had already converted to Christianity could be baptized without question because by virtue of being born to Christian parents, these infants no longer were ethnics.[10] John Hales framed the debate about baptizing the children of ethnics in these terms:

> First of the Baptizing of children born of Ethnick parents . . . concerning the adults, the Synod agreed, that if they made profession of the Christian Faith they might be baptized, *etiam invitis parentibus.* Their reason was, because that after children came to be of years, in case of Religion they depended not from the power of their parents, but might make their own marker. All the difficulty was of infants, and children not yet of discretion to make their choice.[11]

10. Hales, *Golden Remains*, 17 (letter of 3 December 1618).
11. Hales, *Golden Remains*, 17 (letter of 3 December 1618).

The issue regarding baptizing the children of ethnic parents first arose because Dutch merchant families who had "adopted" South Asian infants and children were uncertain of the theological integrity of baptizing these children. The question was framed: "Whether the Children of Ethnick Parents, adopted into the Families of Christians, were to be baptized, if so be they who did offer them to be baptized, did undertake that they should be brought up in the Christian Faith." These adoptive parents would serve as the Christian sponsors of these potential baptismal candidates, promising to rear the children in the Christian faith.[12]

These "adopted" South Asian children possessed various degrees of freedom; at stake in the determination of baptismal candidacy was how free the potential ethnic baptismal candidate actually was. Disqualified from being baptized were children who were apprehended violently or were fraudulently separated from their parents; these children could not be baptized because their Christian sponsorship and adoption was deemed illegitimate. Additionally, adults could not be baptized by force or against their free will; all adults had to be granted the right to embrace or reject Christianity. Hales noted that

> The English, the Professors, those of Hassia, those of Breme, of Zeland, of Freesland thought it necessary they should be baptized, if they were rightfully adopted into Christian Families, and that their parents had altogether resigned them into the hands of the Christians. They grounded themselves upon the examples of Abraham circumcising all that were of his Family; of Paul baptizing whole households, of the primitive Church recorded in S. Austin, who shews, that anciently children that were *exposititii* were wont to be taken up by the Christians and baptized.[13]

The English delegation crafted an affirmative response to the query from South Asia, framing their argument in terms of Re-

---

12. "Letters from the Synod of Dort to the Right Honourable Sir Dudley Carlton, English Embassador at the Hague by Mr. John Hales of Eaton-College," in John Hales, *The Works of the Ever Memorable John Hales of Eaton, Volume 3* (Glasgow: Printer by Robert and Andrew and Foulis, 1665), 27.

13. Hales, *Golden Remains*, 17 (letter of 3 December 1618).

formed covenantal theology wherein the sign of baptism was analogous to circumcision for Jews. The English delegation interpreted Abraham's act of circumcising everyone in his household, whether they were his biological kin or purchased household servants, as biblical proof that the sign of the covenant extended to all persons who were members of a Christian household. Genealogical connections between the Christian head of the household and the members of the household were not a prerequisite to being included in the covenant. Ethnic infants and children, while not born into the covenant because they were not born to Christian parents, could be "adopted" into the covenant and were included by virtue of their membership in the household.[14]

In addition to the Abraham case, this inclusive faction appealed to Augustine who chronicled how Christians rescued abandoned ethnic children, incorporated these ethnic children into their household, and had them baptized. They also took the Apostle Paul as a precedent in his baptism of all members of households; they assumed that since infants and underage children were in an average first-century household, they were also baptized. They argued that since such ethnic infants and children lacked the maturity to request baptism, they needed a Christian sponsor to agree to commit to support and encourage them in living the Christian life. The sponsor had to be a Christian married couple who would adopt the underage child or infant through proper channels, becoming the Christian parents of the baptismal candidate. The baptismal candidate would then become a member of a Christian family.[15]

Opposing the English position were the North Hollanders. Hales stated:

> The North Hollanders themselves, whose business it was, and who moved the Synod in it, were expressly against it; whether they were bought, given, taken in war, or howsoever. Their reasons were, because they are *immundi*; because they are *extra*

---

14. Hales, *Golden Remains*, 17 (letter of 3 December 1618).
15. Hales, *Golden Remains*, 17 (letter of 3 December 1618).

foedus, of which Baptisme is a signe; because Adoption could entitle them only to terrene, not to an Heavenly inheritance, etc.[16]

Joining the North Hollanders were the Helvetians and South Hollanders. They opposed baptizing the children born to ethnic parents. For these Reformed Protestant leaders, baptism was limited to ethnic children of the age of discretion and ethnic adults because these cohorts could be educated in Christian faith and then profess the faith. Infant baptism and the baptism of underage children were considered theologically impermissible since the children of ethnic parents were "not born within the Covenant, and therefore cannot be Partakers" of the sign of the covenant, according to the leaders of this faction. Infant baptism was only open to children born of Christian parents. In this interpretation of the theology of the covenant, Christian genealogy became a requisite for infant baptism. According to Hales, they argued:

> First, whether it were likely that in Abraham's Family, when he put circumcision in act, there were any Infants, whose Parents died uncircumcised. Secondly, whether it were likely that in the Families baptized by Paul, there were any Infants, whose Parents died unbaptized.

The possibility existed, according to this position, that the parents of all male children circumcised in Abraham's household and of the children in the households baptized by Paul were present at the time of the two acts. This possibility created enough doubt for the Reformed Protestant leaders opposing the English inclusionary position to cause them to refuse to support the baptism of children born to ethnic parents. For these leaders, the Reformed theology of the covenant saw baptism as a sign of the promise of salvation; consequently, salvation was passed on from one generation to the next almost in a hereditary manner. It was as if the covenant could be transmitted through the seed of Christians; the children of Christians became born into the covenant. Children of non-Christians or

---

16. Hales, *Golden Remains*, 17 (letter of 3 December 1618).

possibly of just one Christian parent would not be eligible for infant baptism but could only be baptized when they became adults or, at least, adolescents.[17]

The voting members of the Synod ruled that infants and children of ethnic parents were precluded from baptism until they reached the age of discretion. For the ruling faction, Christian parents could only sponsor their own biological children for baptism; Christian adoptive parents or godparents could be the primary sponsors. Whether an ethnic infant or underage child was "rightfully adopted" was immaterial. According to Hales, "their reasons were, because they are *immundi*; because they are *extra foedus*, of which baptism is a sign." For this ruling faction, the adoption by Christians only affected earthly inheritances, not spiritual or heavenly inheritances; ethnic infants were not born into the covenant because they were not born to Christian parents.[18]

As stated above, there existed different classes of ethnics: adults and adolescents; and underage children and infants. Ethnic adults and adolescents could make a decision and thus were candidates for baptism based on their "profession of the Christian Faith," according to the ruling of the voting Dutch delegation at the Synod. John Hales stated: "[C]oncerning the *adulti*, the Synod agreed, that if they made profession of the Christian Faith they might be baptized, *etiam invitis parentibus*." The distinction between the child of age and the underage child evolved around the dependency of the child upon their parents regarding religious affairs. Since the children were abandoning their familial religion for Christianity, the Synod ruled that these children needed to be of age or of the age of discretion wherein they could make a religious choice. In the words of Hales, "their reason was, because that after children came to be of years, in case of Religion they depended not from the power of their parents, but might make their own marker." With adults and children of age, the Synod concluded that there were no questions about the right of these ethnics to receive baptism. There were no questions about the cognitive, moral, and spiritual capacity

---

17. Hales, *Golden Remains*, 18 (letter of 3 December 1618).
18. Hales, *Golden Remains*, 17 (letter of 3 December 1618).

of ethnic adults and children of age. The Synod ruling assumed that ethnic baptismal candidates who were adults or adolescents could comprehend and profess the basic knowledge of Christianity. Preadolescents on the other hand were deemed to lack the maturity to make choices and profess the Christian faith. Ethnic adults and adolescents, however, were mature enough to understand the basics of the Christian faith and could be baptized on their Christian profession of faith.[19]

Baptizing Children of Ethnics during the Late Reformation

The debate at Dort was not the first time this issue had been raised for Protestants. The Classis of Amsterdam had received queries regarding the children of ethnics as early as 1612 from the Global South, specifically from Batavia in South Asia. After the Synod, queries from the Global South continued to be sent to the Classis of Amsterdam, from Brazil in South America in 1637, Curaçao in the Caribbean in 1644, and Luanda in Central Africa in 1644. These queries raised other questions. Should Reformed clergy recognize the baptism of children and adults who participated in the mass baptisms performed by Roman Catholic priests? Should they recognize a Christian lineage of children born to a Christian mother and be willing to baptize this infant regardless of the faith of the father? Should they recognize a Christian lineage of children born to a Christian father and be willing to baptize this infant even if the mother is non-Christian? Does the existence of Christian godparents or sponsors who promise to raise the child of ethnic parents in a Christian household provide access to a Christian lineage or the covenant by "adoption," and thus permit the baptism of children of ethnic parents who willingly allow them to be "adopted"?[20]

A letter from Brazil that was sent in 1637 was addressed by the

---

19. Hales, *Golden Remains*, 17 (letter of 3 December 1618).

20. "Acts of the Classis of Amsterdam," in *Documents of the Senate of the State of New York*, vol. 14, 112 (16 November 1637); *Ecclesiastical Records, State of New York* (1902), 186 (7 November 1644).

Classis of Amsterdam on November 16, 1637. On the issue of baptizing "adopted" Native Americans, Africans, and others in Brazil, the classis basically reaffirmed its exclusionary policy. The classis's concern was that these children needed to be properly interviewed prior to being adopted into Christian families. Letters from Curaçao in the Caribbean and from Angola on the central African coast were read before the Classis of Amsterdam on November 7, 1644. Reverends John Backerus and Jacobus Beth wrote from Curaçao and Angola, respectively. It appeared that each sought for the 1618 exclusionary baptismal decision of the Synod of Dort to be revisited and possibly overturned.[21]

In a letter dated April 17, 1660, Rev. Adrian van Beaumont, a minister in Curaçao, submitted a query to the Classis of Amsterdam regarding the infants and children of African and Native American parents who had been baptized during mass baptisms by Roman Catholic priests. It was contended that since "the parents are actually heathen, although they are baptized in the gross, (by wholesale, by the Papists), the children may not be baptized." The only infants and young children to be baptized were those whose parents had "abandon[ed] heathenism" and "pass[ed] over to Christianity." As enacted by the Synod of Dort, adult Africans and Native Americans were only to be baptized after they had been instructed in the Christian faith and made a profession of faith.[22]

The situation of Rev. Beaumont in Curaçao and Rev. Henry Selyns in New Amsterdam involved African parents who had been baptized and were requesting baptism for their infants and young children, and so differed from the issue that prompted the 1618 Synod of Dort discussion in which Dutch adoptive parents were making the request. Probably, it was the African parents who were also prompting the issue in Angola. For New Amsterdam, Selyns specifically states: "As to baptisms, the Negroes occasionally request, that we should baptize their children."[23]

21. "Acts of the Classis of Amsterdam," in *Documents of the Senate of the State of New York*, vol. 14, 112 (16 November 1637); *Ecclesiastical Records, State of New York* (1902), 186 (7 November 1644).

22. *Ecclesiastical Records, State of New York* (1902), 506.

23. *Ecclesiastical Records, State of New York* (1902), 509.

In the deliberations around baptizing the children of ethnic parents, the contrast between Christian people and non-Christian people loomed large. Framing this distinction in this manner affirmed the validity of the baptism of the Roman Catholic Church as well as other historic Christian churches of the Global South such as the Thomas churches in India, the Copts in Egypt, or Orthodox in Ethiopia. These people would not be categorized as ethnics; each of their millennial-long Christian "heredities" made them non-ethnics. Similarly, the ruling also assumed the validity of the baptism of Catholic Kongolese and Angolan parents since a number of them had been Christian for five generations by 1618; they were hereditary Christians and their infants and children could be candidates for baptism. Key for the era prior to the invention of modern racism was that color was not a defining factor nor was "non-European" heredity for African, Asian, and Native American ethnics. This might be because religious lineage was predominant rather than other distinguishing factors; the situation for Jews and Muslims was the exception. As George M. Frederickson noted, "religion rather than race justified African slavery in the beginning." Of course, later, when race was invented in the West after the 1660s, debates on race would become a defining feature of Protestant discussions about baptism.[24]

While serving in Batavia, Rev. Adriaan Jacobszoon Hulsebos wrote to the classis regarding baptizing the children of ethnics because different practices were being performed within Reformed Protestant congregations in Asia. In Batavia, children born out of wedlock were baptized if their mother had been baptized Christian. In Sri Lanka and the Moluccas, the Reformed churches adopted an inclusionary baptism policy, opening baptism to all people regardless of their parentage or genealogy, as was the Roman Catholic policy.[25]

What were the social and political consequences of ethnic baptism? Did "On Baptizing the Children of Ethnics" enable or prevent Africans, Asians, and Native Americans from possessing rights and

24. Frederickson, *Race*, 38.
25. Hondius, *Blackness in Western Europe*, 148, 219.

exercising freedoms akin to European Reformed Protestants? Did it enable or prevent these denizens of the Global South from occupying a social space inside the same class system erected for European Reformed Protestants or were they excluded from the class system in the countries or enclaves that European Reformed Protestants governed? Did the rights possessed, the freedoms exercised, and the social space occupied by Africans, Asians, and Native Americans within Reformed Protestantism, if any at all, provide a window to a world prior to the rise of modern racism that would warrant interrogation?

Adult Jewish-to-Christian conversion and adult Muslim-to-Christian conversion complicated the transfer of a person from the infidel to the Christian. Such a transition was fraught with suspicion about the authenticity and motive of these Christian conversions. Consequently, those who converted were classified as "New Christians" and granted limited rather than full rights as Christians. The hegemonic polarities that dominated the sixteenth-century and early seventeenth-century Protestant Reformation placed the Christian over against Jew and Muslim. Grounded in religious distinctions and codified in law, these polarities organized Protestant society. Exclusionary practices were based on religious distinctions. These religious distinctions could also have biological referents as in Jewish being both a religious and proto-racial category. However, the African, for instance, was not a racial category in this era. The adult ethnic-to-Christian conversion was eagerly welcomed among Reformed Protestants until the dawn of the era of modern racism. The adult ethnic-to-Christian conversion appeared void of the "pure blood" criteria that marked the discussion of the adult Jewish-to-Christian conversion and adult Muslim-to-Christian conversion as well as the descendants of each cohort. Nor did these discussions appear to anticipate the debates about the inferiority of Africans and the other people of the Global South. In a sense, there was a difference between the infidel-to-Christian converts and their descendants over against the ethnic-to-Christian converts and their descendants. The "pure blood" criteria precluded infidels from switching fully from the infidel race to the Christian race, which led to the limiting of their social roles in a Christian society, even though they could be Christian liturgically and spiritually. For the Reformed Protestant position, the ethnic-to-Christian conversion included being transferred from the ethnic race to the Christian race; consequently a "pure blood" criterion failed to be instituted.[26]

While a fluid aesthetic polarity between white and black existed within Dutch Christianity during this era, it was not codified in the Dutch legal or ecclesial system, nor did the white-black polarity juxtapose Africa and Europe. For Europeans in the sixteenth century as well as into the early to mid-seventeenth century, a diversity of Africans existed: white Africans such as the Arab Africans, brown (tawny/swarthy) Africans such as the Berbers, and black Africans such as sub-Saharan Africans. Religiously, black Africans referred to Ethiopian Christians, other Christians, Muslims (blackamoors), and ethnics. While civilization as a concept would be developed after this period, "civilization" as a contrast between a highly organized society and a primal society distinguished the Ethiopian Empire and such African kingdoms as those of the Kongo and Benin as "civilizations" from hunter-gatherer societies in Africa. During this era, terms that would later mark modern racism were fluid. As noted earlier, the term "slave" lacked exclusive association with any particular color, being applied to southeastern Europeans, Arabs, North Africans, Asian Indians, Chinese, and Native Americans as well as sub-Saharan Africans. The term "Negro," likewise lacking an exclusive association with a specific "race" or color, referred to Native Americans and Asian Indians as well as sub-Saharan Africans. Consequently, "Negro" applied to a variety of people of color. A polarity between white and black as well as Africa and Europe failed to develop in a hegemonic way that would be inscribed in the legal or ecclesial system. Possibly, the Dutch acquaintance with the multicultural Christian world on the Iberian Peninsula influenced their perspectives on people from the Global South, especially Africans.[27]

26. Dennis Austin Britton, *Becoming Christian: Race, Reformation, and Early Modern English Romance* (New York: Fordham University Press, 2014), 3–5.

27. David D. Daniels, "Will African Christians Become a Subject in Reformation Studies?" in *Subject to None, Servant to All: Essays in Christian Scholarship*

DAVID D. DANIELS

Late Protestant Reformation as Global Event

The Synod of Dort debate and the subsequent debates about ethnic baptism reflected the impact of the emerging globalization on
the Protestant Reformation. The ecclesial context of the Synod of
Dort and the late Protestant Reformation possessed the marks of
globalization. During the late Protestant Reformation, European
Protestants resided in a string of locations in the Global South such
as Indonesia, Taiwan (Formosa), Cochin, Malacca, and Sri Lanka in
Asia; Cape Colony, Angola, and Elmina in Africa; Brazil in South
America and Curaçao in the Caribbean; and North American east-
ern seaboard colonies, including New England, New Netherlands,
New Sweden, and Virginia.[28]

Dutch society grew out of an Iberian context that was globalized
due to the forced migration of African peoples to Europe during
the fifteenth century. While the early seventeenth-century Dutch
Reformed Protestant world emerged out of Dutch political struggles
for independence from Spain, Iberian Catholicism, which bore the
greatest marks of globalization, served as an ecclesial context for
Dutch Protestantism. Since Iberian Catholicism included Christians who were native to Europe and Africa, this globalized Iberian
Catholicism created the larger world in which Dutch Protestantism
developed. Governed by the Iberian monarchies, the region that
became Holland was part of an Iberian world marked by globalization. Iberian society was populated by African ethnics and African
Catholics who were descendants of African ethnics who lived on
the Iberian Peninsula during the sixteenth and early seventeenth
centuries. Although a lot fewer Africans lived in Holland than on
the Iberian Peninsula, they were present in Holland. On the Iberian
Peninsula, African Catholics who descended from African ethnics
possessed rights, exercised freedoms, and occupied a space within
the Iberian class system. During the sixteenth century, 150,000 to

in Honor of Kurt Karl Hendel, ed. Peter Vethanayagamony and Kenneth Sawyer
(Minneapolis: Lutheran University Press, 2016), 113.

28. Samuel Hugh Moffett, *A History of Christianity in Asia*, vol. 11: *1500–1900*
(Maryknoll, NY: Orbis, 2005), 86–87, 213–28.

200,000 Africans resided on the Iberian Peninsula. Sub-Saharan African Catholics who descended from African ethnics attended Roman Catholic mass and had their baptisms, confirmations, weddings, and funerals held in the church and officiated by Roman Catholic priests. Marriages occurred between "white" Portuguese nobility and Kongolese nobility. The legal system granted sub-Saharan Africans the right to sue "white" Portuguese and, within sixteenth-century legal history, there were a set of legal decisions with sub-Saharans as the victors. The religious life of "white" Iberians, Afro-Europeans, and African Catholics centered around Catholic lay brotherhoods, or confraternities. Some confraternities were "interracial," even consisting of "white" Portuguese slaveholders and enslaved Africans as members. African-instituted and -governed confraternities existed, with the first and most influential confraternity for sub-Saharan Africans being Our Lady of the Rosary, which was founded before 1494. During the 1500s, they established at least eight branches in Portugal alone. The ordination of Africans to the Roman Catholic priesthood was made possible by the papal brief, *Exponi nobis*, issued by Pope Leo X in 1518. This papal brief suspended the prerequisite that candidates for the priesthood had to be born to Catholic parents. The Catholic priesthood was also opened to African slaves; one priest, Joao, who was ordained during the 1500s, was born to parents who were both enslaved.[29]

The majority of African Catholic priests who were educated in Europe were trained in Portugal. Catering especially to Kongolese Roman Catholics, these theological institutions included the Saint Eloi seminary at the monastery of Saints George and John the Evangelist in Lisbon along with the seminary of Saint Joao in Xabregas. They were also educated at the University of Coimbra as well as the episcopal residence at Evora. By the early 1600s, sub-Saharan African Christians studied at St. Jerome College in Coimbra, St. Augustine College in Lisbon, and St. Anthony College in Lisbon.

29. A. C. de C. M. Saunders, *A Social History of Black Slaves and Freedmen in Portugal, 1441–1555* (Cambridge: Cambridge University Press, 2010 [1982]), 149–50; also see Daniels, "Will African Christians Become a Subject in Reformation Studies?," 104–6.

During the sixteenth century, St. Eloi ranked as the most prominent center for the education of sub-Saharan African Catholics. At times the student body was even "multiracial," composed of sub-Saharan African, south Asian, and "white" Portuguese Catholics. Education was open to all classes of African and Afro-European Catholics, and though it is unclear if all schools were open, no extant laws excluded Africans and Afro-Europeans. Literate Africans and Afro-European Catholics in Europe pushed the literacy rate within Europe up to the range of 10 to 20 percent of the population; educated African and Afro-European Catholic priests increased the literacy rate among Roman Catholic clergy since many "white" European priests were functionally illiterate at the beginning of the sixteenth century. In a sense, the educated African and Afro-European Catholic priests were in the vanguard. Sub-Saharan Africans were members of the Portuguese religious and educational spheres. While the majority of sub-Saharan Africans living on the Iberian Peninsula were enslaved, there existed a recognizable community of freeborn or manumitted African population of approximately 2,580 people in Portugal.[30]

Ascribing to the European distinction between the nobility and the peasantry, the Portuguese plotted Africans on both sides of the class divide. The African Catholic nobility in Portugal were often from the Atlantic-coast African kingdoms of Benin and Kongo. It appears that Portuguese society, stratified by class, accepted African nobles as peers to Portuguese nobility. The African freed-persons traversed the social space above the lowest stratum. As formerly enslaved Africans, African freed-persons constituted a significant community; they were joined to Afro-Europeans, children born often of European fathers and African mothers as well as children born of mulatto parents. In Portugal, at least, there appeared to be four classes: nobles, mulattoes, freed Africans, and enslaved Africans.[31]

Thus, the debate about ethnic baptism at the Synod of Dort debate as well as subsequent debates on ethnic baptism involved

30. Daniels, "Will African Christians Become a Subject in Reformation Studies?," 106–7.

31. Daniels, "Will African Christians Become a Subject in Reformation Studies?," 104–6.

people that the Dutch had encountered in Europe, especially the Iberian Peninsula; ethnics were not merely those who lived far away among an unknown people. The Synod of Dort and the late Protestant Reformation showed marks of globalization. While the queries came from the Global South throughout the late Protestant Reformation, they could have just as easily been prompted by pastoral cases related to ethnics from the Global South who lived in Europe during the seventeenth century.

Charles E. Farhadian's three paradigms offer options on ways to situate "On Baptizing the Children of Ethnics" within the late Protestant Reformation as a topic in the study of world Christianity. Farhadian summarizes these three paradigms in his edited volume *Introducing World Christianity*. The first paradigm, invented in the nineteenth century, which "stressed the Western-initiated Christian mission movement propelled by Western powers" and linked to "American and European civilization," would obscure the historical agency of the Protestants in the Global South. Mission narratives often focus on Protestant missionaries, Dutch merchants, and Dutch colonials serving as catalysts for the exporting of European Christianity to the ethnic world in the Global South rather than the ecclesial issues and theological concerns of the Global South or the Protestants native to the Global South. The second paradigm, in replacing the missionary story during the late twentieth century, "interpreted world Christianity as polycentric in nature, where each center possessed equivalent yet independent authority," with a strong accent on local agency. This paradigm stresses "the demographic shift of Christianity to the global South." Since each center was independent, often the paradigm differentiated Christianity by continent: African Christianity, Asian Christianity, South American Christianity, and so on. In this paradigm, the exchanges and links between Holland and the scattered Reformed Protestantism would escape investigation. Invented during the advent of the twenty-first century, the third paradigm adds an interdisciplinary perspective to the second paradigm, focusing on how "Christianity appears to have led to the transformation of individual and corporate identities." This paradigm focuses on the circulation and migration of people, discourses, institutions, ideas, and technologies, teasing out the "social, cultural, and political consequences" of the circulation of Christianity across different contexts. This third paradigm has much to offer to an interrogation of "On Baptizing the Children of Ethnics" within the late Protestant Reformation as a topic in the study of world Christianity.[32]

Lodging the Synod of Dort within a global Reformed Protestant context, albeit a mere string of outposts scattered globally, highlights how pastoral issues and theological concerns from the Global South set the agenda and terms of the debate. At the Synod, discourses and ideas related to baptism in general, and ethnic baptism in particular, circulated. The theological debate about ethnic baptism prompted by pastoral cases from the Global South signals a turning point in the history of Reformed Protestantism and world Christianity.

At the nexus of Reformed Protestantism from the Global North and Global South in "On Baptizing the Children of Ethnics," Reformed Protestantism became more than a European-oriented ecclesial project solely driven by challenges facing the church in Europe. As a theological topic and ecclesial practice, ethnic baptism destabilized Reformed Protestantism as a European-oriented ecclesial project by introducing the voices, pastoral issues, and ecclesial concerns of Christians from the Global South beyond Europe. In the decades after the Synod of Dort, this shift continued to set topics for debate within Reformed Protestantism. At the Synod of Dort, Reformed Protestantism as a global-oriented ecclesial project began to emerge. After the Synod of Dort, Reformed Protestantism was a "global movement" of scattered Reformed Protestant communities in Africa, Asia, and the Americas along with those in Europe that included people who were native to the various continents, such as the 65,000 Protestants in Jaffna, Sri Lanka, by 1663. Consequently, Reformed Protestant congregational life of the Global South exceeded being a mere additive to European Reformed Protestantism; it participated in co-constituting Reformed Protestantism in light of the Synod of Dort.[33]

---

32. Charles E. Farhadian, ed., *Introducing World Christianity* (Malden, MA, and Oxford: Wiley-Blackwell, 2012), 1–4.

33. Moffett, *A History of Christianity in Asia*, 226.

In this essay we have pondered how best to interpret African Protestants and "On Baptizing the Children of Ethnics" as a document crafted in an era that precedes the invention of modern racism. Prior to the modern racial construction of Africans, Asians, and Native Americans as inferior people ontologically, theologically, legally, and scientifically, how were these peoples constructed as people during the Late Reformation? In this chapter we have pursued an archeological project by excavating how "On Baptizing the Children of Ethnics" and the history of its reception might have conceived of African descendants prior to the rise of modern racism. Bracketing the genealogical exercise of isolating the building blocks in which "On Baptizing the Children of Ethnics" functioned as a contributor to the rise of modern racism, the archeological exercise unearthed theological trajectories during the Late Reformation era that wrestled with the existence of African people, especially African Protestants along with Asian and Native American Protestants.

At the center of these theological questions are questions related to theological anthropology. Yet the questions that would dominate the era of modern racism are not posed. Are ethnics fully human? Do ethnics have souls? Can ethnics be "adopted" into the covenant? Do ethnics possess the intellectual capacity to comprehend the Christian faith sufficiently to profess the faith according to Reformed Protestant standards? Do ethnics possess the moral ability to live the Christian life as a gracious response to election by God? Interestingly, these theological issues would shape the theological agenda of the post-1660s era, but did not shape the theological conversation of the late Protestant Reformation, which ended around 1660. During the late Protestant Reformation, it was presupposed that ethnics were fully human, possessed souls, could be "adopted" into the covenant, and had the intellectual and moral capacity to be Christians. The theologies that questioned the capability between ethnics and the Christian faith would spark or accompany the rise of modern racism, a social and religious system that emerged during the 1660s.

Such an interrogation could offer insights about African and other Protestants during the late Reformation. It could also result in the generation of new topics in the study of the late Reformation. By excavating the social terrain that African, Asian, and Native American Reformed Protestants navigated and the environments they built on these terrains, another dimension of the late Reformation could surface worthy of further scholarly analysis. These interrogations could contribute to shifting the interpretations of Reformed Protestantism during and after the Synod of Dort from being a European-oriented ecclesial project to a global-oriented ecclesial project.

The Synod of Dort occurred prior to the erection of modern racism as a socio-economic-political system. In this chapter we have sought to excavate a religious and social reality of peoples of Asia, Africa, and the Americas prior to the construction of modern racism. While recognizing the existence of colorphobia and prejudice against non-Europeans as well as religious prejudice against Jews and Muslims, we have contended that it was a form of prejudice distinct from the prejudice produced by modern racism with its ontological, theological, legal, and scientific bases.

While the reception of the Reformed Protestant Reformation within Africa, Asia, and the Americas is of interest, how the Reformed Protestant communions in Europe were changed by their interaction with ecclesial issues and theological concerns of the Global South has been the focus here. Reformed Protestantism during and after the Synod of Dort shifted from being exclusively a European-oriented ecclesial project to a slightly more global-oriented ecclesial movement. By interrogating "On Baptizing the Children of Ethnics" within the late Protestant Reformation as a topic in the study of world Christianity, we have attempted to challenge the dominant historiography of the Protestant Reformation in which the Reformation is interpreted as only a European phenomenon, offering other historiographic directions. The categorizing of most religions of the Global South in contradistinction to Judaism and Islam with the related infidel-to-Christian paradigm for conversion placed the religions of the Global South outside of Christian religious hostility. The fact that the majority of the countries represented at the Synod held a positive view toward ethnic infant baptism, supporting the baptizing of the children of ethnics, illustrates how these Reformed Protestants understood first-generation Christians from the Global South as equals on a certain level. Lodging the Synod of Dort and the late Protestant Reformation as a topic within the study of world Christianity can offer a fresh perspective on the study of the Reformation as a movement in Europe and the Global South, recognizing the interdependencies or interconnections within the history of Reformed Protestantism as an emerging global movement.

5 The Protestant Reformations in Asia

A Blessing or a Curse?

PETER C. PHAN

Recent historiography of the sixteenth-century Protestant Reformation has highlighted the staggering multiplicity of its actors, localities, theologies, and institutional forms as well as the manifold reforms undertaken by the Roman Catholic Church, which non-Catholic historians have dismissively labeled the "Counter-Reformation," as if their whole scope and purpose were restricted to fighting the Protestant Reformation.[1] It is now generally recognized that sixteenth-century Europe underwent not *the* Reformation but *many* Reformations, including the Catholic Reformation prior to and concomitant with the Protestant Reformations as well as the reform promoted by the Council of Trent (1545–63).

With regard to the Protestant Reformation, in addition to its center-stage stars—Martin Luther, Ulrich Zwingli, and John Calvin—scholarly focus is also turned on the lesser-known Radical Re-

---

1. Currently two expressions are used to describe the reforms of the Roman Catholic Church in the sixteenth century: "Roman Catholic Reform/Reformation" to indicate significant movements of renewal within the Catholic Church before and during the Protestant Reformation, and "Counter-Reformation," first used in the seventeenth century to describe efforts by ruling authorities to restore their territories to Roman obedience, and now used to refer mainly to the doctrinal and disciplinary measures adopted by the Catholic Church, especially at the Council of Trent, to combat the Protestant Reformation.

formers, such as the Anabaptists (Conrad Grebel, Menno Simons, Jacob Hutter, Melchior Hoffmann, Hans Denck, and Adam Pastor), the Spiritual Reformers, whom Luther nicknamed the *Schwärmer* (Gaspar Schwenckfeld, Sebastian Franck, and Thomas Müntzer), and the Evangelical Rationalists. These Radical Reformers espoused dizzyingly divergent theologies and practices that are opposed not only to the Magisterial (that is, led by academics [*magistri*] and magistrates) Protestant Reformation but also to each other, and that later found expression in various institutions classified under the umbrella term of "Pietism."[2]

Furthermore, in current scholarship the geography of the Reformation is seen to have extended beyond the countries of western and central Europe such as Germany, Switzerland, France, the Netherlands, England, and Scotland. It is expanded to include the Nordic countries (Denmark, Norway, Iceland, Sweden, and Finland), the Baltic countries (Lithuania, Latvia, and Estonia), and Eastern Europe (Prussia, Poland, Bohemia, Moravia, Silesia, Hungary, Slovenia, and Croatia). Attention is also shifted from the role played by the ordained and theologians to that of the laity, especially women, and the peasants.[3]

Acknowledgment of the multiplicity and diversity of the Protestant Reformations does not of course intend to deny the fact that the reformers, though sharply different among themselves, shared a common goal, namely, restoring the church—deeply corrupted, in their view—to its original purity and authenticity by returning to the Word of God enshrined in the Bible as the sole norm for the Christian faith. Rather this recognition of diversity and multiplicity, in addition to being an imperative of historical scholarship, serves as an indispensable vantage point from which to evaluate the Reformation's five-centuries-old global impact and to shape its legacy

2. On the Radical Reformers, see George Huntston Williams, *The Radical Reformation*, 3rd ed. (Kirksville, MO: Truman State University Press, 2000); Michael G. Baylor, ed., *The Radical Reformation* (Cambridge: Cambridge University Press, 1991); and Leonard Verduin, *The Reformers and Their Step Children: Dissent and Nonconformity* (Paris, AR: The Baptist Standard Bearer, 2001).

3. Among recent histories of the Reformations to be noted is Diarmaid MacCulloch, *The Reformation: A History* (New York: Viking, 2003).

for the future of Christianity. A serious challenge to this legacy is the fact that the Protestant reformers' opposing theologies, methods, and means to achieve their reform agenda have unfortunately led to violence and war and to still-ongoing divisions among the Christian churches.

Keeping in mind the diversity and multiplicity of the Protestant Reformation and its differentiation from Roman Catholicism is especially important for understanding its role and impact in Asia. For one thing, only in Asian countries, even in those that are not in principle hostile to Christianity, are Protestantism and Catholicism legally categorized as two different *religions*, alongside other religions such as Hinduism, Buddhism, Judaism, and Islam, and not just two branches of one single religion. Furthermore, in Asia, to the great detriment of Christian missions, historical divisions of Christianity continue to exist, not only between the Roman Catholic Church and the various Protestant churches but also among the different "denominations" within Protestantism, often seen as different "churches" competing with one another for membership and influence, and in the eyes of most Asian governments, as separate "religions."

In light of the foregoing observations the title of my essay on the impact of Protestant Reformations on Asia is intentionally phrased as a question: Are the Protestant Reformations a blessing or a curse for Asia?[4] The answer of course depends on how Protestant missions, past and present, in Asian countries are viewed. To gain a fair and balanced picture of these missions, it is necessary, in the first part, to describe, albeit summarily, the current situation of

---

4. For our present purposes, by Asia are meant primarily South Asia (in particular India, Pakistan, and Sri Lanka); Northeast Asia (especially China, Japan, and Korea), and Southeast Asia (particularly Myanmar, Laos, Thailand, Vietnam, Malaysia, Singapore, the Philippines, Brunei, Indonesia, and East Timor). I will leave out of consideration Western Asia (the Middle East) and Central Asia. Furthermore I will concentrate on countries where the churches issued from the Reformations maintain a significant presence, namely, India, Sri Lanka, China, Japan, (South) Korea, Myanmar, Singapore, the Philippines, and Indonesia. For comprehensive resources on Asian Christianity, see Scott W. Sunquist, ed., *A Dictionary of Asian Christianity* (Grand Rapids: Eerdmans, 2001), and Peter C. Phan, ed., *Christianities in Asia* (Oxford: Wiley-Blackwell, 2011).

Protestant churches in countries of Asia.[5] In the second part I examine the most challenging theological issues facing the Protestant churches in Asia today. The last part indicates the way forward and ahead for the missions of Protestant churches in Asia.

The Protestant Reformations in Asia

As is well known, the Orthodox Church and the Roman Catholic Church had undertaken extensive missionary work in Asia and Latin America, the latter since the fifteenth century with the support of the Spanish and Portuguese Crowns under the *patronato/ padroado real* system. In contrast, the first Protestant reformers were not concerned with mission outside Europe, partly because of their urgent need to consolidate their churches within their own countries and partly because of their belief that the apostles had completed the work of evangelization and that the end of the world was imminent. Of the three founders of the Reformation, only Calvin saw a connection between the church as the *regnum Christi* and the duty of evangelizing non-Christians; he even attempted a short-lived mission by sending a group of Genevans on a Huguenot colonial venture in Brazil in 1557.

Early Protestant Missions in Asia

Historically speaking, the first Protestants to come Asia in the seventeenth century were not missionaries but Dutch traders of the

5. In this essay the churches of the Reformations in Asia refer to (1) the mainline Protestant churches, including especially the Lutheran, the Reformed (Presbyterian), the Baptist, and the Methodist churches; (2) the Anglicans; (3) the Evangelicals; (4) the Pentecostals; and (5) the Independents. I will leave out of consideration the Roman Catholics, the Orthodox, and the so-called Marginal Christians (that is, those who claim to be Christian but do not hold the basic Christian doctrines, such as the Church of Jesus Christ of the Latter-day Saints [Mormons], Jehovah's Witnesses, the Unification Church, Family International, and the Iglesia ni Cristo in the Philippines).

Dutch East India Company whose primary interest was trade and not evangelization. There were Calvinist chaplains accompanying these traders to Indonesia (1601), Formosa (Taiwan, 1642), and Ceylon (Sri Lanka, 1656), but their mission was not to Christianize the natives but to provide for the spiritual needs of their fellow coreligionists. Some of these chaplains—Justus Heurnius in Indonesia, Georgius Candidius and Robert Junius in Taiwan, and Philip Baldaeus in Sri Lanka—did try to evangelize the indigenous people, but their efforts were individual and sporadic.[6]

In terms of organized missions it was not the main reformers who played the key role but the seventeenth-century followers of those who are referred to as the Radical Reformers and who were associated with the Pietist movement. "Pietism," originally a term of abuse and derision used in the 1670s to refer to the followers of Philipp Jacob Spener, describes a highly complex theological and spiritual movement of renewal that was deeply rooted in the traditions of medieval mysticism and the Radical Reformers. It sought to overcome the crisis affecting seventeenth-century Protestantism caused by the church-state system, denominational conflicts, an overemphasis on institutions and orthodoxy, and failures to bring about a reform of Christian life in church and society.[7] The Pietist remedy lies in personal sanctification, interior experience and devotion, and Bible study and prayer, especially in small groups or conventicles (*ecclesiola in ecclesia*).

The Pietist movement had its first home in Germany. It was inspired by the devotional literature of the English Puritans and the writings of Johann Arndt (1555–1621), Philipp Jacob Spener (1635–1705), August Hermann Francke (1663–1727), and Count Nikolaus von Zinzendorf (1700–1760). The main center of Pietism was the University of Halle, founded by Frederick III, Elector of

6. For an account of the early Protestant presence in Asia, see Samuel Hugh Moffett, *A History of Christianity in Asia*, vol. 2: *1500–1900* (Maryknoll, NY: Orbis, 2005), 213–35.

7. It is customary to distinguish between "Reformed Pietism" and "Radical Pietism," the latter, headed by August Hermann Francke and the Petersens (Johann Wilhelm and his wife Johanna Eleonora), promotes anti-establishment, nondenominationalist tendencies and millenarian and apocalyptic views.

Brandenburg, in 1691, where Francke was appointed a professor in 1692. It was here that a plethora of Pietism-inspired activities were organized, such as theological training, orphanages, educational work, Bible societies, and care of Christians outside their native countries (the "diaspora").

Another important activity of the Pietists, which is of interest here, is mission outside Europe, especially in Asia. It is in connection with the University of Halle that the first extensive "foreign" Protestant missions were undertaken, thanks to which the Pietist movement was soon spread to Scandinavia, Russia, North America, and Asia. The occasion for the Protestant mission from Halle to India was the decision of King Frederick IV of Denmark in 1706 to establish a mission in the Danish colony of Tranquebar (Tharangambadi) in southeast India. Unable to find Danish missionaries, the king entrusted the mission to two Halle University Lutheran Pietist professors, Heinrich Plütschau (1676–1752) and Bartholomäus Ziegenbald (1683–1719), whose work marked the beginning of Tamil Lutheran Christianity in India.

Besides the University of Halle, another center of Pietist missionary activity was Herrnhut, an estate of Count von Zinzendorf, who in 1722 welcomed there a group of Bohemian Brethren (the Unitas Fratrum), known in Europe as the "Herrnhutter," who constituted the Moravian Church or the United Brethren. These Pietist Christians believed that their particular task was to witness to Christ to non-Christians rather than establishing new churches in places that were already Christianized. Moravian missionaries constituted the first large-scale and officially organized Protestant missionary movement. Within three decades of its founding, the Moravian Church sent hundreds of missionaries worldwide, including the Caribbean, North and South America, Labrador, Greenland, South Africa, and (Central) Asia.[8] In 1760, fourteen Moravians landed in Tranquebar. Later, twenty-four Moravians were sent to another Danish colony, the Nicobar Islands, in the Bay of Bengal, where, however, their mission foundered due to the eventual deaths of all

---

8. On the German Pietist Danish-Halle mission to Tranquebar (1706–1846), see Moffett, *A History of Christianity in Asia*, 2:236–50.

of them. They were more successful in the northern Danish trading colony, Serampore, near Calcutta (Kolkata), where they went in 1777 but from which they departed in 1803 due the denominational jealousy of the Lutherans.

"The Great Century" (1784–1860)

The nineteenth century has been dubbed by church historian Kenneth Scott Latourette "The Great Century" of Protestant missions. Actually, the Great Century began before 1800, toward the latter half of the eighteenth century. The scene moved from Germany to Britain, with Anglican missionaries serving as "evangelical chaplains" to the British East India Company, notable among whom are David Brown (1763–1812), Claudius Buchanan (1766–1815), and Henry Martyn (1781–1812). Missionary societies were founded, such as the Society for Promoting Christian Knowledge (SPCK, 1698), the Society for the Propagation of the Gospel in Foreign Parts (SPG, 1701), the London Missionary Society (LMS, 1785), and the Church Missionary Society (CMS, 1799), all of which carried out extensive missionary work in Asia during the "Great Century."

But the "father of the modern [Protestant] missionary movement" is no doubt the English Baptist William Carey (1761–1834), a cobbler and self-taught multilinguist. With his famous 1782 tract *An Inquiry into the Obligation of Christians, to Use Means for the Conversion of the Heathens*, Carey successfully led the leaders of the Northampton Baptist Association to establish in 1792 a "society for propagating the gospel among the heathen," the Baptist Missionary Society (BMS). In 1793 Carey and his family arrived in Kolkata, where after a stint as manager of an indigo plantation, he moved in 1799 to the Danish colony of Serampore, some thirteen miles north of Kolkata, where he was joined by Joshua Marshman (1768–1837) and William Ward (1769–1823). In a fruitful partnership governed by the famous "Serampore Covenant," Carey, Marshman, and Ward, dubbed the "Serampore Trio" (Carey characterized himself as Erasmus, Marshman as the theologian, and Ward as Luther), engaged in activities such as Bible translation (in whole or part, into some twenty-four languages and dialects), education (Carey as professor of Sanskrit, Bengali, and Marathi at Fort William College for thirty years and establishing schools for girls), and social reform (promotion of the abolition of the practice of burning widows). The educational work in India was further promoted by Alexander Duff (1806–1882), on behalf especially of upper-class Brahmins.[9]

In the first half of the nineteenth century, Protestant missions were extended to China with the arrival of Robert Morrison (1782–1834), a missionary of the LMS, in 1807. Together with his colleague William C. Milne (1785–1822), also of the LMS, he translated the Bible into Chinese and established the Anglo-Chinese College in Malacca. Following the example of the LMS, the American Board of Commissioners for Foreign Missions (ABCFM), an independent and interdenominational mission society founded in 1811, sent American missionaries to China, especially to work in the medical field. The Netherlands Missionary Society joined the Chinese missions in 1827 by sending the talented Lutheran Karl Friedrich Augustus Gützlaff (1803–1851), who founded the Chinese Union with the goal to distribute Bibles in mainland China. Sadly, the Opium Wars (1839–44; 1856–60) and the Taiping Revolution (1851–64) compromised and destroyed much of the Protestant (and Catholic) missionary work in China.[10]

Meanwhile Protestant missionaries penetrated other Asian countries. The Congregationalist-turned-Baptist Adoniram Jud-

9. The most comprehensive resource on Christianity in India and South Asian Christianity in general is Roger E. Hedlund, ed., *The Oxford Encyclopedia of South Asian Christianity*, 2 vols. (Oxford: Oxford University Press, 2012). An informative one-volume history of Indian Christianity is Robert Eric Frykenberg's *Christianity in India: From Beginnings to the Present* (Oxford: Oxford University Press, 2008).

10. Two very helpful overviews of Christianity in China are Jean-Pierre Charbonnier, *Christians in China: A.D. 600 to 2000*, trans. M. N. L. Couve de Murville (San Francisco: Ignatius, 2007), and Daniel H. Bays, *A New History of Christianity in China* (Oxford: Wiley-Blackwell, 2012). See also Daniel H. Bays, ed., *Christianity in China: From the Eighteenth Century to the Present* (Stanford, CA: Stanford University Press, 1996). The most authoritative and comprehensive treatment of Chinese Christianity is the massive two-volume work: Nicolas Standaert, ed., *Handbook of Christianity in China*, vol. 1: *635–1800* (Leiden: Brill, 2000), and R. G. Tiedemann, ed., *Handbook of Christianity in China*, vol. 2: *1800–Present* (Leiden: Brill, 2009).

son (1788–1850) and his wife were sent by the BCFM to Burma and founded the Burma Baptist Church among the Karens. Later, during the British rule, especially after the third Anglo-Burmese War (1885–86), missions were carried to the Kachins, mostly by Karen Baptist converts. The Anglican Church came to Ceylon (Sri Lanka) in 1802 when the British took it from the Dutch, who had wrested it from the Portuguese in 1796, and ruled for the next three hundred years. For its work the church was largely dependent on the colonial power for material support. Unfortunately, the missions were badly damaged by the controversy in the mid-1840s between the High Church, represented by the Society for the Propagation of the Gospel, and the Low Church, represented by the Church Missionary Society, which was not resolved until the disestablishment of the Anglican Church in 1881.

In 1828, the peripatetic Karl Gützlaff, who had left the Netherlands Missionary Society and turned independent, and Jacob Tomlin of the LMS were the first Protestants to enter Siam (Thailand). They were followed by missionaries of the ABCFM, the Presbyterians (the Presbyterian Board of Foreign Missions), and the American Baptists. The focus of these missions was healthcare and education. Unfortunately, despite the work of able missionaries, mostly Presbyterians, such as Samuel G. McFarland (1830–1897) and Daniel McGilvary (1828–1911), Protestant missions in Thailand did not produce many conversions, except a few in the northeast (Chiang Mai). The main reason for this failure was that most Thais identified being Thai with being Buddhist.[11]

The Dutch Reformed Protestants came to Malacca (Malaysia, including Singapore), whose Christianity had been largely Catholic under the 130-year rule of Portugal, when it was colonized by the Netherlands, which ruled it for 154 years. Next came the Anglican Church when the country fell under British rule in 1819. Because of its close connection with British colonization and because it was perceived as an exclusively white concern, the Anglican Church did

---

11. For a survey of Protestant Christianity in Thailand, see Kenneth E. Wells, *History of Protestant Work in Thailand, 1828–1958* (Bangkok: The Church of Christ in Thailand, 1984).

not make much progress. The most successful Protestants in Malaysia/Singapore were the American Methodists, with the American James M. Thoburn (1836–1922) as the first bishop and the Indian-born Englishman William B. Oldham (1854–1935) as the founder of the Methodist mission in Singapore.[12]

As noted earlier, the first Protestants to arrive in Indonesia were not missionaries but Dutch traders associated with the Dutch East Indies Company. In 1833, the ABCFM sent two missionaries, Samuel Munson and Henry Lyman, to work among the Bataks in Sumatra. Tragically, they were killed by the natives, but their efforts brought about the largest single Protestant denomination in the islands, the Batak Christian Protestant Church. Protestant missions in Indonesia, particularly in the Moluccas, received a boost in the middle of the nineteenth century when there was a renewal of missionary enthusiasm in Holland. Between 1858 and 1861 three missionary societies were founded: the Netherlands Missionary Union, the Utrecht Missionary Society, and the Dutch Reformed Missionary Association. The LMS too entered the field, with Joseph Carel Kam (1769–1833), the "Apostle of the Moluccas."[13]

As the nineteenth century was drawing to a close, Protestant missions made rapid advance in India, thanks in part to the support of Queen Victoria, after the government of India was taken away from the British East India Company and turned into a crown colony. There were mass conversions to Protestant Christianity from the Dalits (the outcasts) and the tribals, as Western missionaries made the momentous decision to shift their targets from the rich, the powerful, and the educated to the poor and the outcasts. In the northeastern states of Meghalaya, Nagaland, and Mizoram the American Baptists and the Welsh Calvinistic Methodists (later changed to Welsh Presbyterians) had great success, mostly through the evangelizing work of the native converts themselves.

12. For a history of Protestant Christianity in Malaysia/Singapore, see Robert Hunt, Lee Kam Hinh, and John Roxborough, eds., *Christianity in Malaysia: A Denominational History* (Petaling Jaya: Pelanduk, 1992).

13. For a comprehensive resource on Christianity in Indonesia, see Jan Sihar Aritonang and Karel Steenbrink, eds., *A History of Christianity in Indonesia* (Leiden: Brill, 2008).

The closing decades of the nineteenth century also witnessed a rebirth of Protestant missions in China with the coming of the English Hudson Taylor (1832–1905) in 1853 and 1866, who founded the China Inland Mission, an evangelical nondenominational organization aiming at the evangelization of all the provinces of China. Equally if not more famous is Timothy Richard (1845–1919), a Welsh Baptist of the BMS, who spent forty-five years in China and was widely praised as evangelist, relief worker (especially during the 1876–79 famine), social reformer, and educator. Another exceptional China missionary is the Episcopal Jewish bishop, Samuel Isaac Joseph Schereschewsky (1831–1906), who went to China under the sponsorship of the Domestic and Foreign Missionary Society of the Protestant Episcopal Church of the United States. A linguistic genius, Schereschewsky spoke thirteen languages and could read twenty; he is best remembered for his translation of the Bible into popular Chinese (a "Bible for the poor"), typed with one finger (the "One-Finger Bible"). In addition to evangelism, Protestant missions in China produced an extensive network of schools, from elementary and high school to university, notably the Hangchow Christian University (Presbyterian), St. John's College (American Episcopal), Nanjing University (Methodist), Shantung Christian University (American Presbyterian and English Baptist), and Yenching University (a union of smaller Presbyterian, Methodist, and Congregational schools). Tragically, as during the Opium Wars and the Taiping Revolution, Christian missions (both Catholic and Protestant) were heavily damaged by the anti-foreign Boxer Rebellion (1900).

In Japan, where Christianity had been banned since the middle of the seventeenth century and was not fully permitted until 1873, Protestant missions were not initiated until 1859, when Japan formally opened three treaty ports of Kanagawa, Nagasaki, and Hakodake to nondiplomat foreigners. The first denominations to arrive were Episcopal, Presbyterian, American Dutch Reformed, and Free Baptist. After the Meiji Restoration in 1868, with the removal of the last anti-Christian edicts in 1873, five major Protestant denominations were actively working in Japan: Presbyterian/Reformed, Congregationalist, Methodist, Episcopal, and Baptist.

Part of the reasons for the early success of Protestant missions in Japan lies not only in the active role of Japanese student groups called "Bands" in evangelism and church leadership, but also in the fact that Christianity was perceived as identical with Western civilization, which would be useful for Japan's projected way to modernization.[14]

Protestant missions also came to Korea thanks to the country's openness to the West. As with Roman Catholicism, Protestant Christianity was first brought to Korea not by expatriate missionaries but by Koreans themselves, the former by Peter Yi Sunghun in 1784 and the latter by Suh Sang-Yun (1848–1926), who in 1883 carried a Korean translation of the Gospel of Luke back to his village and organized a house church. Immediately after Korea signed its first treaty with the United States in 1882, foreign missionaries, mostly Americans, arrived, notably the Presbyterian medical doctor Horace N. Allen (1858–1932), the Presbyterian Horace G. Underwood (1859–1916), the Methodist Henry G. Appenzeller (1858–1902), and the Presbyterian Samuel A. Moffett (1864–1939). These early Methodist and Presbyterian missionaries—the two main Protestant denominations in Korea—carried out evangelism mainly through medicine (Allen's Royal Hospital) and education (Yonsei University and Ewha Woman's University). The two denominations eventually experienced a phenomenal growth, partly thanks to the adoption of the "Nevius Plan" or "Three-Self Plan" (self-government, self-support, and self-propagation) and partly thanks to Korean Christians' support for Korea's struggle for liberation from Japanese colonization (1910–45).[15]

The predominantly Catholic Philippines was introduced to Protestantism after the United States took the country over from Spain in 1898. The first permanent Protestant presence began with the establishment of the YMCA in the following year. Next, a variety of American mission agencies rushed in: Northern Presbyterian,

---

14. A resource on Japanese Christianity is Mark R. Mullins, ed., *Handbook of Christianity in Japan* (Leiden: Brill, 2003).

15. On Korean Protestantism, see Lak-Geoon George Paik, *The History of Protestant Missions in Korea, 1832–1910*, 2nd ed. (Seoul: Yonsei University Press, 1971).

Methodist, and American Baptist. To avoid counterproductive rivalries, these mission boards agreed to a cooperation comity arrangement by adopting the common name of *Iglesia Evangelica* and by dividing up the country for their missions. Manila and the rest of the island of Luzon were divided in half between the Presbyterians and the Methodists, and Panay Island was assigned to the Baptists. These denominations were later joined by the American Episcopalians, among whom Bishop Charles Henry Brent played a key role in missions to non-Catholic Filipinos.[16]

The World Missionary Conference to the Present

There is no doubt that the World Missionary Conference (Edinburgh, 1910) marked a momentous new beginning for Protestant missions worldwide at the beginning of the twentieth century. As is clear from its title, the explicit focus of the conference was Christian mission; its aim was, in W. H. Findlay's words, "to be a Grand Council for the Advancement of Missionary Science." Furthermore, its scope was intended to be global, even though in fact its participation was restricted to the representatives of Protestant and Anglican missionary societies. Nor was the conference geographically all-inclusive; Africa, Latin America, the Pacific Islands, and the Caribbean were absent. With regard to Asia, of 1,215 official delegates to the conference, only nineteen were Asian: eight Indians, four Japanese, three Chinese, one Korean, one Burmese, and one of Turkish origin.[17] Given these restrictions it might be argued

16. For a resource on Protestantism in the Philippines, see K. J. Clymer, *Protestant Missionaries in the Philippines, 1895–1916: An Inquiry into the American Colonial Mentality* (Urbana and Chicago: University of Illinois Press, 1986).

17. The best history of the World Missionary Conference is Brian Stanley, *The World Missionary Conference, Edinburgh 1910* (Grand Rapids: Eerdmans, 2009). Helpful studies of the conference with the focus on mission are Kenneth R. Ross, *Edinburgh 2010: Springboard for Mission* (Pasadena, CA: William Carey International University Press, 2010); David A. Kerr and Kenneth R. Ross, eds., *Edinburgh 2010: Mission Then and Now* (Oxford: Regnum, 2009); and Daryl Balia and Kirsteen Kim, eds., *Edinburgh 2010: Witnessing to Christ Today* (Oxford: Regnum, 2010).

that the World Missionary Conference would not have the intended worldwide influence.

With regard to the impact of the conference on Protestant missions, John R. Mott's slogan "The evangelization of the world in this generation," which may be taken as expressing the ultimate goal of the conference, admirable though it is for its zeal, has been criticized as wildly naïve. No doubt the two world wars, which wrought terrible havoc on Christian missions worldwide, prevented the conference from implementing its "Missionary Science." Despite its potential limitations, however, the conference can serve as a useful benchmark to evaluate Protestant missions in Asia in the twentieth century and beyond.[18]

First of all, some numbers. In 1910, Protestants in Asia (including East, South, and West Asia) numbered 22,119,000 and Anglicans 778,000. In 2010, they numbered 87,379,000 and 864,000 respectively. The growth rate of Protestants in Asia (average annual growth, percent per year, between 1910 and 2010) was 2.68 and that of Anglicans 0.10.[19] In 1910–2010, Christianity as a whole (Anglican, Catholic, Independent, Marginal, Orthodox, and Protestant) grew at twice the population growth (2.68 vs. 1.41); still in 2010 it represented only 8.5 percent of the Asian population (352,239,000 Christians out of the population of 4,166,308,000). (One significant fact, which is of great import for Christian mission and to which we will return, is that the number of atheists and agnostics grew the fastest, from 60,000 in 1910 to 600 million in 2010. Asia became the most nonreligious continent in 2010!) Another important fact is

18. The two most informative sources for twentieth-century Christianity are Todd M. Johnson and Kenneth R. Ross, eds., *Atlas of Global Christianity 1910–2010* (Edinburgh: Edinburgh University Press, 2009), and Patrick Johnstone, *The Future of the Global Church: History, Trends and Possibilities* (Downers Grove, IL: InterVarsity, 2011). On world Christianity, consult the many works by Dyron B. Daughrity, especially *To Whom Does Christianity Belong? Critical Issues in World Christianity* (Minneapolis: Fortress, 2015); Douglas Jacobsen, *Global Gospel: An Introduction to Christianity in Five Continents* (Grand Rapids: Baker Academic, 2015); and Sebastian Kim and Kirsteen Kim, *Christianity as a World Religion* (London: Bloomsbury, 2008).

19. All the statistics, here and below, are taken from *Atlas of Global Christianity 1910–2010*, 134–49.

that in 1910 the majority of Christians in Asia were Roman Catholic and Orthodox; in 2010, it shifted to the Independent and Marginal churches, especially in China. The fastest current growth rates were found in East Asia, especially China, and in South Central Asia. In 2010, the Asian countries with the largest numbers of Christians were, in descending order: China, the Philippines, Indonesia, South Korea, Vietnam, Myanmar, and Japan. In terms of percentage of the population, the Philippines had the highest (86.2), followed by Timor (84.8), South Korea (41.4), Singapore (16.1), and Brunei (15.3). Urban areas in which the number of Christians exceeded one million in 2010 were, in descending order: Manila (11,068,000), Seoul (4,366,000), Jakarta (2,433,000), Shanghai (2,368,000), Mumbai (2,004,000), Pusan (1,835,000), Incheon (1,482,000), Tangu (1,142,000), Tokyo (1,064,000), and Hong Kong (1,001,000).

Statistics, albeit informative, do not tell the whole story, very complex and often underreported, of the presence of the Reformation in Asia. Clearly, the number of spiritual descendants of the Reformation, especially the Protestants, has increased dramatically during the past hundred years, as the figures above show. There are many reasons for this explosive growth, chief among which is, as we will see, the staggering and unexpected rise of Christianity in China after the 1980s. Yet, the percentage of Christians in Asia's total population (more than four billion) remained small in 2010 (8.5 percent, with 352,239,000 members) after centuries of mission. The discomforting question inevitably arises as to whether anything was wrong with Christian evangelization in Asia and whether, with new missionizing methods, a new "Advancement of the Missionary Science" advocated by the Edinburgh Conference will produce in Asia the kind of demographic growth we have witnessed in Africa and Latin America—the three continents forming the Global South. We will take up these questions in the second and third sections of this essay. Meanwhile we will take a closer look at the Protestant churches in Asia in the past century.

In *South Central Asia*, with the end of British colonization and many of the countries constituted along ethnic or religious lines and gaining national independence, Christian churches underwent tremendous political, economic, military, and religious turmoil. The countries with the largest number of Christians in 2010 were, in descending order: India (58,367,000), Pakistan (3,923,000), Sri Lanka (1,714,000), Nepal (935,000), and Bangladesh (859,000). Countries with the highest percentage of Christians (not only Protestants) were, in descending order: Sri Lanka (10.7), India (4.8), Nepal (3.3), and Pakistan (2.3). Among the descendants of the Reformation in South Asia, in 2010 there were 55,100 Anglicans (a huge decrease from 657,000 in 1910), 20,734,000 Independents (up from 101,000 in 1910), 167,000 Marginals (up from 200 in 1910), and 23,998,000 Protestants (up from 856,000 in 1910). Clearly, there has been a tremendous growth among Protestants, Independents, and Marginals.

In terms of church life and missionary activities, there have been five significant trends toward indigenizing Christianity in the South Asian context. First, ecumenically, there has been a movement toward church union for collaboration on national and international levels: the Church of South India (1947), the Church of North India (1970), the Church of Pakistan (1970), and the Church of Bangladesh (1971). In addition, collaboration in mission is also fostered by the formation of National Councils of Churches, which are affiliated with the World Council of Churches. Second, liturgical reforms and the introduction of new worship styles (notably, the production of the *Book of Common Worship* in the Church of South India) provide the people with a rich source of spirituality. Third, a vibrant development of contextualized theology, especially in dialogue with other religions, in particular Buddhism, Hinduism, and Islam, and for the liberation of the oppressed (e.g., Dalit theology), has brought new insights to the understanding and practice of the Christian faith. Fourth, the churches have engaged extensively in the traditional fields of healthcare and education, especially for the outcasts and the tribals.[20] Fifth, Indian churches have organized missionary societies such as Discipling a Whole Nation (DAWN) and the India Mission Association (IMA), an independent evangelical mission-networking organization that linked various conservative-evangelical missionary agencies with more than 41,000 Indian missionaries in 2001. Given the influence of Christianity in South Asia, quite dispropor-

20. See *Atlas of Global Christianity*, 142–43.

tionate to their number, it has recently met with opposition, often violent, from extremist Hindus in India (the Hindutva), Muslims in Pakistan, and Buddhists in Sri Lanka.

In *Southeast Asia*, during the twentieth century all the countries where Christianity had a significant presence, such as the Philippines, Vietnam, and Indonesia, underwent violent struggles for independence from colonial powers, and engaged in the arduous task of nation-building, and Christian churches were unavoidably implicated in these political and economic processes. Given the strong anti-colonial sentiments, foreign missionaries, both Catholic and Protestant, were perceived as agents of Western domination; in Myanmar and Vietnam, they were expelled. Some native Christians called for a mission moratorium. The situation changed substantially for the better in the last decades of the twentieth century. In 2010, there were 537,000 Anglicans (up from 47,300 in 1910), 28,498,000 Independents (up from 2,188,000 in 1910), 1,253,000 Marginals (up from 60 in 1910), and 27,184,000 Protestants (up from 705,000 in 1910). Clearly, the children of Protestant Reformations have been doing extremely well in Southeast Asia in the past century! Countries with the highest number of Christians (not only Protestants) in 2010 were, in descending order: the Philippines (83,151,000), Indonesia (23,992,000), Vietnam (7,796,000), Myanmar (4,002,000), Malaysia (2,530,000), Timor (1,077,000), Thailand (849,000), Singapore (740,000), Cambodia (305,000), and Laos (194,000). Countries with the highest percentage of Christians were, in descending order: the Philippines (89.4), Timor (84.8), Singapore (16.1), Brunei (15.3), Indonesia (12.1), Malaysia (9.1), Vietnam (8.6), Myanmar (8.0), Laos (3.1), and Cambodia (2.0).

Protestantism came to all East Asian countries, except Thailand, through Western colonization—Dutch, British, and American successively. As elsewhere, Protestant missions were carried out chiefly through healthcare and education, the two areas in which notable benefits would be enjoyed by converts. Two issues present significant challenges to Christian missions. First, the relationship between church and state: Though all Southeast Asian countries now recognize religious freedom in their constitutions, religious practice is closely monitored by the government through the registration system and at times suppressed, especially when a particular church, particularly unregistered Pentecostal churches, is perceived as a threat to national security. Second, the process of indigenizing the Christian faith ("enculturation"): To what extent should the Christian faith be adapted to local cultural customs, such as marriage and funeral rituals, and especially indigenous religious practices ("popular religiosity"), such as the veneration of ancestors and sacrifices to spirits, without adulterating the Christian faith and Christian identity?

Lastly, in *Northeast Asia*, the situation of Christianity in the past century is anything if not extremely complex. Seismic political events such as the Boxer Uprising (1900), the establishment of the Communist government in China in 1949, the Japanese occupation of Korea (1910–45), the defeat of Japan in 1945, the Korean War (1950–53), and the Cultural Revolution (1966–76)—just to cite a few—not only transformed the political landscape but also did untold damages to Christian missions. By 2010, however, an astonishing and explosive phenomenon had occurred in the Reformation in Asia: it would be a gross understatement to say that the situation of Protestantism in Northeast Asia had ameliorated. Anglicans numbered 176,000 (up from 43,500 in 1910), Independents 93,002,000 (up from 12,400 in 1910), Marginals 1,662,000 (up from 0 in 1910), and Protestants 35,974,000 (up from 475,000 in 1910). The countries with the highest number of Christians (not only Protestants) in 2010 were, in descending order: China (115,009,000), South Korea (20,150,000), Japan (2,903,000), Taiwan (1,420,000), North Korea (484,000), and Mongolia (47,100). Countries with the largest percentage of Christians were, in descending order: South Korea (41.4), China (8.6), Taiwan (6.0), Japan (2.3), North Korea (2.0), and Mongolia (1.2).[21]

This demographic explosion, especially of the Independents and the Marginals in China, does not mean that Christianity in Northeast Asia is problem-free. On the contrary, there are no places on earth where Christianity is facing more political conflicts and

---

21. Note that the number of Christians in China, as will be seen below, is much debated.

apparently intractable internal problems than Northeast Asia and Western Asia (the Middle East). Of the Northeast Asian countries listed above, only South Korea is one in which the Reformation churches (as well as the Catholic Church) have enjoyed a vigorous expansion. Moreover, Korean churches, especially the Presbyterian Church, the largest denomination in Korea, have sent a large number of missionaries overseas, estimated at 16,000 in 2006, the second-largest number of foreign missionaries after the United States. Part of the reasons for this flourishing is the fact that Korean Protestants, in spite of the apolitical stance of their foreign missionaries, played a decisive role in the struggle against Japanese occupation, especially during the 1919 March First Independence Movement.

By contrast, in Japan, where in 1941, under government coercion, thirty-two Protestant denominations (except the Anglican Church and the Holiness Church) joined together to form the United Church of Christ in Japan (*Nippon Kirisuto Kyōdan*), church growth has been anemic, perhaps due to the fact that chastened by their acquiescence to the country's past military adventures, Christian churches have tended to abstain from political involvement and as a result have little impact on Japanese society.

China represents an extremely complex case of its own. After the Boxer Uprising (1900), xenophobic hostility to Christianity subsided and Protestant missions resumed with great vigor, especially in the five eastern coastal cities, with a new emphasis on social services, particularly through healthcare and education, so much so that 1902–27 has been dubbed the "Golden Age" of Protestant missions in China. Between 1900 and 1925 the number of Protestant missionaries increased fourfold—from two thousand to eight thousand. At the same time, there began a movement toward building an indigenous church, through the "Three-Self" movement, that is, self-administration, self-financing, and self-evangelization, a plan eloquently advocated by the twenty-eight-year-old Chinese delegate Cheng Jingyi at the World Missionary Conference in a speech that was judged by the Boston-based *Missionary Herald* as "without question the best speech" made at Edinburgh. Cheng further proposed that an interdenominational or nondenominational Protestant Church be established in China for the sake of mission.[22] The idea of a "Chinese Church" that is confessionally, ecclesiastically, and institutionally a single church was taken up at the National Christian Conference of the China Continuation Committee of the World Missionary Conference, of which Cheng Jingyi was chairman, in Shanghai in 1922. Out of this all-China conference two organizations were created: the National Christian Council and the Church of Christ in China (*Zhonghua Jidujiaohui*), with a significant degree of Chinese leadership. The Church of Christ in China was not established until 1927; unfortunately, several members of the conservative Bible Union of China refused to join, objecting to its alleged modernist theology, including the Christian and Missionary Alliance, the China Inland Mission, the US Southern Presbyterians, the Anglican Communion, the Southern Baptists, the American Methodists, the Church of the Nazarene, and the Assemblies of God. Thus Cheng Jingyi's and the National Christian Council's dream of one unified Chinese Church was stillborn.

It was also during the first decades of the twentieth century that an extremely significant phenomenon took place, namely, the rise of Independent Chinese Christianity, without any foreign leadership whatsoever, though their founders were influenced to varying degrees by foreign missionaries. These include, with the names of their founders in parentheses: the True Jesus Church (Wei Enbo, 1876–1916), the Jesus Family (Jing Dianying, 1890–1957), and the Christian Assembly, commonly known as the Little Flock (Ni Tuoshen Watchman Nee, 1903–1972). In addition to these Independent churches, there were indigenous Pentecostal-like and Charismatic movements such as the Spiritual Gifts Society (*Ling'en hui*) in Feixian (Southern Shandong), the "Shandong Revival" (started by the freelance Norwegian missionary Marie Monsen), the Christian Tabernacle (*Jitudu Huitang*), initiated by the conservative Wang Mingdao (1900–1991), and the Bethel Worldwide Evangelistic Band, founded by the revivalist preacher John Sung (Song Shangjie, 1901–1944). These Independent churches, with emphasis on speaking in

---

22. For a helpful presentation of the voices of the Asian delegates at the World Missionary Conference, see Stanley, *The World Missionary Conference*, 91–131.

tongues, prophesying, miraculous healing, emotional worship, and apocalyptic expectation, also engaged in enthusiastic evangelism, especially of the western parts of China, with their "Chinese Back-to-Jerusalem Evangelistic Band," dedicated to evangelizing the vast reaches of Xinjang and the far west.[23]

The Golden Age of Protestant missions in China, with its enviable achievements in healthcare and education and its bright future, and Chinese Christianity as a whole, were dashed to pieces by the Communist Party's victory over the Nationalist Party (*Guomindang*) and the establishment of the People's Republic of China in 1949. Missionaries were expelled; church properties nationalized; and religious leaders forced to undergo reeducation, imprisoned, condemned to hard labor, or killed. Ironically, the dream of one unified and nondenominational (Protestant) Chinese Church, long pursued by the National Chinese Council and the Church of Christ in China, and fiercely resisted by the more conservative groups, was realized by a stroke of the pen in 1954, when separate denominational organizations were abolished and all Chinese Protestants came under the oversight of the Three-Self Patriotic Movement (TSPM).[24] (Later, in 1957, the Catholic Church met the same fate, with the founding of the Catholic Patriotic Association.) In the new China, all religions came under the control of the government Religious Affairs Bureau, now called the State Administration for Religious Affairs (SARA).

Protestantism is known as the "New Religion of Christianity" (*Jidujiao xinjiao*), whereas Catholicism is known as the "Religion of the Lord of Heaven" (*Tianzhu jiao*), and they are legally categorized as two different "religions." In 1980, in addition to the TSPM, the China Christian Council (*Zhonguo Jidujiao Xiehui*, CCC) was founded as the umbrella organization for all Protestant churches in China, responsible for activities promoting their internal church life,

23. For an informative account of Independent and Marginal Protestants in China, see Lian Xi, *Redeemed by Fire: The Rise of Popular Christianity in Modern China* (New Haven: Yale University Press, 2010).

24. On the TSPM, see Philip L. Wickeri, *Seeking the Common Ground: Protestant Christianity, the Three-Self Movement, and China's United Front* (Maryknoll, NY: Orbis, 1988).

such as Bible translation, theological education, worship, and church order. Together the TSPM and the CCC are called the "Two Associations" (*liang hui*), the former more political, the latter more ecclesiastical. Through the CCC, registered Protestant churches joined the World Council of Churches. The chief leaders of the TSPM were Wu Yaozong (Y. T. Wu, 1895–1971) and his successor, in 1980, the Anglican bishop Ding Guangxun (K. H. Ting, 1915–2012). Of course, not all Chinese Christian churches accepted being incorporated into the TSPM, notably the Evangelical and Independent groups.

In addition to the historical irony concerning the establishment of a nondenominational church mentioned above, there is another huge historical irony, this time to the chagrin of the Communist Party. The requirement for all churches to register with the TSPM brought about the rise, within both Protestantism and Catholicism, of the so-called underground churches (*dixia jiaohui*), which refuse to register and be controlled by the government. The number of Christians in underground churches, which is hard to count, is likely much larger than that of the official churches.[25] There have been tensions between the TSPM and the CCC on the one hand and unregistered Protestant churches on the other. (Within the Catholic Church such tensions have been much more pronounced, especially due to the ordination of bishops appointed by the Chinese government without the consent of the Vatican. In recent times, however, some progress has been made toward reconciling the registered and unregistered Catholic groups. In general, the relation between the Vatican and the Chinese government is a *pas de deux*, with one step forward and two steps back.)

Two more political events contributed to the devastation of Chinese Christianity: first, the "Great Leap Forward" (1958–66), Mao Zedong's (1893–1976) social and economic campaign to transform China's agrarian economy into a socialist society through rapid industrialization and collectivization. The program caused a

25. In 2010, the State Administration for Religious Affairs (SARA) put the number of registered TSPM Protestants at 16 million. Other scholars believe that SARA intentionally underestimated that number and suggested that the likely number is near 90 million. The Pew Research Center (2011) estimates 50 million to 70 million Christians practice in nonregistered churches.

great famine in which millions, estimated to be between 18 and 45, died of starvation. It also closed over 90 percent of the churches that were still open, especially in the rural areas. The next maelstrom into which Chinese society and Christianity were plunged was the "Great Proletarian Cultural Revolution" (1966–76), also promoted by Mao Zedong, during which Christianity as a whole seemed about to be wiped out in China.

However, in and through these extremely adverse conditions, there occurred the third historical irony, one of immense impact on the descendants of the Reformation. Unable or forbidden to worship in public, Chinese Protestants began to conduct religious services in the homes of believers without government approval. These informal gatherings, generally small in cities but large in rural areas, are called "spontaneous private meetings" by authorities but "house churches" (*jiating jiaohui*) by believers. These house churches in practice function as independent churches, though there are a few networks of house churches stretching over many provinces and even the entire country. These house churches are an enormous boon for Protestantism. In 2009, a one-year government-commissioned study on house churches put the number of Protestants worshiping in house churches between 45 and 60 million, with another 18 to 30 million attending registered churches. House churches generally are either evangelical, emphasizing their historical and doctrinal connections with former Western missionaries and conservative Chinese pastors (for example, Wang Mingdao) and adopting a literalist interpretation of the Bible, or charismatic, with emphasis on personal religious experiences and the gifts of the Spirit, particularly miraculous healing and speaking in tongues.

In addition, there is a large group of new and bewilderingly varied religious movements that are inspired by or connected to Protestantism, especially of the Pentecostal type, and which are usually categorized as "Marginal Christians." These movements, with colorful and biblical-sounding names, can pop up anywhere with charismatic founders, quickly attract a large following, and are not officially registered. These include the Local Church (also known as the Shouters), the Established King Sect, the Lightning from the East, the Lord God Sect, the All Scope Church, the South China

Church, the Disciples Sect (also known as the Narrow Gate in the Wilderness), the Three Ranks of Servants, the Cold Water Sect, the Commune Sect, the New Testament Church (also known as the Apostolic Faith Sect), the Resurrection Sect, the Dami Evangelization Association, and the World Elijah Evangelism Association.[26] The Chinese government criminalizes these as "evil cults" and arrests, fines, and imprisons their leaders and followers, especially those of the Local Church and its offshoot, the Lightning from the East. Ostensible reasons for this suppression are their heterodox beliefs (end-time predictions and deification of leaders), superstitious practices (derived from folk religion and Pentecostal healing practices), and threat to public order (large-scale activities and meetings), but their large size, rapid growth, and avoidance of government control also play a key role. The above-mentioned house churches assiduously distinguish themselves from these groups, which they themselves condemn as heretical, partly because they do not want to be lumped with them as "evil cults," a deadly legal categorization, partly because these groups try to recruit members from them.

Finally, after Deng Xiaoping's economic opening in the late 1980s, there has been an increase of interest in the role of religion, and Christianity in particular, in the "public sphere" or "civil society." As the result of Deng's massive restructuring of the economy, the growth of Chinese Protestantism moved from rural areas to cities, especially those of the southeast coast in the Shandong, Zhejiang, and Fujian provinces. At the same time, there was a group made up of intellectuals, university professors, and upper-class elites who have a great sympathy for Christianity as a system of cultural, moral, and religious principles, which they consider helpful for China's cultural and moral reconstruction. These are dubbed "Cultural Christians" (*wenhua jidutu*), who occasionally attend church services but do not seek baptism. They promote the academic study of Christianity, and currently there are more than twenty university-based centers or institutes for the study of Chris-

---

26. See Fenggeng Yang, *Religion in China: Survival and Revival under Communist Rule* (New York: Oxford University Press, 2012).

tianity. Unfortunately, the impact of these "Cultural Christians" on Chinese Christianity and Chinese society still remains minimal.

With regard to the Chinese government's treatment of Protestants, in general it is quite varied. By and large, Protestants can freely worship at registered churches associated with the TSPM and the CCC. Of course, many—perhaps a larger number—do not, as we have seen above. Government authorities make periodic attempts at forcing them to join the registered churches, mostly with half-hearted measures, sometimes by more severe actions such as confiscation or destruction of church properties, imprisonment of church leaders, and dispersal of the church into smaller communities. As a whole, more tolerance is shown in cities than in rural areas, and the treatment of Christians varies from place to place, depending on the local authorities. The one exception is with the groups that the government calls "evil cults," whose leaders and members the government openly persecutes.

Challenges and Opportunities

I have lingered over the presence of the Protestant Reformation in China partly because in many ways it epitomizes both the challenges and the opportunities facing the Protestant churches and their missions in Asia and partly because it helps answer the question of whether the Protestant Reformations are a blessing or a curse for Asia as a whole. The challenges and opportunities can be divided into two types, those concerning the relations of Protestantism to the outside world (*ad extra*) and those that are internal to the life of the churches (*ad intra*). Limited space will allow me to mention only the most significant ones.

The Reformations Encountering the World of Asia

As mentioned above, Protestantism (as well as Catholicism) entered Asia (except Thailand) on the back of Western colonialism. This colonialist legacy, and the subsequent complicity of some foreign missionaries as well as indigenous Christians, either by collaborating with colonialist powers or by seeking to benefit from privileges attached to their Christian status, such as extraterritoriality, judicial immunity, healthcare, education, and job opportunities, must ever be borne in mind with repentance and humility by both local Christians and foreign missionaries. Governments such as China, Vietnam, and North Korea may be forgiven for being suspicious of Christianity, especially those denominations that have financial and organizational ties with foreign institutions located in the West, especially the United States (and for Catholics, the Vatican). But even in countries that are not in principle hostile to Christianity such as India, Sri Lanka, the Philippines, Malaysia, Singapore, and Indonesia, the history of Western colonialism and its lingering impact on Protestant missions must not be forgotten by Christians engaged in evangelization.

In several countries, harassment, intimidation, arrest, imprisonment, persecution, and even killing of Christians and destruction of church properties are a fact of life. These violent acts are motivated by religious hatred (in some Islamic countries such as Pakistan and Malaysia), political ideology (the Hindutva and anti-conversion laws in India), or concern for state and party security (Vietnam and China). While pressure must be applied and measures taken to defend and protect the right to religious freedom, Christians must not return violence for violence, and when absolutely necessary, must be ready to suffer and even to lose their lives to bear witness to Christ. Martyrdom, not deliberately sought but faithfully accepted, is no doubt the most efficacious form of evangelization.

In broader terms, Protestant churches must face the extremely complex issue of church-state relations. Although most if not all Asian countries recognize the right to religious freedom in their constitutions, the actual practice is fraught with difficulties in many countries such as China, Vietnam, Laos, Myanmar (especially in the case of the Christian Karen), and India (especially in the northeastern majority-Christian states of Meghalaya, Mizoram, and Nagaland). At times, discrimination takes on subtle forms, as in Malaysia recently, where there is an attempt to ban the use of "Allah" to refer to the Christian God. In Islamist countries and in Hindu-majority India, there exist severe restrictions on evangelization, the presence of foreign missionaries, and conversion. This is particularly true with Evangelicals and Pentecostals, who generally practice a rather aggressive form of proselytization without due respect for local customs and religions, and whose churches are mostly unregistered. The challenge for Christians is to seek out ways to collaborate with the government to promote the common good, especially in healthcare, education, and social services, particularly for the benefit of the marginalized and the oppressed such as the Dalits and the Tribals, ethnic and religious minorities, women, and workers, without surrendering to the unjust religious policies of the government and being co-opted by it.

One of the most difficult challenges for Protestant missions is to indigenize Christianity in all its beliefs and practices. By and large, Catholics have been more willing to take on this task of enculturation and more successful than Protestants, except in Bible translation. This is not of course always the case. In China, for instance, except for the efforts of the Jesuits in the seventeenth century, it was the Protestants who were seriously engaged in building a Chinese church on the basis of the three-self principles, and even if they were not successful on their own in bringing about one unified Church of Christ in China, they finally achieved their goal by the Communist Party's fiat through the creation of the TSPM and the CCC. However these two associations are judged, there is no doubt that they have performed an indispensable role in keeping the Protestant churches alive during the harrowing decades following the Communist victory and continue to do so today. To the extent that is possible, the three-self principles should be the guide for creating indigenous churches elsewhere in Asia.

Another important aspect of enculturation is the adoption of cultural customs and popular religious practices. In contrast to Catholics, Protestants have tended to look upon them with suspicion, especially when local customs and practices such as marriage customs, sexual mores, the veneration of ancestors, and sacrifices to the spirits seem at first sight contrary to Christian faith and morality. The challenge is to discern with prudence and humility, in broad consultation with all the local churches, what may and should be adopted and what should be changed and rejected, and avoid imposing Western cultural norms and practices as essential parts of the Christian faith.

Lastly, one recent phenomenon that is presenting serious challenges to Christian missions in Asia is migration. According to one statistical report, in 2013, 232 million people—3.2 percent of the world's population—lived outside their countries of origin. It is predicted that the immigration rate will continue to increase over time. A 2012 Gallup survey determined that nearly 640 million adults would want to immigrate if they had the opportunity to.[27] Global population movements today are so global and immense that our time has been dubbed "The Age of Migration."[28] In 2010 Asia hosted some 27.5 million immigrants. Countries from which these migrants came included India (9 million), Bangladesh (7 million), and China (6 million). Pakistan, the Philippines, Afghanistan, Vietnam, Indonesia, South Korea, and Nepal were also important countries of emigration. Top Asian countries of destination include India (6 million), Pakistan (3 million), Hong Kong (2.5 million), Japan (2.1 million), Malaysia (2 million), South Korea (1 million), Iran (2 million), and Saudi Arabia (2 million).[29] Asian migration is fueled mainly by the search for jobs through labor contract (especially to the Middle East). The majority of migrants are women (the "feminization of migration") whose typical jobs include domestic work, entertainment (a euphemism for the sex industry), restaurant and hotel service, and mail-order marriage. That migrants, and

27. Boundless, "Dimensionalizing Immigration: Numbers of Immigrants around the World." Boundless Economics. Boundless, 21 July 2015. Retrieved from https://www.boundless.com/economics/textbooks/boundless-economics-textbook /immigration-economics-38/introduction-to-immigration-economics-138/dimen sionalizing-immigration-numbers-of-immigrants-around-the-world-544-12641/. There are legions of websites dedicated to the study of migration.

28. This is the title of the best one-volume study of international migration: Stephen Castles, Hein de Haas, and Mark J. Miller, *The Age of Migration: International Population Movements in the Modern World*, 5th ed. (New York: Guilford, 2014).

29. On migration in the Asia-Pacific region, see Castles, de Haas, and Miller, *The Age of Migration*, 147–71.

especially refugees, face a host of enormous problems of various kinds needs no elaboration. What has not been sufficiently studied is the religious life of migrants, especially of Christians in Christian-minority countries (the Middle East in particular). It is here that Christian missions are most urgently needed.[30]

Varieties of Reformations in Asia

Turning now to the internal life of Protestant churches in Asia, it is important to recall that the first sustained initiatives in Protestant missions were not taken by the early reformers but by the eighteenth-century (Moravian) Pietists who stood within the tradition of the Radical Reformers. The Pietist emphasis on personal sanctification, interior experience and devotion, reception of the gifts of the Spirit, and Bible study and prayer, especially in small groups or conventicles (*ecclesiola in ecclesia*), was imported to Britain and the United States and bore fruit in the various Awakening and Revival movements. It is from these movements in Germany, Britain, and the United States that Protestant missions to Asia were undertaken.

Today many elements of this Pietist tradition are alive and well in the various Evangelical, Charismatic, Pentecostal, and Pentecostal-like churches and movements in Asia, which have enjoyed phenomenal growth.[31] Recall the demographic explosion of the Independents and the Marginals in Asia from 1910 to 2010: the former from 2,301,000 in 1910 to 142,737,000 in 2010 and the latter from 290 in 1910 to 3,139,000 in 2010. On the other hand, this demographic explosion has proved to be both a blessing and a curse for Protestant Christianity in Asia (as well as in Africa and Latin

---

30. For a study of migration and theology, see the trilogy edited by Elaine Padilla and Peter C. Phan, published by Palgrave/Macmillan, New York: *Contemporary Issues in Migration and Theology* (2013); *Theology of Migration in the Abrahamic Religions* (2014); *Christianities in Migration: The Global Perspective* (2016).

31. See Allan Anderson and Edmond Tang, eds., *Asian and Pentecostal: The Charismatic Face of Christianity in Asia* (Oxford: Regnum, 2005).

America). Again, space permits only a listing of some of the challenges facing Protestant Christianity *ad intra*.

To most Asians the seemingly unlimited number of Protestant churches and denominations, often in the same city, is a mind-boggling mystery. Worse, as Cheng Jingyi put it succinctly at the World Missionary Conference in 1910, "Denominationalism has never interested the Chinese mind. He finds no delight in it, but sometimes he suffers for it."[32] Ironically, Cheng's dream of a nondenominational, interdenominational, or postdenominational church for China became a reality only thanks to the Communist government. In India and Pakistan denominationalism was overcome by creating church unions, and elsewhere by establishing National Councils of Churches that then joined the World Council of Churches. In countries where such collaboration is absent, the evils of denominationalism are exacerbated by rivalries, "sheep-stealing," and mutual condemnations, which scandalize non-Christians.

Denominationalism is the pivot of a much more complex issue confronting Christian churches in Asia, namely, ecumenism. The World Missionary Council at Edinburgh is generally regarded as the starting point of ecumenical dialogue among Protestants. The Catholic Church gave a strong impetus to work for Christian unity at the Second Vatican Council (1962–65). After bursts of enthusiasm and intense ecumenical activities in the immediate aftermaths of the council, fervor for ecumenism cooled down considerably toward the end of the last century. This state of affairs does much damage to the cause of Christian missions in Asia. Unfortunately, it is largely ignored in Evangelical and Pentecostal missiology and missionizing practice, which give pride of place to church-planting and thus perpetuate denominationalism.

A related, and much more complex, internal challenge for the Reformation in Asia is the dramatic explosion of Independent and Marginal churches and groups, especially in China. Independent churches, as the name implies, represent a new paradigm of being church, which, ironically, represents a form of, to coin

---

32. Quoted in Stanley, *The World Missionary Conference*, 109.

an oxymoronic phrase, "sectarian postdenominationalism." They are "postdenominational" insofar as they minimize traditional doctrines, forms of worship, and church structures, which they regard as too rigid, formal, and authoritarian. On the other hand, in spite of its post-, or pan-denominationalism, they are "sectarian" insofar as, with few exceptions, they tend to be organized as local units ("house churches") along experiential, ethnic, or generational rather than doctrinal lines. Indeed, one group often claims to be the sole true church and is not slow to condemn all the others as heretical. For them, the guidelines for ecumenical unity, or to use a less exacting term, "convergence," as proposed by the World Council of Churches in its Faith and Order Paper No. 214, *The Church: Toward a Common Vision* (2013), have little if any relevance.

The same thing is true of "Marginal" Christians (the preferred term to "sect" and "cult") who, though self-describing as Christian and adopting certain Pentecostal-like practices, reject certain fundamental Christian beliefs such as the Trinity, the divinity of Jesus and his role as God's final revealer and savior, and key sacraments (for instance, the Eucharist and ordination). This is the case of all the movements classified as "evil cults" by the Chinese government and a host of new religious movements in Korea (for instance, the Unification Church), the Philippines (for instance, the Iglesia ni Cristo), and Japan.[33] The fact that these Marginal churches have historical and theological affinity with the Reformation and their phenomenal growth beyond church and government control makes the issue of their Christian identity all the more urgent for Protestantism in Asia.

Regarding evangelization itself, as reported above, many Protestant churches, especially in India, Korea, China, and Japan, have undertaken missions not only nationally but also internationally, "from everywhere to everywhere," reversing the direction of missions from North to South to South to North and South to South.

---

33. On indigenous Christian movements in Japan, see Mark R. Mullins, *Christianity Made in Japan: A Study of Indigenous Movements* (Honolulu: University of Hawai'i Press, 1998).

This is one of most significant contributions of the Reformation, especially in its Pietist heritage, in Asia. Nevertheless there are problems. The first concerns the very concept of mission itself. By and large, mission is taken, particularly in Evangelical and Pentecostal circles, to mean primarily conversion (baptism) and church-planting, and success of missions is measured in terms of numerical growth. Second, there is the category of "sympathizers" who accept the teachings of Jesus but who do not seek baptism, such as the "Cultural Christians" in China and the *Khrist Panthis* ("Christ followers") in India, that is, Hindus who find a home for devotion and worship of Jesus within Hindu religious structures. They are not unlike the "God-fearers" (*yirei Hashem* and *phoboumenoi ton theon*) in antiquity. Third, as mentioned earlier, in the past century the number of atheists and agnostics grew the fastest, from 60,000 in 1910 to 600 million in 2010. As capitalism and consumerism spread to Asia through globalization, this last category is expected to grow exponentially. Fourth, again as mentioned above, a massive number of the Asian population has shifted from rural areas to cities, making person-to-person evangelism for conversion extremely difficult if not impossible. All these factors call for a rethinking of the concept of and strategies for mission.

Finally, in encountering Asia, the Reformation cannot ignore the fact that Asia, despite the growing phenomenon of agnosticism, is a religiously plural world, with believers of different religions living everywhere cheek-by-jowl with one another. Indeed, religious pluralism is perhaps the greatest challenge facing Christian missions in Asia, especially in the encounter with Hinduism and Islam. Theologically, it calls for a radical reassessment of the exclusivist theology of religions that is implicit in the thought of the Protestant reformers, operative in early Protestant missionaries, and vigorously maintained in many Protestant churches active in Asia today. A new theology of religions, one that is responsive to the reality of religious pluralism, will leave no Christian doctrine untouched, from the presence of the Spirit of God and salvation outside Christianity, the role of Christ as the unique and universal Savior, the function of the church as community and symbol of God's grace, to the necessity and goal of mission.

The Way Forward and Ahead

Is (are) the Reformation(s) in Asia a blessing or a curse? The historical survey and theological reflections above do not lend themselves to a clear-cut, either/or answer. As a human enterprise sustained by God's grace, it is unavoidably both, a truth that the Reformation theology of *simul justus et peccator* will have little difficulty admitting. There was of course the ambiguous relation between evangelization and colonization, which was sometimes collaboration, and at other times resistance and subversion. On balance, however, the overall picture is one of more light than darkness.

First, the Reformation has offered an *alternative* religious vision and an *alternative* way of life, one that brings hope and liberation to Asians who are oppressed and marginalized by their own political systems and religions. In particular, the Reformation, especially in its Pietistic tradition with its emphasis on the personal and immediate relation to God, affirms the inalienable value and dignity of the individual over the interests of the group. Second, in addition to bringing the Word of God to Asia, the Reformation brought to the continent vast improvements in education at all levels and for all (girls included), mass printing, Western medicine and healthcare, nationalism, democracy, and human rights. In the process a great number of Protestant missionaries have made innumerable and heroic sacrifices; some have lost their lives, all for the sake of the gospel.

As has been argued by Scott H. Hendrix, the reformers, despite their different agendas that ended up confessionalizing their reforms, were all united in one common goal, namely, re-Christianizing Europe, a process that had suffered serious deficiencies (according to the early reformers), or had utterly failed (as the Radical Reformers thought) during the medieval process of Christianization.[34] It was the genius of the descendants of the Radical Reformers who first initiated the project of Christianization outside Europe, which was later joined by other Protestants.

---

34. Scott H. Hendrix, *Recultivating the Vineyard: The Reformation Agendas of Christianization* (Louisville and London: Westminster John Knox, 2004).

In Asia today this process of "Christianization" is encountering severe challenges without and within. It is even highly debatable whether "Christianization," as envisioned by the reformers, is the right term and goal for Protestant missions in Asia. That Protestant missions should go *forward* and meet all these challenges is not an option but an act of obedience to the Lord and a way to consolidate the legacy of the Reformation in celebration of its 500th jubilee. With regard to Asia, what Aiming Wong writes about the Reformation jubilee and Christianity in China indicates the way *ahead* for Asia as a whole as well. Asians' knowledge of Luther, Melanchthon, Zwingli, Calvin, and Knox, Wong notes, is still rudimentary, and the legacy of the Reformation cannot be established without a profound knowledge of its founders, and I must add, especially with reference to Protestant missions in Asia, the lesser-known but no less important Radical Reformers. As the Chinese character for "crisis" implies, it means both danger and opportunity. Some dangers have been described above; the opportunity is well expressed by Wong: "The Reformation Jubilee can become a historical opportunity for Chinese Christians to draw up a road map for a promising future; the legacy of the great reformers and their spirit could increasingly become a tradition of relevance to Chinese Christianity."[35]

---

35. Aiming Wong, "The Reformation Jubilee and Christianity in China," in *Reformation: Legacy and Future*, ed. Petra Bosse-Huber, Serge Fornerod, Thies Gundlach, and Gottfried Locher (Geneva: World Council of Churches, 2015), 298.

6   Contemporary Challenges

The Reformation and the World Today

VLADIMIR LATINOVIC

To commemorate an event, to honor those who are not among us anymore and remember their actions, brings to mind our own mortality while simultaneously providing us with the necessary strength and motivation to follow their positive example and to avoid the negative one. One such event is commemorated in 2017, when we celebrate the 500th anniversary of the Reformation.[1] One of the questions we should engage with in connection with this anniversary is how much the modern world and the church's current situation differ from that of Luther's time and how Luther himself would react to the issues that our churches face today.[2] For this

1. At the time of writing, there is an intense discussion about what precisely will be "celebrated" and if one should indeed define it as a "celebration." In my opinion, because Luther's legacy does not consist wholly of the Protestant churches, but belongs more generally to all Christian churches and to all humanity, we should observe this commemoration collectively if possible. In the past five hundred years, all churches, almost without exception, have moved in the direction of the Reformation and have adopted many of the changes that Luther called for regarding the Roman Catholic Church. The Reformation influenced all Christian churches in one way or another. I think this is a good reason to call this anniversary a "commemoration."

2. Various studies have engaged with this question in recent years. For example, see Judith Krasselt-Maier, *Luther: Gottes Wort und Gottes Gnade: Bausteine für den Religionsunterricht in der Sekundarstufe II* (Göttingen: Vandenhoeck & Ruprecht, 2012); Ulrich Asendorf, *Luther neu gelesen: Modernität und Ökumenisch*

reason, I will analyze the challenges of the modern era in relation to the Reformation era, in order to see if and to what extent today's churches can benefit from the lessons learned from that time.

Globalization and the Churches

When comparing the Reformation era with the present, it becomes clear that although the world has changed more in the past fifty years than it had in the previous five hundred, the challenges that the churches are facing today are analogous or similar in their structure to those of the past, even if the concrete challenges are not identical.[3] The world and the churches admittedly face great political, demographical, and economical challenges, but the same can be asserted for almost every other era. As in an earlier age, today's churches' main purpose is putting people together with God and each other. In order to fulfill this task successfully, churches must always search for new and accessible ways of responding to the basic questions of the age and respond to the needs of modern people. Thus churches must adapt to the world and if they want to survive can never remain the same.

This willingness to change and update church teachings can be found in the theology of different churches, from Karl Barth's idea of *ecclesia semper reformanda*[4] to the "aggiornamento" of Pope John XXIII, which became a maxim for the Second Vatican Council. The challenge of constantly changing and adapting to the world seems, however, to be particularly difficult in our modern era, and

---

Aktualität in seiner letzten Vorlesung (Neuendettelsau: Freimund Verlag, 2005); Friedrich Hauschildt, ed., *Rechtfertigung Heute: Warum die Zentrale Einsicht Martin Luthers Zeitlos aktuell Ist* (Hannover: VELKD, Lutherisches Kirchenamt, 2008).

3. See Petra Bosse-Huber, Serge Fornerod, Thies Gundlach, and Gottfried Wilhelm Locher, eds., *Reformation: Legacy and Future, A Jubilee Volume* (Geneva: World Council of Churches, 2015).

4. See Theodor Mahlmann, "'*Ecclesia semper reformanda*': Eine historische Aufklärung: Neue Bearbeitung," in *Hermeneutica Sacra: Studien zur Auslegung der Heiligen Schrift im 16. und 17. Jahrhundert*, ed. Torbjörn Johansson, Robert Kolb, and Johann Anselm Steiger (Berlin and New York: De Gruyter, 2010), 381–442.

the church can only follow it one step at a time. Some churches have admittedly been heftily criticized by some sectors of society both because of their traditional (and often conservative) positions and because of the actions of their leaders and members.[5]

The situation of the Christian church in modern society in general has become extremely complicated due to a number of factors. The first factor that has substantially contributed to this situation, and at the same time poses one of the greatest challenges for the churches today, is the phenomenon of "globalization," whose economic and communication processes have led to and still contribute to a worldwide interconnectedness of society.[6] How deep this interconnectedness goes, and what this phenomenon means for our lives, we experienced very painfully through the recent economic crisis. Through this crisis, we grasped the extent to which we live in an interconnected world society, a "global village," in which hardly a single country was not affected. Economically strong countries were immediately affected by the crisis, but economically weak ones were also eventually affected, due to their financial dependence and because they are reliant on the support of richer countries. Even if it does not refer to this situation, the message of 1 Corinthians 12:26, "If one member suffers, all suffer together with it; if one member is honored, all rejoice together with it" (NRSV), is quite fitting.

The swift spread of the economic crisis of the past decade was abetted by the communicative mobility that accompanied it, but it is also simultaneously one of the causes of the globalization phenomenon. The reports of the so-called credit-rating agencies can serve as a good example of how means of communication affected the spread of the crisis: in the hands of the media, these reports

---

5. It seems that the Roman Catholic Church has received most of this criticism. Over the past few decades it was due to sexual abuse scandals as well as unmeasured behavior of some bishops and countless other questions posed at the center of the criticism. See Philip Jenkins, *The New Anti-Catholicism: The Last Acceptable Prejudice* (New York: Oxford University Press, 2003). But some other traditional churches, too, such as the Orthodox Church, are not completely spared from the criticism.

6. See Ulrich Beck, *Was ist Globalisierung? Irrtümer des Globalismus—Antworten auf Globalisierung* (Frankfurt am Main: Suhrkamp, 1997).

exacerbated the growing panic, exactly like the recent situation in Greece, for example, where people wanted to withdraw their money out of the bank in fear, and by doing that actually contributed to deepening the crisis. In this respect, the correlation between "economic" and "communicative" globalization is a critical factor.

Fundamentally, it should be noted that the phenomenon of globalization is not a new one. The first examples of it can be found as far back as the Old Testament. One of these is the story of the Tower of Babel in Genesis 11, in which people attempt to come together and overcome their differences to pursue a common globalizing goal, which in itself is a clear case of globalization. Further examples of globalization can also be found if we take a look at the history of early Christianity. After the rise of Christianity to become the state religion in the fourth century CE through the period of Justinian the Great, globalization processes took place inside the Roman Empire whereby one consistent system (*symphōnia*) with one god and one emperor was adopted, in contrast to the early Roman era, where polytheism was favored as the form of religion and authority.[7] Today's globalization, however, is not contingent on a central power, due especially to technological developments and the global information revolution.

For our context, it is interesting that in the era of the Reformation processes similar to globalization appeared.[8] Comparing today's situation with the sixteenth century, one can see that these processes admittedly have clear differences, but there are also some similarities. At first glance, for example, it is possible to recognize that the Reformation was not global, but primarily locally bound, as evidenced by the different domains of Luther, Zwingli, Calvin, and others. Without supporters in these historic sites (particularly in Switzerland), the Reformation would not have been possible.

7. Jean-Yves Huwart and Loïc Verdier, *Die Globalisierung der Wirtschaft: Ursprünge und Auswirkungen* (Paris: Organisation for Economic Co-operation and Development [OECD], 2014), 24.

8. See Michael Welker, "Protestantismus und Globalisierung," in *Johannes Calvin und die kulturelle Prägekraft des Protestantismus*, ed. Emidio Campi, Peter Opitz, and Konrad Schmid (Zürich: vdf Hochschulverlag, 2012), 57–72.

Initially it concerned the differentiation expressed in *cuius regio, eius religio*, but this situation did not endure for long. This principle would hardly be applicable in Germany or anywhere in Europe today. This is not just due to the demographic changes brought about by migration, but also because the symbiosis of church and state is no longer as strong, or in most cases no longer officially exists, at least not in modern democracies.[9] Particularly in the Orthodox churches, which are organized on the "national model," secularization is felt to be somewhat negative. As opposed to most Orthodox theologians, I categorize this development as somewhat positive, however, as in my opinion the link between church and state in past centuries has caused much damage to both sides.[10] The church has tried to align itself with the state system and thereby has often been institutionalized, and the state has constantly meddled in religious matters that do not affect it.[11] This point was actually one of the key issues on which the Reformation was consciously focused and with which the contemporary church is still grappling. One sees this for instance in the document "500 Jahre Reformation Luther 2017: Perspektiven für das Reformationsjubiläum" from the Evangelical Church in Germany (EKD), which must still call for a "clear distinction between church and state" to be made, implying that it has not yet been fully done.[12]

The church can likewise also benefit in different ways by and large from globalization, as from secularization. Globalization brings with it very many positive aspects, such as the internationalization of science, the intensification of communication, and international improvement of universal human rights and quality of

9. In practice, this symbiosis does, however, still exist in many areas.
10. See Vladimir Latinovic, "Local Church in the Global World: Orthodox Ecclesiology in the Age of Pluralism," *Ecclesiology* 12, no. 2 (2016): 165–82.
11. See Theodoros Nikolau, *Die Orthodoxe Kirche im Spannungsfeld von Kultur, Nation und Religion* (St. Ottilien: EOS Verlag, 2006).
12. Council of the Evangelical Church in Germany (EKD) in Wittenberg and Luther Memorials Foundation of Saxony-Anhalt, *Luther 2017—500 Jahre Reformation: Perspektiven für das Reformationsjubiläum* (Wittenberg: Geschäftsstelle der EKD, 2016), §15.

life for individuals and groups. As the church lives in this world, it is not excluded from these processes and can benefit from them.

The relationship of church and globalization has been broached at numerous church conferences and in many documents, including:

- Antelias (Lebanon 2003)
- Lutheran World Assembly (Winnipeg 2003)
- Evangelical Academy (Loccum 2004)
- World Alliance of Reformed Churches (Accra 2004)
- 96th German Catholic Convention (Saarbrucken 2006)
- World Council of Churches (Porto Alegre 2006)
- Encyclical of Pope Benedict XVI, *Caritatis in veritate* (Rome 2009)

All of these documents unanimously reached the conclusion that globalization is an impending external issue for the life of the church, has a place within the church, and will be worked around positively in almost all churches.

The church can benefit from all the above-mentioned aspects of globalization, especially the intensification of communication. The changes in communication will lead to the Christian message being more easily spread and mission work being simplified. One can mention various charismatic movements as an example of good use of this potential to implement modern methods of communication for their mission in a targeted way. In Pentecostal movements, it has even contributed to an astonishing success in the area.[13] Being challenged and thrust onto the defensive, the traditional church likewise is discovering this capability. Pope John Paul II, for example, employed the media with great success and because of this was often referred to as the "media-friendly" pope. Current Pope Francis also shows great charisma in this regard.[14]

Methods of communication also played a huge role in the

---

13. See pp. 174–79, below.

14. Even if I treasure the meaning of these gestures, I nevertheless wonder whether the boundlessness brokered by the media will at some point lead to certain saturation. What I do know for certain is that the next pope will not have an easy job attempting to achieve his level.

spread of the ideas of the Reformation. The capability and speed of the spread of information at that time were very different from modern communication methods, but their significance was just as great as it is today. One can even argue that because information at that time generally took longer to spread, it held more weight and had a greater influence. For this, the use of modern communication methods was of singular importance. Luther's theses, for example, only had their great influence at that time because they were printed and spread widely without his knowledge.[15] The papal nuncio of that day in Germany, Aleandro Girolamo, reported on the situation a few years after the publication of Luther's theses:

> Every day it rains Lutheran works in German and Latin; even here a print works is being maintained, where such a craft had been hitherto unknown. Nothing else is being sold here except Luther's works, even at the Royal Court, as the people keep together stupendously and have an abundance of money.[16]

From this example, we can see quite clearly how the most modern technology of the era (print) was used to spread the Reformation ideology. A further good example of the speed of the dissemination of information is the exchange of letters between the Ecumenical Patriarch Jeremias II and the Tübingen theologians that took place between 1573 and 1581.[17]

A further aspect that played an important role in the dissemination of the Reformation ideology was that the Reformation was

15. On the subject of publication of Luther's theses, see Volker Leppin, *Martin Luther: Gestalten des Mittelalters und der Renaissance*, 2nd ed. (Darmstadt: Wissenschaftliche Buchgesellschaft WBG, 2010), 117–20.

16. Girolamo Aleandro, *Die Depeschen des Nuntius Aleander vom Wormser Reichstage 1521*, ed. Paul Kalkoff (Halle: Verein für reformationsgeschichte, 1886), 44.

17. See Council of the Evangelical Church in Germany (EKD), *Wort und Mysterium: Der Briefwechsel über Glauben und Kirche 1573 bis 1581 zwischen den Tübinger Theologen und dem Patriarchat von Konstantinopel* (Witten: Luther Verlag, 1958); and George Mastrantonis, *Augsburg and Constantinople: The Correspondence between the Tubingen Theologians and Patriarch Jeremiah II of Constantinople on the Augsburg Confession* (Brookline, MA: Holy Cross Orthodox Press, 2005).

organized according to the principle of small networks.[18] Through the already mentioned tenet *cuius regio, eius religio* that it introduced in the Imperial State and the Peace of Augsburg, which made it possible for the newly formed Reformation churches to develop free from the influence of Rome, and because there was no center to the entire movement, Rome found it very difficult to fight the Reformation. The national churches that emerged could adapt to the concrete situation locally. The great strength of these churches was that they were contextual in comparison with the Catholic Church. This "contextuality," among other things, contributed to the people of these churches having their own understanding and easily identifying with the churches.

Today, this purpose to be contextual is especially important because the process of globalization has contributed to a multireligious, multicultural situation in many countries. Because of this multireligiousness, the many Christian churches preside over the task of coming to grips with other denominations or religions, but also more intensely with other religions and cultures.[19] Through ecumenical and interreligious dialogue, diverse denominations and religions learn to better communicate with each other. The experiences that are collected through this process can also be used in social spheres. Here lies the great potential for ecumenical dialogue, for the world, too, can learn from these experiences and can use them for the common good.

There are other areas that I see in which the church from its long experience of over two thousand years can render a contribution

18. Even today small networks play an important role in the missions of individual Christian churches, such as the Pentecostals. For more, see below.

19. From the Roman Catholic side, the encyclical of Paul VI, *Evangelii nuntiandi,* needs to be mentioned, but also the work of individual theologians such as Francis X. d'Sa, Director of the Institute for the Study of Religion in Pune, India, among many others. See, for instance, Peter C. Phan, *Being Religious Interreligiously: Asian Perspectives on Interfaith Dialogue* (Maryknoll, NY: Orbis, 2004). A general overview of Roman Catholic teaching for the past five decades is found in Francesco Gioia, ed., *Interreligious Dialogue: The Official Teaching of the Catholic Church from the Second Vatican Council to John Paul II, 1963–2005* (Boston: Pauline Books and Media, 2006).

to society. One of them concerns the growing inequality of wealth. Globalization has unfortunately helped to accelerate the growing economic inequality that makes a few much richer at the expense of the many. Because power today lies in the hands of the few, one can talk about the "end of the free world," in that decisions are no longer made with the agreement and in the interests of the people, but in the interests of capital, which is increasingly held by a few. "Democracy,"[20] the rule of people, has unfortunately become "Moneycracy," the rule of money. This goes so far as to affect health systems and the food industry.[21] Capitalism, which is closely tied to globalization, has led to the necessities of the people being disregarded, or viewed merely as consumers to whom one wants to sell products. In addition, this connection between capitalism and globalization has had consequences for the environment and the approach to natural resources, and has led to a readiness to endanger the whole planet for short-term profit or to start economically motivated wars.[22]

The church has long nurtured prophetic voices in its midst that have been critical of the inordinate amassing of wealth and have called for a more just system of distribution of resources. In light of this tradition it is no wonder that the head of the largest Christian church, Pope Francis, wrote his first two letters dedicated to this subject. His apostolic letter *Evangelii gaudium*, which was published on November 24, 2013, included a strong criticism of capitalism and its consequences.[23] His encyclical *Laudato si'*, which was published

20. The meaning of this term is "popular government" from the Greek words *dēmos* (people) and *kratia* (governance).

21. One only needs to think of what the sugar lobby did to the USA in the course of the past decades.

22. The examples of Iraq and Libya are very fitting here, where the theft of natural resources was the ultimate goal under the cloak of democracy and human rights. See the interview of Noam Chomsky by Stephen Shalom and Michael Albert, "On Libya and the Unfolding Crises," at https://chomsky.info/20110330/.

23. Pope Francis, "*Evangelii gaudium*: On the Proclamation of the Gospel in Today's World," at https://w2.vatican.va/content/francesco/en/apost_exhortations /documents/papa-francesco_esortazione-ap_20131124_evangelii-gaudium.html. Paragraph 53 of the document states: "Human beings are themselves considered consumer goods to be used and then discarded. We have created a 'throw away' culture which is now spreading." See also Pope Francis, "*Ad participes Conven-*

May 24, 2015, was primarily concerned with addressing the current global ecological crisis, but it connected this crisis with global economic inequality and the plight of the poor.[24] The reactions to both of these letters have been varied thus far. While many believers and most theologians received them with great zeal, politicians (particularly those in the US) have been much more reticent or even critical of these papal utterances.[25] This is perhaps to be expected, as both letters were addressed mainly to laypeople and the pope pointed to every individual believer's responsibility.[26]

Migration and the Multireligious Reality

A second great challenge in addition to globalization processes that the church faces in our time is the question of migration, which is very closely connected to the phenomenon of globalization and mutually affects it. More people, with their religions, are on the move thanks to increased methods of rapid transportation that are shrinking the globe. Global social, political, and economic forces are making more of these moves take the form of long-term or even permanent migrations. Such long-term migration causes different elements of religions to align, exchange, and repel each other more. In more extreme cases, this leads to the formation of "patchwork religions" that reflect the present multireligious situation.[27] Inter-

---

tus Internationalis pro pastorali considerando proposito Adhortationis Apostolicae 'Evangelii Gaudium,'" Acta Apostolicae Sedis Commentarium Officiale 106, no. 10 (October 3, 2014): 766–69.

24. Pope Francis, "*Laudato si'*: On Care for Our Common Home," at http://w2 .vatican.va/content/francesco/en/encyclicals/documents/papa-francesco_20150524 _enciclica-laudato-si.html. Paragraph 49 states: "Today, however, we have to realize that a true ecological approach always becomes a social approach; it must integrate questions of justice in debates on the environment, so as to hear both the cry of the earth and the cry of the poor."

25. The encyclical *Laudato si'* in particular was heavily criticized by lobbyists in the US. Many politicians also expressed very negative views of it.

26. Pope Francis, *Evangelii gaudium*, 1.

27. Patchwork religions originate when people put together their own beliefs and life philosophy from different denominations or even religions.

denominational or interreligious marriages are but one expression of this multireligiousness.[28]

Migration, especially for economic reasons, is one of the main reasons that we live in a multireligious society. The effects of this can be felt in different areas in everyday life such as in education or in the domestic arena. The question is no longer whether we want to live in a multireligious society, but how we shape this preexisting situation. This is particularly the case in large cities, where increasing numbers of people from a migrant background live and work. This cultural and religious diversity is not just found in the United States, but also in the European Union and therefore also in Germany. People of almost one hundred nationalities with different religious and cultural backgrounds live together here: Roman Catholic, Protestant, and Orthodox Christians, as well as Jewish communities and Buddhist groups, which are becoming more and more popular, especially among the "higher" classes. Also, not to be forgotten are Islamic communities, which have over the intervening years grown to be the second-largest religious community in Germany, as well as in the whole of Europe, mainly due to a large family structure.[29]

From a historical viewpoint, members of other religions had already existed in this part of the world since medieval times in Europe and therefore also in the Reformation era. They were present in this geographical area, of course not in such quantities, and with more or less tolerance on the part of the Christians. Until the Reformation, the Roman Catholic Church was, except for an insignificant number of Orthodox Christians, the dominant *de facto* religion in these countries. Through the Peace of Augsburg (1555), the second communion of Lutheran Protestantism was introduced into the legal system and then through the Treaty of Osnabrück (1648) the number increased to three with the Reformed Church. It is scarcely possible in Germany today to find a purely Christian population in a

28. See, for instance, Erika B. Seamon, *Interfaith Marriage in America: The Transformation of Religion and Christianity* (New York: Palgrave Macmillan, 2012).

29. The situation in Germany has arisen due to economic factors after World War II, including the shortage of workers. As well as immigrants from Italy and Yugoslavia, countries with Christian backgrounds, many "Gastarbeiter" (guest workers) came from Turkey, which resulted in interreligious diversity.

single small village, let alone a large city. This new situation has been influenced substantially by the stance of the Christian church on non-Christian religions. One can see the signs of change even in the Orthodox Church, which is one of the more conservative Christian communions,[30] but also in other churches, particularly in the Roman Catholic Church, in which there was an enormous turnaround after the Second Vatican Council,[31] which led to an intensification of the interreligious dialogue. The pinnacle of this dialogue formed the World Day of Prayer for Peace in Assisi in 1986 and 2011, where representatives of all major world religions were present.

This newly discovered awareness concerning the inevitability of the multireligious society and world in which we live and in which the church must exist has also led to a number of official statements from the various Christian churches. The resulting documents have sought to help laypeople and church leaders alike to deal with multireligious situations in a Christian way. In 2003, the German Roman Catholic bishops published a recommendation with the title "Guidelines for Multi-Religious Celebrations of Christians, Jews and Muslims," and in 2011 "Christian Witness in a Multi-Religious World: Recommendations for Conduct" was jointly published by the World Council of Churches, the Pontifical Council for Interreligious Dialogue, and the World Evangelical Alliance.[32] These are but two examples of such efforts.

With reference to these documents, it is clear that the church is

30. The Orthodox Church has, for example, long been engaged in dialogue with Islam. See George C. Papademetriou, *Two Traditions, One Space: Orthodox Christians and Muslims in Dialogue* (Boston: Somerset Hall, 2010).

31. See Vatican II, "*Nostra aetate*: The Declaration on the Relation of the Church to Non-Christian Religions" (1965), at http://www.vatican.va/archive/hist_councils /ii_vatican_council/documents/vat-ii_decl_19651028_nostra-aetate_en.html.

32. Sekretariat der Deutschen Bischofkonferenz, *Leitlinien für multireligiöse Feiern von Juden, Christen und Muslimen. Eine Handreichung der deutschen Bischöfe* (Arbeitshilfen 170) (Bonn: Deutschen Bischofkonferenz, 2003); and World Council of Churches, Pontifical Council for Interreligious Dialogue, and World Evangelical Alliance, "Christian Witness in a Multi-Religious World: Recommendations for Conduct," at https://www.oikoumene.org/en/resources/documents/wcc -programmes/interreligious-dialogue-and-cooperation/christian-identity-in-plural istic-societies/christian-witness-in-a-multi-religious-world.

aware that it must position itself in today's multireligious situation if it is not to be isolated from society. This particularly concerns the areas in which church and state work together, e.g., in healthcare and education. Central to this are kindergartens, where interreligious pluralism has played an important role for some time. A common celebration of Christmas between Protestants and Catholics in nursery school in Germany is old hat today, and it is not just secular educators in the field looking for a way to fashion this celebration in an interreligious way, but also religious educators.[33]

On the question of how to deal with religious pluralism as a Christian, one is often presented with rigid alternatives: either adhere to a strict exclusivity and regard all non-Christian religions as a mission,[34] or regard other religions as having a degree of salvific efficacy.[35] There are, however, multiple possibilities between these. One example is the attempt at Christian inclusivity advocated by Karl Rahner, who spoke and wrote about "anonymous Christians"[36] who belong to other religions.[37] Another is the attempt at relativism, advocated by John Hick, in which no religion approaches an absolute claim to truth, but all have a share of the truth.[38]

33. See Friedrich Schweitzer, Anke Edelbrock, and Albert Biesinger, *Interreligiöse und Interkulturelle Bildung in der Kita* (Münster: Waxmann, 2011).

34. A good example of this would be Cardinal Meisner's prohibition of Catholic religious teachers from celebrating festivals with Jews or Muslims or praying with them. See Statement of the Archdiocese of Cologne, "Richtlinie des Erzbischofs zu multireligiösen Feiern in Schulen" of December 6, 2006, at http://bildungsklick .de/datei-archiv/50009/stellungnahme_des_erzbistums_061206.pdf. Also compare Spiegel Online at http://www.spiegel.de/panorama/katholische-kirche-kardinal -meisner-untersagt-multireligioese-schulfeiern-a-452948.html.

35. This is exactly what the Second Vatican Council told Catholics, in that it allowed other religions at least partial recognition of the truth through council decisions such as *Lumen gentium* and *Nostra aetate*. This has recently been disputed by some authors, however. See, for example, Ralph Martin, *Will Many Be Saved? What Vatican II Actually Teaches and Its Implications for the New Evangelization* (Grand Rapids: Eerdmans, 2012).

36. See Karl Rahner, "Christianity and the Non-Christian Religions," in *Theological Investigations*, vol. 5 (Baltimore: Helicon, 1966), 115–34.

37. With this he means that although only Christianity comprises the whole revelation, other religions also participate in it.

38. See John Hick, "Gotteserkenntnis in der Vielfalt der Religionen," in *Hori-*

Neither of these attempts means, in my opinion, that one has to relinquish the Christian ideal and cannot stay true to one's roots. Exactly the contrary is true. This deference for the dignity of one's fellow human being is much more in line with the spirit of the Christian message. Certainly, some see the new multireligious situation as a threat to the continuity of the Christian church. In my opinion, however, the church can again only benefit from this, and even rise to the challenge. Competition is always a good thing, and that is not just true for the economy, but also for religion. The existence of multireligiousness in a country, for example, contributes to the church in this country being motivated to face the problems of the era actively and to continually contemplate others in a new light. Meanwhile, the church has come a long way and has discarded the view that other religions are enemies or objects of Christian mission. Despite a bad prognosis that the relevance of religion in society is diminishing, there is still hopefully a long way to go for the church.

However, if one looks at the present religious situation in Europe with respect to multireligiousness, it is clear that Europe today is a less and less Christian continent.[39] As well as those belonging to other religions, the number of professed atheists is also growing.[40] In Germany, for example, almost a third of the total population is not religious.[41] This number is comparatively much higher in the former East Germany; here we can refer to figures of around 75

---

zontueberschreitung: Die Pluralistische Theologie der Religionen, ed. Reinhard Bernhardt (Gütersloh: Gerd Mohn, 1991), 60–80; and John Hick, *An Interpretation of Religion: Human Responses to the Transcendent*, 2nd ed. (New Haven: Yale University Press, 2005).

39. Press releases from the German Bishops' Conference, "Wege für Kirche und Gesellschaft in säkularisierter Zeit: Ein Zwischenruf aus Ostdeutschland für Europa," cited in a lecture by Bishop Dr. Joachim Wanke, Erfurt, at the annual reception of churches in Brussels, November 18, 2009.

40. Currently this number stands at around 700 million across the globe.

41. However, this does not mean that they are all avowed atheists; some of them have various reasons for not being involved in the church (church taxes, disappointment over the abuse scandal, papal visit, etc.) and others simply do not have much of an interest in the more in-depth questions of life, as their own prosperity is their focus.

percent of citizens being unaffiliated with any religion.[42] Christians must ensure that in future they stay part of this multireligiousness and that they do not become extinct or become a small minority in what was hitherto the world's largest Christian continent.

"New" Atheism

One of the biggest challenges for the church today is New Atheism. This phenomenon is, in my opinion, particularly dangerous for the church because due to its militant nature it represents a type of "anti-church."[43] New Atheism itself originated from the Anglo-American linguistic area, or more precisely from the US.[44] It then settled mostly in Great Britain where it found its main representative, the biologist Richard Dawkins.[45] The impact of the emergence of New Atheism lies mainly in religious fundamentalism in the US, in both its Islamic and Christian forms.[46] The latter has become known throughout the world, for example, through the theory of the origins of the universe known as creationism, which should, according to the view of some evangelical groups, be taught and is sometimes taught in the schools there instead of the theory of evolution.[47]

New Atheism in many ways mirrors fundamentalism in its close-minded approach. That Dawkins has founded this ideology

42. See Judith Könemann, "Neuer Atheismus—Intellektuelles Spiel oder gesellschaftliche Realität?" *Ökumenische Rundschau* 59, no. 4 (2010): 480–91.

43. See Thomas Schärtl, "Neuer Atheismus, Zwischen Argument, Anklage und Anmaßung," *Stimmen der Zeit* 3 (2008): 147.

44. See Könemann, "Neuer Atheismus," 481.

45. See Richard Dawkins, *The God Delusion* (Boston and New York: Houghton Mifflin, 2006).

46. Since the terrorist attacks of September 11, 2001, intolerance and the problems of the modern world have been blamed on religion (mostly Islam).

47. "Creationism" is defined as the literal interpretation of the biblical story of creation, which originated as an alternative to Darwin's theory of evolution and starts from the premise that the world began through the direct interference of God. See, for instance, Henry M. Morris, *The Scientific Case for Creation* (San Diego: Creation-Life Publishers, 1977), and Henry M. Morris and Gary E. Parker, *What Is Creation Science?* (San Diego: Creation-Life Publishers, 1982).

supposedly on pure science is quasi-logical. Other prominent representatives of New Atheism are (or were) also mostly scientists. Along with Dawkins, the names of Daniel Dennett, Christopher Hitchens, Sam Harris, Michel Onfray, and Piergiorgio Odifreddi can also be mentioned.[48] For a long time New Atheism was limited to the works of these (and other) individuals. This has, however, changed recently. In the meantime, different organizations have come into being that support New Atheism institutionally as a program. The Giordano Bruno Foundation is especially prominent here. It is composed in turn of regional groups with over two thousand prominent members (professors, politicians, etc.) from a total of twenty-five countries. In Germany there is also such a group called Humanistischer Verband Deutschlands (Humanist Association of Germany) that actively promotes the agenda of New Atheism.

New Atheism is not a methodologically positive system, but is based on the negation of the existence of God. The aim is "the replacement of religion by naturalistic concepts."[49] Depending on how this aim is implemented, one can distinguish between argumentative, denunciatory, and cultural atheism.[50] The beliefs of Dawkins share all three: that faith is one of the world's greatest evils, comparable to the smallpox virus, but harder to eradicate.[51] There are many other similar arguments made by representatives of New Atheism against religion, equally measured and equally offensive. Odifreddi believes, for example, that religion is nonsense that only spiritual dwarves would believe.[52]

---

48. See Daniel Dennett, *Breaking the Spell: Religion as a Natural Phenomenon* (New York: Penguin, 2006); Christopher Hitchens, *God Is Not Great: How Religion Poisons Everything* (New York: Hachette Book Group USA/Warner Books, 2007); Sam Harris, *Waking Up: A Guide to Spirituality without Religion* (New York: Simon & Schuster, 2007); Michel Onfray, *Atheist Manifesto: The Case against Christianity, Judaism, and Islam*, trans. Jeremy Leggatt (New York: Arcade, 2007); Piergiorgio Odifreddi, *Perché non-possiamo essere cristiani (e meno che mai cattolici)* (Milan: Longanesi, 2007).

49. Könemann, "Neuer Atheismus," 482.

50. See Schärtl, "Neuer Atheismus," 147–48.

51. Richard Dawkins, "Is Science a Religion?" *Humanist* (January/February 1997): 26.

52. There are numerous prominent examples of these "spiritual dwarves" in

When one considers all of this, one asks oneself to what extent it makes sense to call this movement "New Atheism" when its content and methods can hardly be distinguished from "old" atheism. Both essentially assert that there is no God and both use science to prove their theories. They remain, despite all effort, what they are—theories. The existence of God cannot be proven, just as the nonexistence of God cannot be proven. Religious people decide to believe in God for nonscientific reasons and their faith is independent of proof, or should be at least. Ultimately, with New Atheism, however, one can also talk about a form of faith because one believes in evolution[53] or the Big Bang Theory,[54] and one does not believe in God, none of which can be proven.[55] On this point Christianity and atheism do therefore have something in common, and this could possibly serve as a good basis for the start of a serious dialogue.

When one looks at the phenomenon of atheism with reference to the Reformation era, the differences are very clear. In the Reformation era, there were very few if any atheists who would have labeled themselves as such. However, it was not long after the Reformation that Baruch Spinoza, Julien La Mettrie, and Baron d'Holbach laid the first foundations for modern atheism. There is still a debate as to whether one can connect these philosophical developments with the Reformation.[56] In my opinion, and also ac-

---

science, including Max Planck, Albert Einstein, Johannes Kepler, Nikola Tesla, and Owen Gingerich among others, all of whom were religious.

53. One must naturally recognize that the theory of evolution is more than just a hypothesis, but has not yet been completely proven scientifically, meaning it is therefore still a "theory." What I mean by this is that of course the precise so-called "missing link"—the link between apelike ancestors of humans and humans—has not yet been found, even though it has been claimed many times in the press.

54. The Big Bang Theory, the basic concept for modern cosmology, has the big problem of explaining thermodynamic equilibrium in the universe.

55. I am aware that most physicists would not agree that either evolution or the Big Bang Theory is a matter of faith.

56. See Michael Hunter and David Wootton, eds., *Atheism from the Reformation to the Enlightenment* (New York: Oxford University Press, 1992), 3; and Denis J. Robichaud, "Renaissance and Reformation," in *The Oxford Handbook of Atheism*, ed. Stephen Bullivant and Michael Ruse (New York: Oxford University Press, 2013), 194–97.

cording to the views of some other modern researchers,[57] one can make this conclusion. The authority of the Catholic Church was starting to be weakened by the Reformation, so that there was not so much fear of asking questions, including about the existence of God. In addition, the Reformation also contributed to many elements of popular piety as well as the cult of relics and Eucharist worship disappearing, which weakened the tie between the people and the church. Ultimately, the Reformation led to belief being seen as a personal matter rather than a state one, which was one of the key prerequisites for the development of atheism, but also one of the causes of the soon-approaching secularization.

If we compare today's situation, looking at the church with regard to the phenomenon of atheism, with that of the Reformation era, it is clear that the situation has changed. This is because today's atheism has a very concrete form.[58] Luther wrote very often about "nonbelievers," but by this he meant those of other religions rather than those who profess an atheist way of life.[59] To the question of how one should deal with these "nonbelievers," a quotation from Luther that Dietrich Bonhoeffer reportedly cited can be very helpful: "the curse of a godless man can sound more pleasant in God's ears than the Hallelujah of the pious."[60] Even if we don't use this label for nonbelievers or those of other religions, in my opinion the statement can be a signpost for the church as to how to deal with such persons. We have to recognize the value of those who do not share our life philosophy or religious views.

Guided by this insight, I am ready to argue that although the New Atheism has mostly been judged to be negative by religions

57. See, for example, Alec Ryrie, "Atheism and Faith in the Age of the Reformation," presentation given at the University of Durham on November 7, 2013, online at https://www.dur.ac.uk/research/ils/videos1314/alecryrie/.

58. The first of this, of course, is that which originated in the former communist block and was entrenched within this system. The second is New Atheism, which we have to deal with today.

59. See Armin Pfahl-Traughber, *Antisemitismus in der Deutschen Geschichte* (Berlin: Verlag für Sozialwissenschaften, 2002), 34.

60. Quoted by John W. Doberstein in his introduction to Dietrich Bonhoeffer, *Life Together*, trans. John W. Doberstein (New York: Harper & Row, 1954), 9.

and religious representatives, in my opinion there are also some positive aspects from which the church can benefit. Primarily, New Atheism demands that the faithful question themselves and reconsider their own position. One can compare this, for example, with the so-called heresies of early Christianity: if they had not existed, the content of our theology would be much poorer today.[61] A further positive consequence that New Atheism brings with it is the fact that it constantly spurs reflection and therefore never lets us "fall into a slumber" of complacency.[62] New Atheism also forces theology to reconsider its traditional classifications and the terms with which it describes God and to form new types and methods. There are also obvious parallels with the Reformation era here, because the answer was also a "sign of the times." For example, Christian statements of faith were translated into a language that the people could understand[63] and at the same time theology adapted to the needs of the people. Unfortunately the church as a whole also made the painful discovery through the Reformation of what can happen when it refuses to undertake reforms.[64]

Through learning from criticism on the part of "others," we ourselves can learn better and know better how to deal with these "others." In dealing with atheists, the words of Christ are definitive: "But if anyone strikes you on the right cheek, turn the other also" (Matt. 5:39, NRSV). Even if the atheists don't meet religion or the religious person with complete respect, Christians are encouraged to face them and every other person with respect. A 2011 study

61. Of course, there is no such thing as heresy. This word was simply used for all of those who had a different opinion, which is also a part of the original meaning of the word *hairesis*—choice.

62. There is currently an interesting German research project on the theme, "The 'Return of Religion' and the Return of the Criticism of Religion—The 'New Atheism' in Recent German and American Culture," being conducted by Prof. Dr. Harmut Zinser in the Institute for the Scientific Study of Religion at Freie Universität in Berlin.

63. Luther's translation of the Bible into German is the preeminent example of this.

64. The split in Western Christianity in the sixteenth century can be seen, in my opinion, as an immediate consequence of the refusal of the Church in Rome to reform.

from the German Protestant Centre for Religious and Ideological Issues (EZW) with the title "Dialog und Auseinandersetzung mir Atheisten und Humanisten" has a helpful suggestion:

> Atheists and non-believers should be classed neither as a threat to their beliefs, nor as people lacking in religious vocation. Rather keep inquiring what [the atheist or non-believer] believes in, what he doesn't believe in, how he answers essential questions in his life, justifies ethical decisions and overcomes life crises.[65]

One must of course stay true to one's own values and one can (with respect) also exercise criticism toward New Atheism. In my opinion, approaching New Atheism is especially problematic, as atheists only take to be valid that which can be tested and proven with scientific methods. This aspect seems to me to be too simplistic. Our reality is much more complex than that which can be seen with a mere (scientific) eye. One can of course try to explain phenomena such as love, poetry, or music scientifically, but this explanation cannot capture everything about them. It is the same way with religion. One can of course argue that religion is merely an invention of primitive people, but one cannot explain why it has survived into today's modern era.[66] The prognosis from the viewpoint of some atheists, that religion as an outdated phenomenon will play less and less of a role for modern people, has evidently proven not to be true. If anything, atheist systems, especially those in Russia and Eastern European countries, have collapsed.[67] At the same time, in these countries we are experiencing a strong return to religion. Not just there but worldwide we are experiencing a growth in Christianity,

---

65. Uta Gerhardt, "Woran glaubt, wer nicht glaubt? Überlegungen zum Dialog mit Atheisten und Konfessionslosen," in *Dialog und Auseinandersetzung mit Atheisten und Humanisten*, ed. Reinhard Hempelmann (Berlin: Evangelische Zentralstelle für Weltanschauungsfragen Texte, 2011), 93.

66. Even if it is so, it does not necessarily mean that religion is insignificant. Voltaire formulated this very well in his thought, "If God did not exist, it would be necessary to invent him."

67. Here I find an example of graffiti very fitting, in which the first line read "God is dead" (Nietzsche) and a reply below that read: "Nietzsche is dead" (God).

particularly in the expansion of local churches. When one examines this expansion phenomenon more closely, it becomes particularly clear that modern people, despite modernization and the new forms of atheism, are still open to religion.

The Pentecostal Challenge

Finally, there is another challenge that must be faced in modern times, in the form of the Pentecostal and Neo-Pentecostal or Charismatic churches. In contrast to the first three challenges we have discussed here, this is a challenge decidedly from within Christianity. The term "Pentecostal" can be understood or applied to different charismatic movements that have a Christian-religious basis. It is not a matter of just one single group, but a variety of autonomous organizations and individual groups that have tended to distinguish themselves from traditional Orthodox, Roman Catholic, and Protestant branches of the Christian church. The term itself suggests that these churches emphasize the ministry of the Holy Spirit in their theology. This tendency goes back to the first Pentecostal groups, which had deep roots in the Wesleyan Methodist Holiness movement.[68] While Methodism originated in Great Britain, the Pentecostal movement began primarily in North America in a much more culturally mixed environment, and with strong African American influences.[69]

---

68. See Donald W. Dayton, *The Theological Roots of Pentecostalism* (Grand Rapids: Baker, 1987). It is important to note that John and Charles Wesley, who were the most important founding figures of Methodism in England in the eighteenth century, were both Anglican priests, and that Methodism had deep roots in Anglicanism, and through it to both the Eastern Orthodox and Catholic streams of Christian tradition. See Edgardo Colón-Emeric, *Wesley, Aquinas, and Christian Perfection: An Ecumenical Dialogue* (Waco, TX: Baylor University Press, 2009); and S. T. Kimbrough Jr., ed., *Orthodox and Wesleyan Spirituality* (Crestwood, NY: St. Vladimir's Seminary Press, 2002).

69. For basic introductions to the global Pentecostal movement, see Allan Anderson, *An Introduction to Pentecostalism: Global Charismatic Christianity* (Cambridge: Cambridge University Press, 2004); and Cecil M. Robeck Jr. and Amos Yong, eds., *The Cambridge Companion to Pentecostalism* (New York: Cambridge Univer-

The origin of the Pentecostal movement lay at the beginning of the twentieth century. The enormous growth of this movement was perceptible beginning in the 1950s and not only in the US and Africa,[70] but also in Latin America, which up to this point had been traditionally Catholic.[71] The Pentecostal churches in Latin America have become major competition for the traditional Roman Catholic Church. In some studies, it is claimed that Pentecostals will exceed the Catholic Church in terms of number of members by the year 2030.[72] When considering if such a prognosis should be taken seriously, one also sees that in the past one hundred years the number of members has risen to 605 million. In percentage terms, this means that the number of Christians who belong to various Pentecostal movements 1900–2009 rose from 0.18 percent to 26.6 percent. In comparison with this, the number of members of the Catholic Church rose from 47.8 to only 49.9 percent over the same period.[73]

The reasons for this growth of Pentecostal churches are of particular interest. Several factors in fact have contributed to this expansion. The main reason is that these churches responded to the requirements of modern people, which qualifies them as a phenomenon of the modern era. Pentecostals also often bypass lengthy processes of catechetical training or leadership formation. In my opinion, they tend in this regard to reflect much of today's lifestyle. At present, everyday life is shaped by accomplishing as much as

---

sity Press, 2014). On the African American roots of Pentecostalism, see Walter J. Hollenweger, *Pentecostalism: Origins and Development Worldwide* (Peabody, MA: Hendrickson, 1997); and Cecil M. Robeck Jr., *The Azusa Street Mission and Revival: The Birth of the Global Pentecostal Movement* (Nashville: Thomas Nelson, 2006).

70. In Africa alone today there are around five thousand different Pentecostal groups. See Ogbu U. Kalu, *African Pentecostalism: An Introduction* (New York: Oxford University Press, 2008).

71. See Michael Huhn, "Religiöse Landkarte aufgemischt," *Jahrbuch Mission* 42 (2010): 143.

72. See Antje Schrupp, "Im Namen des Heiligen Geistes: Die Pfingstkirchen erobern die Dritte Welt," at http://www.antjeschrupp.de/pfingstkirchen.

73. See Giancarlo Collet, "Implikationen der globalen Transformation des Christentums für die röisc-katholische Kirche," *Berliner theologische Zeitschrift* 27 (2010): 73.

possible in a short space of time. Some would say that people who often nourish themselves with fast food need a kind of "fast food religion." Without wanting to insult these churches or their leaders, I agree with this in part because one has to note that, for most Pentecostal churches, the spiritual or aesthetic requirements for their believers and their theological basis are of a low threshold[74] and therefore very accessible, whereas the teachings of the "traditional" churches are difficult to comprehend and enforce for many people these days.[75] In my opinion, neither is particularly good. The aim has to be much more in balance than in either extreme. In contrast to traditional Christian churches, Pentecostal churches fit extremely well into the modern capitalist world order. Differing from the Orthodox Christians for instance, many Pentecostal spiritual leaders and teachers represent "prosperity theology," according to which God does not only want spiritual well-being for all people, but also physical and material economic prosperity.[76]

A further advantage of Pentecostals in today's world is that they do not have a centralized system. In comparison with the Catholic Church, where all the decisions are made centrally in Rome, Pentecostal churches are much more adaptable. The disadvantage of centralization is also that it is difficult to orient the different countries and mentalities through faith, but centralization is not the only problem that the traditional church has. The Orthodox churches, for example, do not have this problem with centralization, as they were conceived as national churches. However, this is simultaneously their weakness in comparison to the Pentecostal churches. The local Orthodox churches are too closely tied to each respective nation. By way of example, in Greece with few exceptions it is Greeks who are members of the Orthodox Church. In Serbia, it is almost exclusively Serbians, and so on. In the pluralistic society in which we live today, this ecclesiological concept has no future

74. This does not have to be a negative. Jesus, too, expressed himself in very simple terms in order to be accessible to everyone.

75. Few people are prepared to spend more than 250 days of the year fasting (Orthodox Church) or attend mass every day (Roman Catholic Church).

76. On the so-called Prosperity Teaching, see Kate Bowler, *Blessed: A History of the American Prosperity Gospel* (New York: Oxford University Press, 2013).

without giving up its exclusive status. The message of Jesus must be made accessible to all.

In comparison, Pentecostal churches do not place importance on particular nations and assimilate very well in a multireligious situation. However, this does not mean that Pentecostals completely ignore the mentalities of various nations. They originate from the tradition of the appropriate nation but this is not of central significance for them.[77]

A further reason for the great success of the Pentecostal churches is that they place much more emphasis on the emotional rather than intellectual "perceptions," in contrast to most "traditional" Christian churches. An example of this is that music plays a big role in Pentecostal church services, which are strongly shaped by emotionality and more open to ecstatic aspects of the ministry of the Holy Spirit. This is what gives their services great appeal. Ultimately the social dimension should also be considered as influential in this success. Pentecostal churches answer modern problems such as poverty, isolation, unemployment, drugs, family issues, and others by keenly referring to prayer and faith in God among their members, while also emphasizing their own responsibility. This then greatly improves the life of the individual, not necessarily through a miracle, but through abstinence and discipline in their way of life.[78]

When one looks at the Reformation era, it seems that there are few parallels between today's situation with the Pentecostal churches and that time. But if one looks at what I have just mentioned about Pentecostal movements being particularly attractive to modern people's current lives, then these parallels can easily be

77. While Pentecostal churches are mostly organized along national lines, they have strong international networks and a pronounced international identity. See Anderson, *An Introduction to Pentecostalism*, and Amos Yong, *The Spirit Poured Out on All Flesh: Pentecostalism and the Possibility of Global Theology* (Grand Rapids: Baker, 2005).

78. A good example of this is the smoking ban that is advocated in most Pentecostal churches. See Walter J. Hollenweger, *Die Pfingstkirchen: Selbstdarstellungen, Dokumente, Kommentare* (Berlin and Stuttgart: Evangelisches Verlagswerk, 1971), 363.

found. Topicality was exactly what the reformers made a mark with in their time and what made them so attractive for the people.[79] Today, the churches that originated from the Reformation are seen as traditional churches, and the role of "modern" (contemporary) churches is played by Pentecostal churches. One could say that the reformers of that time are the Pentecostals of today. This currentness is seen most clearly in the media used to spread Pentecostal churches' Christian message. The use of modern communication methods and technologies is a contextual specification of this "modern" era.[80]

It is true that the Pentecostal movement is not consistent with all achievements of the modern era. Pentecostals often represent a traditional worldview, which means they also often have a conservative view of women.[81] Further criticisms of Pentecostals from the side of the other (traditional) Christian churches are well known: that they are financed by the US and are thereby global political tools, that they are ecstatic and unpredictable, that they are not interested in societal matters, and that they will not take part in ecumenical dialogue.[82] Many of these criticisms are now dated,

79. Both Adolf von Harnack and Karl Holl saw Luther as the father of modernity and the Enlightenment. See Peter Grove, "Adolf von Harnack and Karl Holl on Luther at the Origins of Modernity," in *Lutherrenaissance Past and Present*, ed. Christine Helmer and Bo Kristian Holm (Göttingen: Vandenhoeck & Ruprecht, 2015), 106–26.

80. In Brazil, for example, Pentecostals have thirty TV channels. See Huhn, "Religiöse Landkarte aufgemischt," 146. In Serbia where I was born, the Pentecostals imported the nation's first 3D movie camera and showed films for free with a short introductory film about Christ or their church.

81. Although women can become pastors in many Pentecostal churches, the majority of the pastors are still men. See Estrelda Alexander and Amos Yong, eds., *Philip's Daughters: Women in Pentecostal-Charismatic Leadership* (Eugene, OR: Pickwick, 2008); Estrelda Alexander, "Beautiful Feet: Women Leadership and the Shaping of Global Pentecostalism," in *Spirit and Power: The Growth and Global Impact of Pentecostalism*, ed. Donald E. Miller, Kimon H. Sargeant, and Richard Flory (New York: Oxford University Press, 2013), 225–41; and Charles H. Barfoot and Gerald T. Sheppard, "Prophetic vs. Priestly Religion: The Changing Role of Women Clergy in Classical Pentecostal Churches," *Review of Religious Research* 22 (1980): 2–17.

82. See Steve Brouwer, Paul Gifford, and Susan D. Rose, *Exporting the American Gospel: Global Christian Fundamentalism* (London and New York: Routledge,

however, as a new generation of Pentecostal leadership globally is bringing about changes. Whatever their weaknesses might be, Pentecostal churches show us that there is still an inner strength in Christianity and they remind us that the greatest strength of Christianity is its adaptability, while simultaneously preserving its own identity.

Conclusion

The above-analyzed challenges, as well as many others that for reasons of space could not be explored here, signify a test for the churches, which they must pass in order to play a further role in society. In this test, they must, in my opinion, answer by summoning their teachings and experience, but also by keeping current their doctrinal statements. In this respect, the principle of *ecclesia semper reformanda*, which originated with the Reformation and is mentioned above, is of great significance to us all.[83] This principle is not just valid for Reformation churches, but for all churches, particularly traditional ones, who have a clause of immutability in their self-conception.[84] With the aid of different historical examples, one can see that although these churches are sometimes very slow to proceed with reforms, all do change eventually.[85]

1996); Nils Bloch-Hoell, *The Pentecostal Movement: Its Origin, Development, and Distinctive Character* (London and New York: Allen & Unwin, 1964); and Cecil M. Robeck, "The Challenge Pentecostalism Poses to the Quest for Ecclesial Unity," in *Die Kirche en Ökumenischer Perspektive: A Festschrift for Cardinal Walter Kasper on His 70th Birthday*, ed. Peter Walter, Klaus Krämer, and George Augustin (Freiburg: Herder, 2003), 306–20.

83. See Mahlmann, "'*Ecclesia semper reformanda.*'"

84. For a Roman Catholic interpretation of *semper reformanda*, see Walter Kasper, *Weil Taufe Zukunft Gibt: Wegmarken für eine Weiterentwicklung der Taufpastoral* (Ostfildern: Matthias Grunewald Verlag, 2011), 18.

85. For the Roman Catholic Church, this reform (or at least the beginning of the reform) came with the Second Vatican Council, which in a way formed an adoption of reformation. For the Orthodox churches, there is the Great and Holy Council, Pentecost 2016. For more about this council, see Viorel Ionita, *Towards the Holy and Great Synod of the Orthodox Church: The Decisions of the Pan-Orthodox*

With regard to all the possible and likely positive consequences of the above-analyzed challenges for the church, I will finish with the words of Juan Carlos Monedero, a young Spanish political scientist: "What doesn't hurt doesn't change and what doesn't change dies."[86] The painful challenges and experiences are therefore good for the church, because it can only change under pressure and through this better fulfill its purpose in the world. I hope that the individual Christian churches grasp this fairly swiftly,[87] before it is too late for some of them. The Christian church as a whole on the other hand will always remain, for even the gates of hell will not prevail against it (Matt. 16:18).

Meetings since 923 until 2009 (Basel: Friedrich Reinhardt Verlag, 2009); and John Chryssavgis, "At Last, a Council for the Ages? The Great Council of the Orthodox Church in 2016," *First Things*, March 3, 2014, at http://www.firstthings.com/web-exclusives/2015/03/at-last-a-council-for-the-ages.

86. Juan Carlos Monedero et al., "Venezuela: A 'Critical Evaluation' of the Bolivarian Process III—Summary," *Venezuelanalysis.com: News, Views, and Analysis*, at http://venezuelanalysis.com/analysis/4610.

87. I primarily mean my own Orthodox Church here, which has done the least in the way of modernization and adapting to the modern world. The "Holy and Great Council of the Orthodox Church" held in Crete in June 2016 also did very little in this regard.

Contributors

Charles Amjad-Ali is the Martin Luther King Jr. Chair of Justice and Christian Community (emeritus) at Luther Seminary, St. Paul, where he was also the director of its Islamic Studies Program, and the first holder of the Desmond Tutu Chair of Ecumenical Theology and Social Transformation in Africa at the University of Western Cape in South Africa. From 1985 to 1995 he was the director of the Christian Study Centre in Rawalpindi, Pakistan, which focused on Christian-Muslim dialogue, peace advocacy, and human rights work. An ordained presbyter of the Church of Pakistan, he holds a BA from Oxford University and Karachi University, an MDiv and PhD from Princeton Theological Seminary, and a postdoctoral certificate in Islamic law and history from Columbia University. In 1995 he received an honorary doctorate in theology from the University of Uppsala, Sweden. Recent publications include *Dreaming a Different World: Globalisation and Justice for Humanity and the Earth*, *The Challenge of the Accra Confession for the Churches*, which he edited along with Allan Boesak and Johan Weusmann (2010); *Leaving the Shadows? Pakistani Christians and the Search for Orientation in an Overwhelmingly Muslim Society*, cowritten with Theodor Hanf, (2008); and *Islamophobia or Restorative Justice: Tearing the Veil of Ignorance* (2006). He has also published over four hundred academic articles around the world.

Joel Morales Cruz is adjunct professor of theology at Lutheran School of Theology at Chicago, and adjunct professor of religion at Elmhurst College. He has also served as an instructor at Seminario Evangélico de Puerto Rico and Elmhurst College. A graduate of Moody Bible Institute (BA) and Gordon-Conwell Theological Seminary (MA), he holds a ThM and PhD from the Lutheran School of Theology at Chicago. He is the author of *The Mexican Reformation: Catholic Pluralism, Enlightenment Religion and the Iglesia de Jesus Movement in Benito Juarez's Mexico (1859–72)* (2011) and *The Histories of the Latin American Church: A Handbook* (2014). Dr. Cruz is a member of the Evangelical Lutheran Church in America.

David D. Daniels is the Henry Winters Luce Professor of World Christianity at McCormick Theological Seminary. The author of numerous articles, he serves on several editorial boards and has been an advisor for several projects of historical documentation and social research. He holds a BA from Bowdoin College, an MDiv from Yale University, and a PhD from Union Theological Seminary in New York. An ordained bishop in the Church of God in Christ, he has been a participant in a number of international ecumenical dialogue projects, including the World Alliance of Reformed Churches and Pentecostal International Dialogue.

Rebecca A. Giselbrecht is director of the Center for the Academic Study of Christian Spirituality (CASCS) and senior research and teaching associate in practical theology at the University of Zurich. She is also an affiliate assistant professor of history and spirituality at Fuller Theological Seminary, as well as a Sozialdiakonin (associate pastor) of the Evangelisch-reformierte Kirchen der Schweiz. She is a graduate of Moody Bible Institute (BS), the University of Applied Science, Rorschach (CAS), and Fuller Theological Seminary (MAGL, MDiv, PhD). She is coeditor of *Sacrality and Materiality: Locating Intersections* (2015) and *Hör nicht auf zu singen: Zeuginnen der Schweizer Reformation* (*Keep Singing: Female Testimony in the Swiss Reformation*) (2016).

Dale T. Irvin is president and professor of world Christianity at New York Theological Seminary. A graduate of Thomas A. Edison

University (BA), Princeton Theological Seminary (MDiv), and Union Theological Seminary in New York (PhD), he is the author of several books, including *History of the World Christian Movement*, a three-volume project he has written with Scott W. Sunquist, and numerous articles. He is also a founding editor of *The Journal of World Christianity*. He is an ordained minister in the American Baptist Churches USA.

Vladimir Latinovic is a lecturer at the Eberhard-Karls University of Tübingen. He formerly served as a teaching fellow at the Faculty of Catholic Theology and as a research fellow at the Institute for Ecumenical and Interreligious Studies in Tübingen (founded by Hans Küng). A graduate from the Faculty of Orthodox Theology at the University of Belgrade (MA), he obtained his PhD at the University of Tübingen in 2014 with a dissertation titled "Christology and Communion: Emergence of Homoousian Christology and Its Repercussions for the Reception of Eucharist." A lay member of the Serbian Orthodox Church, he serves as director and vice-chair of the Ecclesiological Investigations International Research Network.

Peter C. Phan is the inaugural holder of the Ignacio Ellacuria Chair of Catholic Social Thought at Georgetown University, Washington, DC. Previously he taught at the University of Dallas and at the Catholic University of America, where he held the Warren-Blanding Chair of Religion and Culture. He holds three earned doctorates: the STD from the Universitas Pontificia Salesiana, Rome, and the PhD and the DD from the University of London. In addition, he has been awarded two honorary doctorates: in theology from the Catholic Theological Union, Chicago, and in humane letters from the College of Our Lady of the Elms, Chicopee, Massachusetts. He is the author of more than twenty books and the editor or coeditor of more than twenty other volumes, and has published over three hundred essays covering almost every aspect of Christian theology, interreligious dialogue, and world Christianity. He is also the recipient of numerous awards, including the John Courtney Murray Award given by the Catholic Theological Society of America, in recognition for outstanding and distinguished achievement in theology.

Index